The *Yoder* Case

LANDMARK LAW CASES

&

AMERICAN SOCIETY

Peter Charles Hoffer
N. E. H. Hull
Series Editors

TITLES IN THE SERIES

The Bakke *Case*, Howard Ball
The Vietnam War on Trial, Michal R. Belknap
Reconstruction and Black Suffrage, Robert M. Goldman
Flag Burning and Free Speech, Robert Justin Goldstein
The Great New York Conspiracy of 1741, Peter Charles Hoffer
The Salem Witchcraft Trials, Peter Charles Hoffer
Roe v. Wade, N. E. H. Hull and Peter Charles Hoffer
The Reconstruction Justice of Salmon P. Chase, Harold M. Hyman
The Struggle for Student Rights, John W. Johnson
Igniting King Philip's War, Yasuhide Kawashima
Lochner v. New York, Paul Kens
Religious Freedom and Indian Rights, Carolyn N. Long
Marbury v. Madison, William E. Nelson
The Pullman Case, David Ray Papke
The Yoder *Case*, Shawn Francis Peters
When the Nazis Came to Skokie, Philippa Strum
Slave Law in the American South, Mark V. Tushnet
Affirmative Action on Trial, Melvin I. Urofsky
Lethal Judgments, Melvlin I. Urofsky
Clergy Malpractice in America, Mark A. Weitz
Race and Redistricting, Tinsley E. Yarbrough

SHAWN FRANCIS PETERS

The *Yoder* Case

Religious Freedom, Education, and Parental Rights

UNIVERSITY PRESS OF KANSAS

Published by the University Press of Kansas (Lawrence, Kansas 66049), which was organized by the Kansas Board of Regents and is operated and funded by Emporia State University, Fort Hays State University, Kansas State University, Pittsburg State University, the University of Kansas, and Wichita State University

Library of Congress Cataloging-in-Publication Data

Peters, Shawn Francis, 1966–
The Yoder case : religious freedom, education, and parental rights / Shawn Francis Peters.
p. cm. — (Landmark law cases & American society)
Includes bibliographical references and index.
ISBN 0-7006-1272-6 (cloth : alk. paper) — ISBN 0-7006-1273-4 (paper : alk. paper)
1. Yoder, Jonas—Trials, litigation, etc. 2. Amish—Legal status, laws, etc.—United States. 3. Educational law and legislation—United States. 4. Freedom of religion—United States. 5. Educational law and legislation—Wisconsin. I. Title. II. Series.
KF228.Y63P48 2003
342.73′0852—dc21 2003007159

British Library Cataloguing-in-Publication Data is available.

Printed in the United States of America

10 9 8 7 6 5 4 3 2 1

The paper used in this publication meets the minimum requirements of the American National Standard for Permanence of Paper for Printed Library Materials Z39.48–1984.

CONTENTS

EDITORS' PREFACE

Can a state or the federal government compel a person to perform acts in violation of his or her genuine lifelong religious beliefs? Could the state of Wisconsin tell Amish parents that they had to send their children to secular schools? Does the clause of the First Amendment guaranteeing the free exercise of religion protect us against such commands, or does it bow to the claims of the government? This last question was not new to the high court when it heard *Wisconsin v. Yoder* (1972). The U.S. Supreme Court had already issued rulings in cases involving religious minorities' refusal to salute the flag, for example. But these and other rulings were contradictory and confusing. Was there an absolute right to conscience, to worship as one chose? Or did the state's interests in universal education prevail over parents' wishes concerning their children's religious training? Was there a wall between church and state that protected both from the commands of the other? Or was the United States founded under the principle that "we are a religious people, whose institutions presuppose a supreme being," as Justice William Douglas wrote in his majority opinion in *Zorach v. Clauson* (1952).

From small beginnings sometimes great cases come. The desire of the Amish families of New Glarus, Wisconsin, to school their children in their own Old World pietistic traditions, and to protect them from the dangers of the secular world, pitted them against the local school authorities and, ultimately, the state of Wisconsin. Its supreme court would ultimately vindicate the Amish parents' wishes, but not before the community was rocked with disagreement over three parents' decision to "go to law" at all. What was more, counsel for the parents came not from within the Amish community but from outside it. The National Committee for Amish Religious Freedom was not characteristic of Amish ways and in fact represented a wide array of religious and lay leaders who wanted the state to fund parochial education rather than simply allow parents to choose appropriate schools based on their religious beliefs. William Ball, who successfully defended Yoder and the other two parents, would later be criticized for using the case to advance purposes entirely contrary to his original clients' view of the world.

These are a few of the many issues in this wonderfully informative, deeply sympathetic, and beautifully written book. Shawn Peters is a prize-winning historian and an expert on religious minorities and the law. Here he was able to interview participants in the case and gain access to other firsthand accounts. Peters's account of the simple and abiding faith of the Amish, the tortured decision of some to break ranks and bring a lawsuit, the conflicting and at times inept efforts of Wisconsin bureaucrats to force the children to attend school, the tactics of counsel on both sides, the motives and arguments of the many individuals and groups that intervened in the case, and the difficult choices the judges faced at every stage of the litigation from 1968 to its final resolution in 1972 give a human face to the story. The First Amendment's clauses on religion are among the most complicated in our constitutional lexicon, but Peters explains in plain and powerful prose what the arcane doctrines of First Amendment jurisprudence meant to ordinary men, women, and children. In a fine concluding chapter, he follows the course of the law and the fate of the principals after *Yoder*.

This is far more than a narrative of dry facts. Peters has strong opinions. But he is fair to all sides, and many readers will come away from this book agreeing with him about the heroism of a small group of people fighting for their rights in a world that seemed to have little respect for their traditions.

INTRODUCTION

The nation's cities and college campuses were not the only areas in America rattled by protests in 1968. During that tumultuous year, even places like New Glarus, Wisconsin — a picturesque and normally tranquil village populated by only a few thousand souls — experienced forms of civil unrest.

The three men at the heart of the conflict in New Glarus were plainspoken farmers, and they worried little about the great social and political issues that sparked massive public demonstrations throughout the United States in the late 1960s. But if Wallace Miller, Jonas Yoder, and Adin Yutzy didn't concern themselves with the carnage in Vietnam or the struggle of African Americans to attain full social and political equality, they shared with student radicals and civil rights activists an unwillingness to yield to coercion by the state. Quietly but firmly, the three men resisted governmental authority because they were steadfast in their uncommon religious beliefs. Miller and Yoder belonged to the Old Order Amish faith; Yutzy had been a longtime member of their church but had drifted away and joined a nearby Conservative Amish Mennonite congregation, which shared many of the same core doctrines.

The discord began in the fall of 1968, when the New Glarus Amish broke away from the local public school system and established schools of their own. After he realized that the defection of several dozen children would cost the school district thousands of dollars in state aid, the local school superintendent devised a scheme that was designed to soften the fiscal blow. He approached several Amish parents and asked them to keep their children in the public schools for the first few weeks of the new school year — just long enough for the youngsters to be tallied in the annual public school census, which determined how much per-pupil state aid the district would receive. The Amish, however, were too scrupulous to participate in this bit of trickery. They balked, and the local public school system lost almost $20,000 in state funding.

Local authorities retaliated against the Amish by charging Miller, Yoder, and Yutzy with violating Wisconsin's compulsory school attendance statute, a law with roots stretching back to the nineteenth century. The district attorney alleged that the three Amish farmers had broken the law because they had failed to keep their children enrolled in school. It seems that the Amish children, in keeping with their faith's traditions, had stopped attending school once they turned fourteen.

The charges put the Amish in an awkward position. The defendants believed that they had done nothing wrong, but they were extraordinarily reluctant to resolve their disagreement with local authorities through litigation. The Amish feel that "going to law" violates their faith's tradition of nonresistance. It was only after several months of indecision that Miller, Yoder, and Yutzy agreed to permit themselves to be represented by counsel in court.

When the case went to trial the following spring, the attorney defending the Amishmen, William Ball, fashioned a two-pronged strategy. First, he argued that application of the school attendance statute to the Amish violated their right to the free exercise of religion. To comply with the law, he claimed, the Amish would have to forsake their religious beliefs, which proscribed school attendance beyond the age of fourteen. At the trial, Ball asserted that the First Amendment clearly protected the Amish from being forced to sacrifice their religious freedom. An argument focusing on parental rights formed the second prong of Ball's defense strategy. He claimed that the state's action was unconstitutional because it violated the right of the Amish defendants to direct the upbringing of their children.

Ball grounded these arguments firmly in judicial precedent. He asserted at the trial (and throughout the appeals that followed) that two U.S. Supreme Court opinions supported the claims of the Amish in the Wisconsin school attendance case. The high court's opinion in *Sherbert v. Verner* (1963) provided strong judicial safeguards for religious liberty, and its ruling in *Pierce v. Society of Sisters* (1925) furnished stout protections for the rights of parents. These two landmark opinions were Ball's precedential touchstones in *Yoder*, and he invoked them repeatedly as the case made its way through the courts.

But not all judicial precedent favored Ball and his clients. Throughout the New Glarus case, the state of Wisconsin pointed out that Amish parents living in other states had made similar challenges to the constitutionality of school attendance laws, and they had lost each time. (In the most recent of these cases, resolved just two years before the Wisconsin case went to trial, the Kansas Supreme Court had ruled against an Amish father.) It also referred to language in several U.S.

Supreme Court opinions that explicitly acknowledged the right of states to enforce education regulations, including statutes mandating school attendance. Some of these passages appeared in the same opinions that defense attorney Ball cited to bolster his arguments in favor of the Amish.

Ball attempted to refute the state's claims by mounting an exhaustive defense. He brought in expert witnesses from as far away as Philadelphia to testify on behalf of his clients. Their ranks included John Hostetler, the nation's leading scholarly authority on the Amish, and an expert on school regulation from the University of Chicago. Although the state's case was far less impressive (Hostetler's testimony alone lasted longer), a judge found the three Amishmen guilty of a misdemeanor and ordered them to pay a token fine of five dollars. But Ball and the New Glarus Amish had better luck when they appealed to the Wisconsin Supreme Court in 1971. With only one justice dissenting, it reversed the convictions of Miller, Yoder, and Yutzy.

To the consternation of the state legislature, which passed a resolution asking attorney general Robert Warren to drop the case, the state of Wisconsin appealed this decision to the U.S. Supreme Court. Although his critics suggested otherwise, Warren was not bent on punishing the New Glarus Amish. He simply feared that accommodating them might open the floodgates to a torrent of similar claims from members of other religious or secular groups. If that happened, he worried, the state's ability to regulate education — and thus ensure that all children received adequate schooling — might be swept away.

The U.S. Supreme Court's opinion in *Wisconsin v. Yoder* left Warren bitterly disappointed. Citing the protections of religious liberty conferred by the First and Fourteenth Amendments, the justices affirmed the lower court's ruling in favor of Miller, Yoder, and Yutzy. The application of the compulsory attendance law to the New Glarus Amish was unconstitutional, Chief Justice Warren Burger wrote in the Court's majority opinion, in part because the record of the case amply demonstrated that its impact on their religious liberty was "not only severe, but inescapable, for the Wisconsin law affirmatively compels them, under threat of criminal sanction, to perform acts undeniably at odds with fundamental tenets of their religious beliefs."

Many critics have insisted that the U.S. Supreme Court botched *Yoder*. A legion of scholarly observers has argued that the justices plainly flouted the First Amendment's establishment clause by conferring special judicial protections on members of a single religious faith. Others have concluded that the high court, by focusing its attention on shielding the religious liberty of Amish parents, neglected the interests of those most affected by the outcome of the case—Amish children. And some commentators have faulted the justices for failing to recognize the importance of the state's long-standing interest in furnishing and regulating education.

But more than a few observers have lauded Chief Justice Burger's opinion in *Wisconsin v. Yoder* as a signal moment for religious liberty. One Wisconsin newspaper hailed the decision as "a victory for religious freedom and proof that the Bill of Rights is indeed a living, vital document," and the *Washington Post* praised it for promoting diversity and "underlining the country's commitment to the First Amendment." Legal scholars have rendered similar judgments. One applauded the Court's ruling in the Wisconsin case as "a shining symbol of religious tolerance." Another, writing in the late 1990s to commemorate the opinion's twenty-fifth anniversary, called it "perhaps the wisest of [the Supreme Court's] modern religion clause opinions."

As is suggested by these conflicting critical assessments, the legal issues raised by *Yoder* were far from clear-cut. Indeed, they were so tangled that they continue to spark spirited debates among legal scholars. The academics involved in these exchanges remain intrigued by such matters as the coherence of the opinion's reasoning, its consonance with previous Supreme Court decisions, and its influence on how the courts have treated subsequent religious liberty and parental rights claims. It is perhaps a testament to *Yoder*'s complexity that these debates have continued long after the opinion lost much of its vitality as judicial precedent. (After chipping away at it for several years, the Supreme Court essentially demolished *Yoder*'s religious liberty holding in its controversial opinion in *Oregon v. Smith* [1990].)

The facts of the case have attracted far less scrutiny. Typical scholarly accounts of *Yoder* have provided only brief and largely perfunctory summaries of the case's origins before moving on to the presumably more significant matter of assessing its place in the pantheon of American constitutional law. This is unfortunate, for the facts of *Yoder* are illuminating in their own right. A full exploration of the backgrounds, motivations, and strategies of the people who shaped the case can provide a revealing perspective on how a relatively small and obscure dispute can develop into a conflict of national importance. It also can furnish an extraordinary glimpse of how the lives of litigants in such cases can be changed in unexpected ways by their decision to pursue the abstract vindication of their rights in a legal decision.

Perhaps the most astonishing fact of the *Yoder* case is that it involved the Old Order Amish. It would be difficult to imagine a more unlikely group, religious or otherwise, triumphing in a landmark legal case and leaving an indelible mark on constitutional law. The Amish live in rural communities and go to remarkable lengths to distance themselves from the trappings of modernity. They dress in distinctively plain clothes, drive horse-drawn buggies rather than automobiles, and agonize over the use of telephones. What's more, the Amish generally avoid relying on the courts to resolve disputes. "Going to law" is anathema to them.

Yoder made its way through the courts only because the Amish warily permitted a group of advocates from outside their faith — men with whom they had only a fleeting connection — to pursue the case on their behalf. Early on, the New Glarus Amish relinquished control over the case to the National Committee for Amish Religious Freedom (NCARF), a coalition of clergy, attorneys, and scholars led by William Lindholm, a Lutheran pastor from Michigan. This outside organization, not the Amish themselves, funded and directed their entire legal defense. It seems doubtful that the case would have made it to trial, much less reached the U.S. Supreme Court, without the indefatigable efforts of attorney William Ball and his colleagues in the NCARF. Their intellectual and fiscal resources propelled the case to the highest court in the land.

The curious alliance between the New Glarus Amish and their champions cast a long shadow over the *Yoder* case. Critics questioned the motives of the NCARF, pointing out that some of its members, including Ball, were involved in contemporaneous efforts to secure public funding for private and parochial schools. One journal went so far as to accuse Ball and his NCARF colleagues of "using the Amish" to develop judicial precedent that would bolster the stature of nonpublic education and augment efforts to secure public funding for it. Critics of Ball's motives also pointed out that he and other conservatives frequently had attacked statutes mandating school attendance as mechanisms for foisting the doctrines of secular humanism on unsuspecting Christian schoolchildren. Ball's well-known positions on such issues fed suspicions that the Amish had been manipulated into allowing *Yoder* to become a stalking-horse for men pursuing a conservative political agenda.

If the relationship between the New Glarus Amish and the NCARF merits examination, so does the impact of *Yoder* on the people whose rights ostensibly were at issue in the case. What happened in New Glarus in the aftermath of the school attendance dispute confounded the expectations of just about everyone involved in it. William Ball and other defenders of the Amish often claimed that nothing less than the survival of the New Glarus settlement was at stake in *Wisconsin v. Yoder.* They repeatedly argued that the New Glarus Amish would flee their community if the courts ruled against them and thus burdened their religious practice. As it happened, almost all the Amish did leave New Glarus—but after the U.S. Supreme Court ruled *in favor* of their faith. What made the wholesale exodus of the New Glarus Amish even more remarkable was that it appeared to be linked to their involvement in the *Yoder* case. Far from preserving their community, the litigation sparked discord that contributed to its disintegration.

This book endeavors to tell the full story of *Wisconsin v. Yoder.* It does so in part by examining the abstract legal questions raised by the case: How broad are the protections of religious liberty afforded by the First Amendment? Does the state have a valid interest in compelling school attendance? Where do the rights of parents end and those of children begin? The book also examines the backgrounds and beliefs of the people who brought these issues before the courts, most notably the Old Order Amish defendants and the attorney who represented them. If nothing else, this examination demonstrates that *Yoder* was the product of an awkward and probably ill-conceived alliance. The case wedded a meek people who treasured isolation and spurned the political realm with zealous advocates devoted to shaping public policy. Given the peculiarity of that union, it is not surprising that the *Yoder* case left behind an ambiguous practical and jurisprudential legacy.

CHAPTER I

Building a Community in New Glarus

Early in 1964, Old Order Amish families began taking over modest farms in the countryside surrounding New Glarus, Wisconsin, a village located about twenty-five miles south of Madison, the state capital. Although some of the Amish intended to raise hogs on their new properties, a few were willing to try their hands at dairy production, a mainstay of the state's agricultural economy. Harry Miller was typical of the latter group of Amish settlers. Miller had raised beef cattle in Iowa, but before moving to Wisconsin he had sold those animals and purchased dairy cattle. Miller had high hopes for his new herd, but he worried that the weather might limit his ability to grow crops such as corn and oats. (He knew that the previous growing season had been mediocre in southern Wisconsin; rainfall totals had been below average, and farm production had suffered.)

The new arrivals — who wore simple, plain clothing and clattered through the town's icy streets in horse-drawn buggies — hailed from the northeastern Iowa community of Hazleton. When asked what had drawn the Amish across the Wisconsin border, a local real estate agent pointed to the reasonable price of land in the area. The first farms bought by the Amish sold for roughly one hundred dollars an acre, making them a bit more affordable than comparable land being offered for sale in Iowa at the time. Other observers speculated that the Amish, whose faith had been born in Switzerland during the Reformation, probably felt comfortable moving to an area that had been settled by Swiss immigrants in the 1840s and still billed itself as "America's Little Switzerland."

Everyone seemed to agree that what attracted the Old Order Amish to New Glarus was probably not as powerful as what had driven them away from Iowa. Throughout the early and mid-1960s, Amish families in the Hazleton area were embroiled in a protracted and bitter dispute with state and local authorities. At issue were efforts by school officials to force unwilling Amish youngsters to abandon the one-room schools operated by their faith and to attend local public schools. The imbroglio in Hazleton would garner headlines throughout the country in the fall of 1966, when authorities attempted an ill-advised roundup of Amish youngsters. (Nearly all the news stories on this disastrous maneuver were accompanied by a dramatic photograph of the children galloping into a cornfield to avoid being apprehended.) As the 1960s wore on and the strife in Hazleton worsened, a steady stream of beleaguered Old Order Amish families sold their farms and moved to southern Wisconsin. There they hoped to find fertile soil, moderate weather, and an environment where they could raise their children without excessive interference by the state.

With few regrets about escaping the increasingly tense situation in Hazleton, a group of Amish settlers wrapped up their affairs in Iowa and moved to their new farms in Green County, Wisconsin, during the first weeks of 1964. There were a few rocky moments for the newcomers: one recently settled Amishman groused that people sometimes drove past his farm and gawked at members of his family "as if we were freaks." But such incidents seemed to be the exception rather than the rule. Recognizing that the Amish traveled by horse and buggy, not automobile, local authorities reinstalled hitching posts at the municipal parking lot behind the village firehouse. The village president proudly called this a "gesture of goodwill toward the new arrivals."

Recalling the arrival of the Amish in New Glarus, one longtime resident maintained that some members of the close-knit community were wary of the newcomers. As he remembered it, a few villagers were particularly concerned about the legendary insularity of the Amish. Some village residents, supposing that the Amish were completely self-sufficient, believed that they simply would not patronize local businesses and thus would harm the local economy. These fears — which were not uncommon in communities near Amish settlements — proved to be largely groundless; even the resourceful Amish had to venture beyond the confines of their community to buy items such as hardware and farm implements. "As it ended up," the resident recalled, "they became very good customers of many local stores."

In fact, the arrival of the Amish appeared to boost one crucial aspect of the New Glarus economy: tourism. Acceptance of the Amish was easier when it became clear that their presence made the tiny village a more attractive destination for visitors from Chicago, Milwaukee, and Madison. The newcomers "were much more favorably regarded after tourists began coming to New Glarus to see the Amish," one resident asserted. "They were a very big tourist draw. On any given day, a tourist could come to New Glarus and walk the streets and see numerous buggies coming into or leaving town."

The Amish also contributed to the local economy by selling goods. Trumpeting his wife's skill in the kitchen, a modest sign near William Hershberger's farm announced "Home Baked Amish Bread—Next Farm." Elizabeth Hershberger's modest career as a baker had begun in Iowa, where her cookies had won a blue ribbon at a local fair. Spurred by that success, she continued to bake after the family moved to New Glarus in 1964. In time, she was regularly producing a variety of baked goods for sale, including doughnuts, pies, dinner rolls, and several varieties of bread. A steady demand for her products kept her busy. "Sometimes I bake every day," she explained to one visitor. "When sales slow up a little, then I cut down so I don't have too much in stock." Although regular customers provided much of the bakery's business, she made numerous sales when tour buses occasionally stopped at the farm.

The Hershbergers' unassuming bakery became the first in a series of battlegrounds between the New Glarus Amish and the state of Wisconsin. After visiting it on four separate occasions, an agriculture department inspector ordered that the business be closed because it was operated out of rooms not devoted solely to baking. A disappointed Elizabeth Hershberger initially prepared to close the bakery. "The Bible says we have to be subject to our magistrates," she explained. But when news of the state's action spread, she received so much encouragement to defy the inspector's order that she decided to keep baking. Her only compromise was to remove the outdoor sign advertising the bakery. After the squabble generated a series of articles in local newspapers (all of them sympathetic to the Amish), the state eventually relented, and the Hershbergers received a license to keep the bakery open. The license cost fifteen dollars per year.

Although it seemed relatively minor at the time, the dispute over the Hershbergers' bakery was not a good omen for anyone who hoped that turmoil would not follow the Amish from Hazleton to New Glarus.

The licensing quarrel demonstrated that Wisconsin authorities were not eager to bend generally applicable laws for the Amish. It also showed just how stubbornly the Amish would resist conforming to measures that appeared to jeopardize their simple way of life.

The distinctive clothing worn by the Old Order Amish immediately set them apart from their neighbors in New Glarus. Described by one scholar as "the foremost tag of Amish identity," wide-brimmed hats were worn by men and boys whenever they ventured outdoors. Throughout the year, the Amishmen in New Glarus dressed in plain suits consisting of trousers (held up by suspenders, not belts), dress shirts, and coats. They shaved until marriage, then grew beards — but not mustaches — afterward. (Because of mustaches' historical association with soldiering, the pacifist Amish frowned on them.) The women and girls dressed extraordinarily plainly as well, outfitting themselves in simple dresses and head coverings. Like all Amish garments, the head coverings were not merely ornaments, for they signified the wearers' "subjection to God and to man." Women tucked their uncut, braided hair beneath these caps.

In an era when fashions were becoming more and more outlandish, the unadorned clothing worn by the Amish stood out in New Glarus. What many villagers failed to understand was that dress served a crucial symbolic function in the Amish community. "The garb not only admits the individual to full fellowship," anthropologist John Hostetler, a leading scholarly authority on the Amish, wrote, "but also clarifies his role and status within his society." Varying sizes of hat brims and crowns, for instance, signaled an Amishman's place within the congregation, as well as his particular community's degree of ideological strictness. (Narrower brims indicated more progressive congregations.) The Amish themselves seemed perfectly content to wear austere clothing. "Sinful man continually designs fashions that are not pleasing to God," one member of the faith explained. "God designs clothes to cover the body, not display it."

The religion brought by the Old Order Amish to New Glarus in the mid-1960s had not changed a great deal since its birth some three centuries earlier during the Reformation. Among the Protestant faiths to arise from that tumultuous period was Anabaptism, practiced by pious dissidents who made a particularly radical break with the Catholic hegemony that had long dominated political and religious life in Europe. Adhering to what has been termed "a primitive, early type of Christianity," they rejected infant baptism and disavowed state control of the church. Disciplined and deeply committed to their faith, the Anabaptists attempted to live in accordance with the ethical principles outlined by Jesus in the Sermon on the Mount. In doing so, they espoused nonresistance and "renounced oaths, reveling and drunkenness, the use of the sword whether in war or civil government, economic rewards, and personal adornment," according to Hostetler. The faith proved to be especially popular in and around Zurich, where its adherents were known as Swiss Brethren.

The Anabaptists who lived and worshipped in Switzerland, Germany, and the Netherlands paid a heavy price for their dramatic repudiation of religious orthodoxy. They endured relentless and brutal persecution during the sixteenth century. Adherents to the faith were routinely tortured, imprisoned, and murdered for their purported heresies; some were sold into bondage and forced to toil in slave galleys. In many cases, local governments and Catholic and Protestant religious leaders organized their persecution, a few even going so far as to bankroll "Anabaptist hunters" to suppress their activities.

The persecution suffered by these early martyrs has not been forgotten by the modern-day Amish. "We plain people often refer to our ancestors, the Anabaptists," one Amishman recalled in the late 1980s. "Willingly, they offered up their lives and accepted death. Hardly a sermon is preached in our churches today without some mention being made of our forebears and what they suffered." Copies of the *Martyrs Mirror*, an immense and sometimes gruesome volume chronicling the abuse of the Anabaptists, could be found in many Amish homes in New Glarus. Accounts of their suffering also appeared in the *Ausbund*, an Amish hymnal. As one member of the faith noted, the purpose of such remembrances was to remind the Amish not to "shrink from hardships, from self-denial, from sacrifice, from a life of discipline and restraint."

In 1632, a group of Mennonites—so named because they followed Menno Simons, a former priest who had embraced Anabaptism—in the Dutch city of Dordrecht adopted a "confession of faith" outlining their central beliefs. Divided into eighteen articles and written in relatively simple, direct language, the "Dordrecht Confession" touched on a number of interrelated issues, including baptism, marriage, and, perhaps most important, the maintenance of discipline within the church. According to the confession, those who abandoned the church's teachings were to be excommunicated and shunned. Church members were not to have any contact with these apostates; they could not even be welcomed to the dinner table. Shunning was intended to be rehabilitative, not punitive, in that it was meant "to bring [those who were banned] to a knowledge of their sins and to repentance." It was hoped that the ordeal of shunning would not ruin apostates but rather simply convince them "of the error of [their] ways." In time, they could be welcomed back into the fold of the church, but only after they had acknowledged their mistakes and fully repented. The church, by ridding itself of "leaven" and thus maintaining its ideological purity, would benefit from shunning as well.

Late in the seventeenth century, conflicts among Swiss Anabaptists erupted in part over the banning and shunning of excommunicated members of the faith, a practice known as *Meidung*. At the heart of the dispute over shunning was the minister Jakob Ammann, a charismatic elder who widely and zealously advocated shunning as a means of enforcing church discipline. Expelling and then shunning those who failed to live up to their commitment to the church, Ammann believed, would keep the faith unblemished. Nothing if not confrontational, Ammann visited Switzerland and neighboring Alsace to investigate the practices of individual Mennonite congregations and to press ministers for their views on *Meidung*. Thanks to his equivocal position on shunning, Hans Reist, another Anabaptist preacher, became a focal point of Ammann's ire, and the two men traded bitter charges of apostasy and malfeasance. Ammann and Reist failed to reconcile, and Ammann's group splintered off. They were known as the Amish.

Although *Meidung* was the focal point of the emergence of the Amish, Ammann's reforms — all of them intended to keep the faith as cohesive and ideologically pure as possible — went far beyond his advocacy of shunning. In addition to proscribing attendance at state-sponsored churches, he championed changes in Anabaptist methods of worship. For instance, most members of the faith took communion only once a year, but Ammann contended that they should do so twice yearly, and he believed that these services should be complemented by the ordinance of foot-washing. Ammann also had strong feelings about personal adornments. Clothes were to be fastened with hooks and not buttons; beards were to be untrimmed; and hats, dresses, stockings, and other garments were to be uniformly plain.

Persecution and a shortage of land made it difficult for the Amish to establish large, unified settlements in Europe. The New World offered fewer obstacles, and in time it became an attractive destination for members of the faith. Drawn by abundant land and the promise of religious freedom, the Amish began migrating early in the eighteenth century. A steady exodus of Ammann's disciples from Europe commenced when two families arrived in Berks County, Pennsylvania, in the 1730s. Hoping to escape oppression, approximately one hundred more Amish families followed during the rest of the eighteenth century. In time, thriving congregations began to develop in several Pennsylvania counties.

They were primarily an agrarian people. A few early Amish settlers in Pennsylvania worked as millers and tanners, but most gravitated to the simplicity and relative isolation of farm life, harvesting wheat, apples, and other crops. Steering clear of burgeoning cities such as Philadelphia and Baltimore and settling in rural areas allowed the Amish to distance themselves from the innumerable perils of what they called "worldliness." For members of the faith, the call for separation from the corruption of the world at large came most clearly from Romans 12:1–2, which advises, "Be not conformed to this world, but be ye transformed by the renewing of your mind that ye may prove what is that good and acceptable and perfect will of God." No single admonition from the Scriptures was more central to the lives of the Amish who fled Europe for the New World in the eighteenth century, and it would remain a basic tenet of their faith for the remainder of the millennium. "The principle of separation," Hostetler wrote, "conditions and controls the Amishman's contact with the outside world; it colors his entire view of reality and being." Simplicity and gentleness were crucial as well.

Over time, individual Amish church districts developed their own rules for living, known as *Ordnung*. These unwritten strictures varied somewhat from settlement to settlement. But nearly all the Amish who settled in the New World shared a well-defined set of core beliefs, with an unwavering commitment to separation from the world being among the most important. They held true to the Anabaptist assertion that only through voluntary baptism in adulthood could a person acknowledge fidelity to the church. They would not swear oaths, nor would they hold public offices. Furthermore, if state authorities persecuted them for espousing such beliefs, the Amish would not resist.

Approximately three thousand Amish emigrated from Europe to America between 1817 and 1860. Although some of these new arrivals poured into established settlements in Pennsylvania, most ventured into the frontier and set up Amish communities in Missouri, Ohio, Indiana, and New York, where land often was cheaper and more available. Growth came with a price. Some of the newcomers who arrived in the mid-nineteenth century were more liberal than their predecessors, and they often seemed less willing to distance themselves from the hazards of worldliness. Breaking with tradition, a few progressive Amish communities erected meeting houses and began to conduct Sunday school programs; others modified the ceremony of adult baptism. Such innovations appalled conservative members of the faith, who viewed the changes as not merely breaks with tradition but also serious challenges to church discipline. Disagreements over baptism procedures and a range of other issues — everything from adornment in clothing and the embellishment of household furnishings to the use of lightning rods — generated friction between traditionalists and progressives in several Amish communities, and by 1862, "the Amish church was in considerable confusion," according to one account. Many larger settlements were rent by factionalism.

Ongoing disputes between traditionalist and progressive Amish resulted in what has come to be known as the "Great Schism." Over time, those who resisted change became known as "Old Order Amish," and those who were open to innovation were called "Amish Mennonites." (Many eventually became full-fledged Mennonites.) As the nineteenth century ended, about a third of the Amish in the United States — roughly five thousand people — lived in Old Order Amish communities. Having largely turned their backs on the modern world, these conservative Amish continued to found new settlements, including a number in the Midwest. Railroad companies, hoping to foster population growth in remote areas serviced by rail lines, sometimes provided an impetus for such midwestern Amish settlements by furnishing free transportation to fledgling communities.

Everywhere they settled, the Old Order Amish clung to their traditions. They continued to work the land carefully, and their clothing remained simple. Men sported long beards, wore broad-brimmed hats, and fastened their garments with hooks rather than buttons; women wore "prayer coverings" on their heads and donned plain dresses. On the farm and in the home, the Amish did their best to live without the technological advances that were transforming American life. Forsaking electricity, tractors (for field work), and automobiles, they maintained essentially preindustrial communities. "We are not conformed to this world," one Amish minister explained. "That includes our dress, but it surely includes our way of making a living. We can believe it also includes our way of traveling on the road, and our way of working in our fields."

Like most of their coreligionists, the Amish who flocked to New Glarus in the 1960s worked the land. Farming was the primary occupation of the adult men who came to the settlement from Iowa and other states (including Indiana and Ohio) in the early and mid-1960s. They toiled long hours in the fields "not . . . merely for economic reasons," Hostetler noted, but also because "the cultivation of the soil [was] a moral directive" within their church. It was arduous work, and men from outside the faith usually did not last long as hired help. Typically, the Amish farmers awoke well before dawn — sometimes as early as 4 A.M. — to milk their cows and perform other chores. The milking had to be done early to meet the schedule of the local milk truck, which picked up containers from most farms well before breakfast. After stopping for that meal, farmers usually headed out to their fields. Weather permitting, they did everything from plowing and planting seed to harvesting crops and haying. Those who owned livestock tended to their animals as well. Eating an early supper (often between 4 and 5 P.M.) allowed the men to perform chores around their homes and then return to the fields, where they labored until darkness fell. Exhausted, the settlement's farmers usually drifted off to sleep by 9 P.M.

For the most part, the early Amish settlers in New Glarus did their farming and dairying without relying too heavily on labor-saving technology. According to University of Wisconsin professor Harvey Jacobs and his colleague Ellen Bassett, men and women such as those who formed the Amish colony in New Glarus were "very selective in adopting new technologies — weighing the probable impact of new technological developments against the norms and beliefs of their community." Even the most progressive early settlers did not want to succumb to worldliness by equipping themselves with modern farm implements; doing so, they feared, was sure to jeopardize their separation from modern society. Amishmen in New Glarus did not utilize tractors for field work, nor did they use milking machines to expedite their dairy operations. Many, however, later came to use portable electric generators and bulk milk tanks operated by diesel engines. "Because of our religious beliefs of using the farming methods of our forefathers, we do not use tractors," Amishman Harry Miller explained during the early months of the New Glarus settlement. "But we use power units for certain things."

The religious beliefs of the Amish in New Glarus led them to avoid operating many modern technological devices themselves (automobiles being the most obvious example). They had few qualms, however, about accepting aid from neighbors whose religious faiths did not proscribe such activities. Fred Gingerich, for instance, planned to install a half-ton feed grinder on his farm with an old-fashioned block and tackle. His non-Amish (or "English") neighbor Paul Klassy saved him from this back-breaking chore by offering to do it with his forklift. Klassy was happy to help. The Amish were "about the finest people I've ever known," he explained. "They are real friendly neighbors and really know the farming business."

By the end of 1965, there were more than sixty members of the Amish faith working near New Glarus and the neighboring village of Belleville. (That number would approach one hundred by the end of the decade.) One of the more notable arrivals from Hazleton, Iowa, was Adin Yutzy, who had been among those repeatedly fined during the schooling controversy there. By the fall of 1965, Yutzy had accumulated more than five hundred dollars in fines and court costs for failing to enroll his children in an accredited school. With a resolution to the schooling controversy nowhere in sight, in January 1966 he sold his property in Hazleton and auctioned off much of his personal belongings and farm equipment. The county sheriff observed the sale and took enough of the proceeds to cover Yutzy's penalties. At the auction, Yutzy told a newspaper reporter that he planned to avoid further trouble by moving east to New Glarus.

It seemed apparent that Yutzy left Iowa simply to escape conflict with school authorities, but he said that a desire to own land also played a big part in his decision to move. Although he had been a tenant farmer in Hazleton, he could afford to buy a farm in New Glarus, where land prices were lower. Yutzy's wife seemed confident that the family would have no trouble cooperating with authorities in its new community. "When we're in Rome," she said, "we try to do as the Romans do."

Not everyone in New Glarus was so confident that the Amish would get along with the rest of the community, particularly if the inscrutable newcomers failed to adhere to local laws and customs, as they had in Hazleton. When the Amish began arriving in New Glarus, the village president alluded to the turmoil in Iowa and stated his desire not to see it repeated in southern Wisconsin. The Hazleton controversy also was on the mind of school superintendent Ray Habeck. As Amish families began to make plans to move to New Glarus, he warned that they "must follow state law regardless of religion." Habeck later met with some of the Amish settlers and discussed school regulations with them. Afterward, he sounded somewhat more optimistic about the prospect of the Amish and local authorities finding common ground. "I do not foresee any points of controversy," he said. "We have agreed to try and cooperate fully." At first, it seemed that Habeck's efforts were going to pay off; there were few reports of any conflicts regarding the Amish and the public schools. According to one story that made the rounds in New Glarus, the chief problem with the schools experienced by the Amish was the size of the lockers — they were too small to hold the large hats worn by Amish boys.

Harry Miller contended that no one among the initial band of Amish settlers in New Glarus was looking to duplicate the strife that had driven them from Hazleton. "We plan to cooperate to the fullest extent that our religion allows," he said, "and will try to be good neighbors." Miller claimed that the Amish families planned to do nothing more disruptive than settle into their farms, work their new land, and practice the rituals that bound them so closely to their faith.

Amish families in New Glarus took turns hosting their faith's biweekly worship services, which lasted several hours and usually were followed by a modest common meal and a lengthy period of socializing. Willie Plank had the honor of welcoming worshippers into his home one Sunday in June 1965. To get ready for the event, Plank and his family cleaned their home from top to bottom and rearranged the furniture to create more room for their guests. When the appointed day arrived, the service drew members of the nearby Amish community as well as visitors from Indiana and Ohio, making for "a good attendance," according to one Amishman. Supper followed, and "singing was held later."

The worship services hosted by members of the Amish community in New Glarus usually began with several hymns, including the *Loblied*, or "Hymn of Praise," which always came second. One could judge the relative conservatism of an Amish church by the time it took to sing this hymn — the lengthier the song, the more conservative the Amish singing it. That the Amish in New Glarus were "on the conservative side," as one of them put it, was evidenced by the fact that their version of the *Loblied* sometimes lasted close to twenty minutes. There followed sermons, Scripture readings, and prayers, all rendered in a mixture of English, German, and a dialect known as Pennsylvania Dutch. A benediction and announcements — which usually included a reminder of where the next service would be held — rounded out the service.

Members of the faith took communion in the fall and spring of each year. The New Glarus Amish prepared carefully for these important ceremonies. Two weeks before the scheduled date of a communion, they readied themselves by participating in a preparatory service. At this meeting, ministers reviewed the community's *Ordnung* and pointed out practices deemed too worldly for members of the church. "Each member is asked whether he is in agreement with the *Ordnung*, whether he is at peace with the brotherhood, and whether anything 'stands in the way' of entering the communion service," an observer of the faith wrote. "Faults are confessed and adjustments are made between members who have differences to settle." In addition to clearing the air in this manner, the Amish prepared for communion by fasting and meditating.

The communion services held by the Amish in New Glarus were lengthy, typically lasting from morning until late afternoon. These solemn occasions were open only to those who had been baptized, so children did not attend; they were left at home, sometimes in the care of unbaptized younger adults. Guest ministers and bishops often presided at the communion rites. They were called on to deliver what one observer termed "specially long sermons" that were known "to test the physical endurance and capacity of the ones preaching." When these marathon addresses ended, bread and wine were dispensed to those in attendance.

The communion services included another crucial ceremony — paired and reciprocal foot-washing. As one Amishman later explained, this practice held a profound spiritual meaning for the Amish, in part because it dramatically reflected "Jesus' revolutionary concept of humility," one of the main underpinnings of their faith. This part of the ceremony began with a minister reading from John 13, which describes the washing of the disciples' feet. Equipped with buckets of water and towels, the assembled men paired with the person sitting nearest them for the washing. When the pairs finished, they kissed and exchanged blessings. Women performed this same cleansing ritual, but in a separate room.

The ordained men who directed such ceremonies stood as the leaders of the Amish community in New Glarus. Two ministers, one bishop, and one deacon gave the congregation what was called a "full bench." In a community suffused by religion, these were prestigious posts, but campaigning for them was unthinkable among men who treasured humility. The congregation picked ministers and deacons in a process termed "the lot." When it came time to select a new minister in the fall of 1965, the names of six widely esteemed men — Andy Plank, Harry Miller, Willis Miller, Abe Kramer, Levi Yoder, and Yost Hoschstetler — were put forward by members of the congregation. A slip of paper was placed among some songbooks, and each candidate selected a volume. Levi Yoder's songbook contained the paper, signaling that he had been selected by God to assume the role of minister. He was not paid for his duties. He was expected to take his cue from a passage in Corinthians in which the apostle Paul states, "When I preach the gospel, I may make the gospel of Christ without charge, that I abuse not my power in the gospel."

Ministers rarely needed to exhort the Amish to come to the aid of their coreligionists. Generous neighbors always stepped into the breach when an Amish family in New Glarus met misfortune. Early in 1968, for instance, a fire gutted Willis Miller's barn. Miller lost not only the structure but also the approximately six thousand bales of hay stored in it. The Amish community rallied to Miller's aid. A few weeks after the conflagration, several Amish families participated in what one neighbor described as "log-cutting frolics" to provide Miller with the lumber needed to rebuild the barn. When the actual rebuilding took place in early March, Miller and his neighbors were aided by three dozen Amish who had chartered a bus from Arthur, Illinois, where Miller had lived before moving to Wisconsin. Because they lived more than 250 miles from New Glarus, Miller's erstwhile neighbors left their homes at 1 A.M. to get to the barn raising on time.

CHAPTER 2

Amish Schooling and the Seeds of Conflict in New Glarus

When he lived in Plain City, Ohio, Jonas Yoder earned his living by raising ducks. The animals produced mountains of excrement, and local authorities became convinced that their waste was polluting a neighboring creek. Yoder was scrupulous about tending to his birds, and an investigation cleared him of wrongdoing; it turned out that the real culprit was probably a nearby chemical plant. In time, Yoder came to believe that the industrial facility had done more than simply befoul the waterway. After one of his daughters died at age five of bone cancer, he suspected that her illness had been caused by the pollution spewing from the chemical plant.

In the wake of that tragedy, Yoder moved to New Glarus, as did several of his coreligionists from Plain City, including Wallace Miller. Yoder plunged into his farmwork almost as soon as he arrived in Wisconsin early in 1966. Many local Amish had taken up dairying, but Yoder chose to start raising hogs in an old dairy barn on his property. According to a neighbor, he established a "contract-type setup" with a local processing company: it supplied the hogs, feed, and other equipment, and Yoder furnished the labor. Like most members of his faith, he was a diligent worker, toiling long hours to feed his animals, clean up after them, and ready them for slaughter.

A non-Amish neighbor who respected Yoder's work ethic later said that he could be lighthearted as well. "Jonas truly loved life and all it held," Kim Tschudy recalled. "He had a good sense of humor and an easy laugh." Yoder's children took after their father, and they got along well with youngsters of all faiths, including Tschudy's son. A spirit of generosity complemented the family's affability. When the Yoders butchered a hog and made pork sausage, they always shared several delicious pieces with Tschudy and his family. They were similarly bighearted with the hard candy made by Yoder's wife every Christmas.

In the mid-1960s, a few dozen Amish children attended the public schools in New Glarus. In general, the Amish youngsters seemed to get along with their classmates and teachers. "They were like any other kids," recalled one instructor who taught Amish students in her physical education classes. "They weren't shunned, they weren't outcasts. . . . They were nice kids. It was fun having them in class." When Yoder's two daughters joined the Amish contingent in the public schools, he took the girls aside and instructed them not to participate in physical education classes.

Yoder articulated several serious objections to his daughters' participation in gym classes. In keeping with their faith's traditions, Amish girls dressed modestly, sporting loose-fitting, ankle-length dresses. To participate in physical education classes, however, they would have to wear the short and somewhat tight uniforms mandated by their school. Yoder was uncomfortable with his daughters wearing such immodest clothing; he felt that it was inappropriately modern and worldly. For similar reasons, he also objected to the requirement that his daughters change and shower with other girls following physical education classes.

At their father's urging, the Yoder girls stopped attending gym classes at their public school. Soon after, a group of New Glarus Amishmen submitted a letter to the local school board spelling out the Yoder family's reasons for objecting to the physical education regulations. (Although it seems that Yoder's daughters were the only Amish youngsters to withdraw from gym classes, their action appeared to have broad support among the Amish community.) The letter noted that the Amish, in keeping with their interpretation of the Scriptures, did not "indulge in the world's methods of pleasure seeking, amusements, and entertainments." The letter went on to directly address the matter of girls' physical education uniforms, changing, and showering:

> The Scriptural sense of modesty includes orderliness and consistency. Modest apparel expresses a sense of propriety and indicates the choice of a virtuous mind. To avoid the change of suits of apparel which are so common in the world today gives credence to uniformity in the church. Church regulations are a solution to the problem of worldliness in attire. Christian propriety calls for one

to be modestly dressed when in public and causes one to shun the unrestrained boldness manifest in present world practices. Recognizing these Biblical ideals, we believe that the accepted standards of the church are in accordance with Scriptural requirements.

These injunctions were detailed in Deuteronomy 22:5, which mandates that "the woman shall not wear that which pertaineth to a man," and Romans 12:1–2, perhaps the single most meaningful passage in the Bible for the Amish. Citing it, the local Amishmen reminded the school board that under absolutely no circumstances would they or their children be "conformed to this world."

Throughout 1966, the Yoders and their supporters in the Amish community clashed with local school authorities over the gym uniform issue. At first, the board's position seemed firm: it issued an ultimatum warning Yoder that his girls would have to wear standard gym uniforms and shower if they wanted to attend public school in New Glarus. In time, however, negative publicity forced board members to grudgingly forge a compromise whereby Amish children would be permitted to wear more modest, homemade gym uniforms.

Although it momentarily calmed the roiling waters in New Glarus, the compromise reached by school authorities and Amish leaders did not put an end to debates over the physical education requirements in Wisconsin's public schools. As the Wisconsin Legislative Council later reported, the publicity surrounding the New Glarus conflict "aroused the interest of many people," including legislators in nearby Madison. Responding to the controversy sparked by Jonas Yoder, state representatives Frederick Kessler and Kenneth Merkel introduced legislation early in 1967 to exempt children from gym classes if they could demonstrate that participation "conflicts with their religious practices." Merkel warned that if lawmakers failed to pass such a measure, they would "move the clock backwards and create a situation where the Amish may be forced to leave this state. This would be a black mark on the record of a great state."

School officials in New Glarus were quick to protest Merkel's efforts. Kenneth Glewen, who had replaced Ray Habeck as school superintendent, voiced the fears of many state authorities who opposed bending school regulations to accommodate the Amish. Catering to them, Glewen warned, might set a precedent that could be invoked by members of other groups who disagreed with school regulations. Wisconsin's schools surely would be thrown into chaos if thousands of students and parents were able to follow the lead of the Amish and gain exemptions from the myriad rules that helped keep the schools running smoothly.

In a letter to Merkel, Glewen decried the measure designed to exempt the Amish from physical education requirements. He argued that it would "open the way to many other such bills which would make school administration difficult if not impossibly legal." Many insincere students would attempt to exploit the various bills' provisions, Glewen cautioned, and it "would be very impractical to check each case out" to establish whether the exemption claim was valid.

The New Glarus school board made a similar plea to Merkel. In a joint letter, the board's five members warned that carving out an exemption from the physical education requirements for the Amish would have the disastrous effect of encouraging members of countless other groups to seek similar accommodations. They claimed that "passage of this bill would result in serious harm to the operation and discipline of the New Glarus School District, and to all public school systems in the state. . . . We feel it would be a Pandora's box in furthering demands by any group seeking evasion from certain state approved curricula."

In their letters to Merkel, both Glewen and the school board asserted that local school administrators — not lawmakers in Madison — were in the best position to work out conflicts over the application of school regulations. Giving local authorities the latitude to resolve such issues on a case-by-case basis made far more sense, they argued, than enacting a sweeping law that might create more problems than it solved. Clearly piqued by Merkel's efforts on behalf of the Amish, Glewen urged the legislator to stop "maneuvering for a small minority" and allow problems to be "solved on a local level." The school board echoed his concerns, maintaining that the physical education exemption bill might be construed as a "veiled threat to the authority of local school districts."

Early in March 1967, the Amish themselves weighed in on Merkel's bill. Hoping to better understand why they had battled so vigorously over the physical education requirements, the assemblyman traveled to New Glarus and spoke with Reuben Hershberger and Levi Yoder.

Hershberger reviewed for Merkel the particulars of the dispute over gym uniforms and its eventual resolution. Merkel learned that the Amish had reluctantly agreed to compromise with the school board "because they had no choice," he later wrote. Hershberger was still uneasy about children of his faith having to comply with the regulations. "This would be a free country again," he told Merkel, "if we did not have to take that." In their conversation in New Glarus, as well as in a subsequent letter, Hershberger and Yoder informed the legislator that they and their fellow Amish supported his bill.

In November 1967, Merkel and Kessler amended their bill and offered changes reflecting the breadth and intensity of the Amish opposition to the physical education requirements. Their amendments acknowledged several specific objections voiced by the Amish parents who had battled the New Glarus school board. Recognizing the origins of the dispute in Green County, the amendment mandated that "when parents object to gym clothes prescribed, the school board shall exempt the pupil from attendance or permit wearing of clothes deemed suitable by the parents." They also provided an exemption for a student from "any physical education course which is co-educational when his parents so request." The last of the additions proposed by Merkel and Kessler held that "when parents object on religious grounds to common dressing rooms or common showers, the school board shall exempt the pupil from attendance or furnish separate dressing rooms and separate showers."

A far more sweeping measure considered by the state assembly in 1967 complemented the efforts of Merkel and Kessler. Intended to help minimize the kinds of conflicts that had arisen between the Amish and school authorities in communities such as New Glarus, Assembly Bill 358 provided that "Amish and Mennonite children shall be compelled to attend school only to 8th grade or 16 years of age." The Amish in Wisconsin and other states, fearing the worldly influences of public high schools, had long objected to formal schooling beyond eighth grade, and they strongly backed this proposed change in state law.

A group of more than a dozen residents of the Amish settlements in New Glarus and Blair, Wisconsin, appeared before the assembly's education committee and called for passage of the bill. Yost Hoschstetler reminded the committee that members of his faith "respect all laws" and thus would comply with state education regulations. He hoped, however, that Wisconsin law could be changed to accommodate Amish beliefs and practices. Speaking for Amish families throughout the state, Hoschstetler beseeched legislators to "give us a chance to bring up our children as they have been" raised for generations by allowing them to leave school after eighth grade. Amos Yoder, an Amishman from Blair, seconded Hoschstetler's comments, telling the committee, "We think an eighth grade education is adequate."

But not everyone favored Merkel's bill. Two men offered impassioned testimony against it, expressing the concerns shared by many school administrators, state authorities, and private citizens who opposed exempting the Amish from generally applicable school regulations. These opponents of accommodation worried that the strictures imposed on Amish children by their parents severely limited the youngsters' freedom to pursue careers or lifestyles of their own choosing. They feared that bending school regulations for the Amish effectively would permit the children's right to learn to be subsumed by their parents' religious fervor.

Fred Blum, a Madison physician, forcefully voiced these concerns in his testimony. Urging the legislature to reject Merkel's exemption bill, he asserted that many Amish youngsters hungered for more education but were held back by the rigid religious beliefs of their parents, who insisted that they limit their formal schooling. "The kids don't have a choice [to continue their schooling] themselves," he said. "The choice is being forced upon them." New Glarus resident Robert Schneider made much the same point. The Amish lifestyle "is forced on the children," he said, and the youngsters were given no choice but to abandon their budding intellectual interests. Both men claimed to have spoken with Amish youngsters who expressed disappointment over being forced by their parents to abandon school after completing the eighth grade.

Despite the dogged efforts of Merkel and other sympathetic lawmakers, the Wisconsin legislature failed in its 1967 session to take action on behalf of the Amish. Much to Merkel's dismay, both the compulsory education and the physical education bills were tabled.

Merkel's efforts on behalf of the Amish probably were doomed by his lack of stature in the legislature. While noting that the Republican lawmaker was well liked by his colleagues for his unfailing courtesy and good humor, one longtime capitol reporter described Merkel as "an oddity" who habitually championed hopeless causes. A member of the John Birch Society, Merkel occupied a "lonely role as the patient and dogged defender of conservative principles and purposes," the reporter noted. Indeed, Merkel railed against sex education in the public schools, urged the United States to withdraw from the United Nations, and praised Senator Joseph McCarthy as a "great man." More a gadfly than a deal maker, he was unable to generate sufficient support among his colleagues for the Amish bills.

The exemption bills also foundered because they failed to garner much support among educators or the public at large. School administrators like Kenneth Glewen predicted that relaxing regulations for the Amish might leave the schools open to accommodation claims from members of countless other groups. These professionals had little enthusiasm for measures that promised to increase their administrative burdens and lessen their control over students. Their concerns were complemented by broader fears regarding the potential impact of exemption laws on Amish children. To critics like Fred Blum and Robert Schneider, Merkel seemed willing to sacrifice the rights of Amish children in order to protect the religious liberty of their parents.

The failure of Merkel's efforts in the state legislature, along with the rancor of the dispute over gym uniforms, seemed to have a catalytic effect among the Amish in New Glarus. It helped convince them that the surest way to safeguard their children from the dangers of worldliness was to open schools of their own, institutions that would be operated in accordance with the strictures of their faith. Even before the gym uniform controversy had been fully resolved, members of the community formed a school board and announced plans to establish Amish schools in the New Glarus area.

The New Glarus Amish were reluctant to provide their children with extensive formal schooling. Amish parents generally understood that their children would benefit from some instruction in subjects such as arithmetic and reading; basic skills in those areas, they acknowledged, would prove useful as the children assumed greater responsibilities on farms and in their church communities. Schooling that went much beyond the elementary level, however, was perceived as a grave threat to the faith. Many Amish parents resisted sending their teenage children to school because they believed that the youngsters "should be under the supervision of their parents or of a community member, learning the skills necessary to succeed economically and socially within the boundaries of the Amish community," according to one account. The Amish believed that if their children attended public schools for too long, the youngsters would be inculcated with worldly values that might undermine their church. With individual communities establishing their own standards, Amish families did not adhere to a hard-and-fast age limit for schooling; many, however, took their children out of school as early as age fourteen.

A reliable overview of the Amish stance toward public education was furnished in 1950, when Amish leaders in Lancaster County, Pennsylvania, issued a summary of their faith's position on public school attendance. In a joint statement, the local bishops' council and education committee maintained that the Amish valued education. "We believe that our children should be properly trained and educated for manhood and womanhood," the Amish leaders stated. "We believe that they need to be trained in those elements of learning which are given in the elementary schools. Specifically, we believe that our children should be trained to read, to write and to cipher." More extensive schooling was unnecessary, if not downright harmful, and members of the Amish community were determined to resist it. The church leaders asserted that for Amish youngsters who were age fourteen and older, schooling in public institutions "has a tendency to cultivate sentiment which may lead to a drifting away from the church." The public schools bred "indolence" and harmed students' "spiritual and emotional welfare," often leading them to become "unduly entangled with things that are not edifying." The way to shield young members of the faith from such pernicious influences was to cut off their formal schooling after eighth grade.

As was true for most aspects of their lives, the Amish grounded their approach to schooling in the lessons of the Scriptures. When the Amish leaders in Lancaster County released their policy on public education in 1950, they were careful to note that their stance was "based upon our interpretation of the Bible which we believe to be the inspired word of God and which we believe to be the complete rule of our living." In citing the Bible to support their views on education, they referred to passages from Deuteronomy, Genesis, Ephesians, Romans, I Corinthians, and James.

The Amish leaders also pursued a more secular line of reasoning when they attempted to justify their position on education: they assailed Pennsylvania's compulsory school attendance law as unconstitutional. Any laws requiring Amish youngsters to attend school beyond eighth grade, they maintained, "are an interference with the religious rights and liberties which were promised to our forefathers when they came to America and which are granted to us by the Constitution of our State and our Nation."

To shield their children from the myriad dangers of public education, parents in numerous Amish communities throughout the country began establishing their own schools. "School building peaked in the late sixties," one observer of the faith wrote, "as the parochial school movement continued to spread among the Amish." In 1965, approximately 5,000 youngsters were being taught by 174 teachers in a total of 150 Amish schools across the country. Five years later, those numbers had skyrocketed. The number of Amish schools had more than doubled (to 303) by 1970, as had the number of teachers (to 375). The number of students in Amish schools had nearly doubled as well, reaching nearly 10,000. (This trend continued in the early and mid-1970s, although not quite as dramatically; by the middle of the decade, more than 12,000 Amish pupils attended about 400 schools nationally.)

In the summer of 1968, members of the newly formed Amish school board in New Glarus notified the local superintendent of schools of their intention to have a school up and running in time for the upcoming academic year. The Amish also contacted Archie Buchmiller of the Wisconsin Department of Public Instruction to determine whether they would have to adhere to any specific state guidelines in establishing their school and hiring teachers to staff it. Buchmiller undoubtedly pleased the Amish by informing them that, aside from stipulations relating to the length of the academic year, state regulation of private schools was minimal. There were no specific qualifications for teachers in such institutions, and school buildings merely had to comply with the state industrial commission code.

Encouraged by their contacts with Buchmiller, members of the

Amish school board issued a statement in August 1968 announcing that the Amish would be breaking away from the public school system "to provide a less modern form of education" for young members of their faith. For the convenience of students, the new Pleasant View Parochial School District, as it was called, would feature two schools. Classes would be conducted in Roman Miller's home in Exeter township, as well as in a new one-room building on property belonging to Willis Miller in Primrose township. The school district would start operating on September 15, according to the announcement, and would conduct a 180-day school year, as mandated by state law. Enrollment during the fledgling school district's first year of operations was expected to be approximately forty students. (As it turned out, twenty-three youngsters enrolled at the Primrose school, and another thirteen studied at Miller's home.)

The Amish erected an extraordinarily simple school in Primrose. The plain, one-story building featured a modest cloakroom but lacked both electricity and running water. Students who needed access to lavatory facilities had to walk outside and use one of two adjoining outhouses. Buchmiller noted that although the structure in Primrose was probably the only one-room school built in Wisconsin in the 1960s, it was in compliance with state building regulations. He stated that running water was not required (although a fresh supply had to be nearby) and that coal or wood stoves were adequate for heating. As long as "illumination is maintained at the desired level," he said, electric lights were not necessary.

To staff the new schools, the Amish looked both within and beyond their immediate church community. In August 1968, they advertised their need for a teacher in *The Budget*, a newspaper published in Sugar Creek, Ohio, and read in Amish settlements across the country. Those interested in the position were encouraged to contact Jonas Yoder by mail. Minnie Weaver, a young Amish woman from Ohio, eventually moved to Wisconsin and assumed teaching duties at the Primrose school. Weaver taught all eight grades there, providing instruction for more than six hours a day in subjects ranging from arithmetic and spelling to geography and social studies. Rachel Miller, one of Wallace Miller's children, taught the classes held at Roman Miller's home. She later said that she taught some of her courses in the Pennsylvania Dutch dialect "because the boys and girls don't understand High German."

After the schools were up and running, several Amish parents explained why they had decided to form the new school district. Not surprisingly, Jonas Yoder felt compelled to remove his girls from public school in part because he so adamantly opposed the physical education requirements enforced by the school district. "We have nothing against the gym classes themselves," he said, "but we don't like what our children would have to wear to the class." He added that the local public high school "just doesn't fit for us" because "eight grades in our own school is all we need." Speaking more broadly about his faith, he commented, "We don't want our children involved in worldly things. In the public schools they have physical education, science, television, things like that — temptations for a different world. I don't want to condemn anybody, but we want to hold what we've got. We want to hold our religion. That's all we're working for."

Other members of the Amish community offered similar justifications for establishing their own school district. Roman Miller maintained that the Amish hoped to use the schools to provide more intensive training in German, the language in which their worship services were conducted. Wallace Miller revealed that the Amish were unhappy with their children being exposed to the theory of evolution in public schools. "Basically, public schools are too modern for us," he said. "We like things a little bit more old-fashioned." Although they obviously were displeased with the operation of the local public schools, the Amish went out of their way to be gracious as they broke away and set up parochial schools. In their statement announcing the establishment of schools in Primrose and Exeter, members of the Amish school board expressed their "hope that formation of this new school district will cause no disruption of public school services."

The potential for discord between the Amish and local authorities lurked just beneath this apparently placid surface. The Primrose school, in keeping with Amish practice, offered classes through eighth grade, but the state compulsory attendance law required students to be enrolled until age sixteen, at which age most students would be in tenth grade. In a story on the establishment of the Amish schools, a local newspaper reported that "Yoder and the Millers did not seem too inclined to go along with" the measure mandating school attendance up to age sixteen. Wallace Miller, in fact, bristled at the idea of having to comply with the law. "We don't think there is anything in the Constitution about that," he said.

Superintendent Glewen spoke at length about the opening of the Amish schools in New Glarus. Most of his public comments were charitable and suggested that he understood and respected the motivations of the Amish. But even as he made diplomatic statements about the Amish and their decision to take their children out of the public schools, Glewen was calculating the impact that the defections would have on the public school system. Shortly after the Amish announced that they would form the Pleasant View Parochial School District, the superintendent reported that the resulting drop in enrollment would cost the local public schools about $18,000 in aid from the state. With education funding allocated on a per-pupil basis, fewer students meant less money. This was a matter of no small concern for Glewen. Though sympathetic to the Amish, he understood that the reduction in state aid caused by their exodus from the school system would have to be absorbed by the taxpayers of the school district. Property taxes, he knew, would have to be increased to make up for the shortfall.

Glewen clumsily attempted to preserve the state funding by proposing a deal to the Amish. Glewen suggested that they hold off beginning classes at the schools in Primrose and Exeter until after the third Friday in September, when public school enrollments were tallied. Glewen's plan was to have the three dozen Amish students attend public school just long enough to be counted for purposes of state aid. Though it might have seemed clever to Glewen, this ruse was totally unacceptable to the Amish; they viewed such chicanery as the worst kind of worldliness and refused to go along. "It would not have been right to sit in their schools," Reuben Hershberger later said, "just so they could collect the money." Jonas Yoder joked that Glewen advanced such an ill-conceived scheme because the school district "already had [the money] spent."

Glewen targeted the Amish after they rebuffed his offer. At a September 1968 school board meeting (it happened to be the same one at which the board announced that the school tax levy would be increased), the superintendent reported on his work as the district's truant officer. Confirming one of the worst-kept secrets in the community, Glewen said that he knew of at least seven Amish students who were under age sixteen but had failed to enroll in either the public or the Amish school districts. These were instances of truancy, the superintendent explained, because Wisconsin's compulsory attendance law mandated enrollment until students reached their sixteenth birthdays. As a result, he had contacted the district attorneys in Green and Dane Counties to see if prosecution might be warranted. (Although New Glarus was located in Green County, some members of the local Amish community lived just over the border in adjoining Dane County.) Glewen was well aware of Amish beliefs regarding education, but he claimed that his hands were tied. "As truant officer of this district," he said, "I must impose the same laws on all students."

Given the timing of his decision to investigate the Amish for truancy, there seems little doubt that Glewen took action at least in part to retaliate for their refusal to participate in his scheme to inflate the local public school census. But he also was influenced by legitimate concerns over maintaining discipline in the local schools. Glewen feared that the authority of school officials could be undermined if they permitted the Amish to flout the state's compulsory attendance law. Other children might interpret this leniency as a signal that it was permissible to disregard all kinds of school regulations.

Glewen also felt compelled to pursue the truancy charges because he worried over how Amish children might be affected if their schooling ended at age fourteen. Like most public school educators, the superintendent believed that, whatever their religious beliefs, all youngsters needed to receive at least a high school education to prepare them for the professional and social responsibilities of adulthood. Permitting Amish children to skip two critical years of high school, Glewen believed, would leave them woefully unprepared to face such challenges if they became disenchanted with their religious faith and chose to live outside its insular communities.

Suspecting that the Amish in the New Glarus area were not complying with Wisconsin's compulsory school attendance law, Glewen visited the Amish schools at Primrose and Exeter and checked their attendance rolls against the public school district's enrollment lists. This bit of detective work indicated that seven Amish youngsters had completed eighth grade in public school but were not enrolled in either of the Amish schools. On August 30, 1968, just after the Amish refused to allow their children to be counted in the public school census, Glewen dispatched warning letters to several fathers whose teenage children were apparently truant. Jonas Yoder, Eli Hershberger, Wallace Miller, and Fred Gingerich were among those receiving admonitions from the superintendent.

After discussing the applicability of the compulsory attendance law with Max Ashwill, an attorney with the Department of Public Instruction, Glewen sent a second round of warning letters on September 18. The superintendent stated that Ashwill had "informed me that no law is now in existence that permits youth from Amish parents to be excused from the Compulsory Attendance Laws. Therefore, this law must apply." After extensively quoting the relevant passages of the Wisconsin statute, Glewen indicated that the Amish fathers would be prosecuted if they failed to comply with the law. "If no action on this matter is taken by you," he wrote to Jonas Yoder, "I shall be forced to notify the District Attorney's office of this situation."

In addition to firing off letters to the Amish parents, Glewen met privately with several of them and, as he later put it, "indicated to them what my position was in regards to the truancy problem . . . and what action I would take." Glewen's visit to the farm owned by Adin Yutzy, the father of Vernon Yutzy, typified his interactions with the Amish parents. When the superintendent spoke with the youngster's mother and tried to determine his whereabouts, "she indicated that they were not sending their son to school, that he was at home," as he later said. Other parents implied that their children were "at home and working" rather than attending school. The Amish parents in question, Glewen said, "don't deny that their children are not in school."

Glewen discussed the truancy issue with several members of the Amish school board, including Wallace Miller, whose daughter Barbara was among those not attending school. Miller explained in detail why his daughter and the other six Amish youngsters in question were not enrolled in school. He offered forceful objections grounded in his understanding of both temporal and spiritual laws. Glewen later said that Miller, citing Amish disapproval of worldliness, had maintained "that he was right in not sending his child to school because it was against their belief." Moreover, Miller had suggested that "he felt that the First Amendment to the Constitution of the United States gave them this freedom to practice their religion, and in this case [he] felt that this was part of his religion that his child should not attend school beyond the eighth grade." Enforcing the compulsory school attendance law against the Amish would violate their constitutional rights, Miller told Glewen.

His patience exhausted, Glewen filed criminal complaints against three Amish fathers in Green County Court on October 23, 1968. In filing the complaints, Glewen asserted that Jonas Yoder, Wallace Miller, and Adin Yutzy had violated Section 118.15 of the Wisconsin Statutes, which outlined the state's compulsory school attendance law. The measure read in part:

> Unless the child has a legal excuse, any person having under his control a child between the ages of 7 and 16 years shall cause such child to attend school regularly, during the full period and hours, religious holidays excepted, that the public or private school in which such child should be enrolled is in session, to the end of the school term, quarter or semester of the school year in which he becomes 16 years of age.

Glewen claimed that the three fathers had violated the law because their children — Frieda Yoder, Barbara Miller, and Vernon Yutzy — were under age sixteen but "were not enrolled in either the parochial school or the public high school in our district," as he later put it.

The Amish fathers reacted calmly to Glewen's formal accusations. After he learned that he had been charged under its provisions, Jonas Yoder acknowledged that the state's compulsory school attendance law made sense — but not for Amish children. "I can see why the law came out like that," he said. "The city people need something for their children to do. We don't." Asked about the possibility that he, Wallace Miller, and Adin Yutzy would fight the charges in court, Yoder initially was noncommittal, telling a reporter, "We'll just see what happens." For his part, Miller reiterated their objections to the public schools, and he also touted the system that the Amish had established to educate their children and prepare them for adulthood. "We don't like modern forms of education, such as television watching, and some of these schools teach evolution," he said. "We feel that is strictly against Bible teaching." He went on to argue that the Amish system of education, which did not provide classroom training beyond eighth grade, was more than adequate. "After eighth grade," he explained, "the best education is at home with the parents on the farm."

Prompted by Glewen's complaint, Green County district attorney Louis Koenig filed formal charges against the three Amishmen in mid-November. The alleged offense was a misdemeanor, and it carried penalties ranging from a minimum of a five dollar fine to a maximum of a fifty dollar fine and three months in jail.

CHAPTER 3

Compulsory Schooling and the Parameters of State Power

The action taken by Green County authorities against the New Glarus Amish marked the beginning of another chapter in the tangled history of compulsory school attendance laws. In the late nineteenth and early twentieth centuries, such measures ignited controversy in several states. In Wisconsin, the enactment of a law mandating school attendance precipitated a fierce dispute over the role of public education in American society and the parameters of parental rights and state power. In the 1960s, social and religious conservatives revived these debates and challenged the state's right to compel public school attendance. In the New Glarus case, their interest in this issue would dovetail with ongoing efforts by the Amish to remain separate from the modern world and preserve control over the schooling of their children.

As historian David B. Tyack has observed, there were a number of justifications for the compulsory school attendance laws enacted throughout the United States in the nineteenth century. Much of the impetus for such measures sprang from the common belief that free public schooling could socialize diverse peoples — the nation's swelling ranks of immigrants in particular — and inculcate them with the virtues of American citizenship. Reformers such as Horace Mann coupled this rationale with a claim that, as Tyack put it, "schooling created economic benefits for the society as a whole through greater productivity and for individuals through greater earnings." For Mann, laws mandating school attendance thus served a dual purpose: they fostered civic responsibility and moral character, and they boosted worker productivity. Both industry and the body politic benefited when the state compelled universal education.

Massachusetts, where the venerable Mann served as education secretary, passed the nation's first compulsory school attendance statute. In 1852, legislators there prescribed a total of twelve weeks of school attendance for all youngsters between the ages of eight and fourteen. Although the law was riddled with loopholes, parents who failed to comply with the measure faced a hefty fine (twenty dollars). A smattering of states followed Massachusetts's example over the next twenty years: Vermont (1867), New Hampshire (1871), Michigan (1871), Washington (1871), and Connecticut (1872). By 1890, twenty-seven states had enacted statutes designed to mandate school attendance in some manner.

Few contemporary scholars have been impressed by the effectiveness of these early school attendance statutes. Tyack wrote that in many places "the laws were dead letters." Educators in some areas, he noted, were unaware of their existence or ambivalent about their enforcement. The statutes sometimes foundered because public opposition to them ran strong. B. G. Northrup, a state education official in Connecticut, noted that at least six main objections were voiced to the attendance statute enacted in his state. Among them were charges that the law increased the power of the state and interfered with the right of parents to direct the upbringing of their children. To Northrup, an advocate of the school attendance law, neither claim stood up to close scrutiny. "The child has rights which not even a parent may violate," he wrote of the latter charge. "He may not rob his child of the sacred right of a good education."

Nowhere were these debates more vociferous than in Wisconsin. Opponents such as state school superintendent Edward Searing maintained that statutes mandating school attendance were terribly impractical, in that the state lacked the means to rigorously enforce them. Moreover, any law requiring school attendance was "something essentially un-American," he said. Citing his own feelings as a father, Searing articulated one of the central objections voiced by opponents of compulsory attendance measures throughout the nineteenth and twentieth centuries: he claimed that the laws compromised his rights as a parent. "The mere consciousness of the existence of a law compelling the attendance of my children would be intolerable," he explained. "I want no statute laws telling me how to feed, dress, or to educate my children."

After years of dawdling, Wisconsin's legislature lurched into action in 1879 and passed a tepid compulsory attendance law. The measure required twelve weeks of school attendance for all children aged seven to fifteen. School attendance in the state rose slightly the following year, but the overall impact of the law was minimal because it lacked meaningful provisions for enforcement. The attendance law was ignored in many parts of the state, and calls for its amendment or outright repeal became common.

Others urged the state legislature to strengthen the law, chief among them state authorities charged with regulating child labor. Despite vehement opposition from business and agricultural interests, Wisconsin had passed its first law restricting child labor in 1877, just two years before the enactment of its feeble law mandating school attendance. It prohibited children under age twelve from working in hazardous factories during the school year. Labeled "ridiculously inadequate" by one critic, the child labor measure suffered from the same defect that crippled the attendance law — it lacked teeth — and as a result, it went largely unenforced. Although exploitative factory owners were partly to blame for the law's failure, it was clear that the child labor law also suffered because of the impotency of the state's school attendance statute. The officials who oversaw the child labor measure's enforcement believed that it would be far easier for the state to keep youngsters out of factories if it devoted resources to ensuring that they were kept inside schoolhouses.

Wisconsin's school attendance law finally underwent a significant revision in 1889. It came in the form of a measure popularly known as the Bennett Law (after the Iowa County legislator who introduced it, Republican Michael Bennett). Its provisions included a definition of truancy, beefed-up mechanisms for enforcing school attendance, and an outright ban on the labor of children under age thirteen. In response to Governor William Hoard's concern that students were receiving too much instruction in foreign languages, the law included a requirement that children in all the state's schools be taught "reading, writing, arithmetic, and United States history, in the English language."

The school attendance statute ignited a political firestorm. The state's Lutherans and Catholics loathed the Bennett Law because it threatened to eliminate teaching in German at parochial schools, and they waged a spirited campaign to secure its repeal. In a widely publicized joint statement, three Catholic bishops assailed the revamped attendance statute, arguing that the measure abrogated the "sacred, inalienable rights of parents" to educate their children as they saw fit. Governor Hoard vigorously countered the arguments put forward by such critics, dismissing the notion that the statute had anything to do with the Catholic Church. Hoard maintained that it was a matter involving only "the citizen and the state," with the former playing a subordinate role to the latter. "The parent," he said, "is subject to the state in all matters pertaining to the necessities of the state."

The Bennett Law proved to be Hoard's undoing. His support for the measure led to his defeat by Milwaukee mayor George Peck in the gubernatorial election of 1890. At the new governor's urging, the legislature passed an anti-truancy law described by one observer as "mild enough to meet the demands of those most opposed to state direction of education." The new attendance statute eliminated the Bennett Law's much-maligned English language requirement, reduced the age requirement by one year (from fourteen to thirteen), and generally loosened oversight of school-age children by the state. The measure was a bitter disappointment to reformers, for it failed to acknowledge any connection between school attendance and child labor.

As Tyack has observed, opposition to compulsory school attendance laws ebbed as the 1890s wore on. "States passed new laws with provisions for effective enforcement," he noted, "including requirements for censuses to determine how many children there were, attendance officers, elaborate 'pupil accounting,' and often state financing of schools in proportion to average daily attendance." This trend even held true in Wisconsin, where lawmakers made piecemeal revisions to bolster the compulsory attendance law. In 1897, for instance, the age requirement for school attendance was restored to fourteen, and in 1903, legislators enacted a provision requiring youngsters aged fourteen to sixteen to attend school unless they were regularly employed. Among other improvements, more truant officers were put on the job throughout the state, and their authority was broadened. What's more, in a nod to the connection between school attendance and child labor, factory inspectors gained the power to act as truant officers.

The 1960s were a time of immense turmoil for public education in the United States. Public schools struggled to find the resources necessary to cope with skyrocketing enrollments caused by the postwar baby boom. They also grappled with the implications of the social and political upheavals that racked the country throughout the decade. Radical critics issued challenges "to change the curriculum and the very nature of schooling," according to one historian of education. Although much of this pressure for reform emanated from liberals inspired by the civil rights and antiwar movements, political and religious conservatives weighed in as well, criticizing what was taught in public schools and how the state regulated those institutions. The compulsory school attendance laws that had sparked such controversy in the late nineteenth century were one of their primary targets.

Members of the John Birch Society — perhaps the largest and most prominent ultraconservative organization in the United States in the 1960s — took a keen interest in education. Like many on the political far right, Robert Welch, the organization's founder, harbored an abiding suspicion of the public schools, and he regularly railed against their corrosive effect on American society. Welch believed that by touting the tenets of secular humanism and communism, the schools were inculcating children with un-American values. In doing so, he concluded, the schools usurped the rights of parents. Welch warned in a widely distributed pamphlet that "parents — not the State — have the ultimate responsibility for the education of their children."

Adamant foes of "big government," Welch and his ideological kin often criticized the public schools for their rigid enforcement of ill-conceived regulations, including laws mandating school attendance. Writing in the John Birch Society journal *Public Opinion* in 1967, Medford Evans lamented the pitiable state of public education in America. As he cataloged the excesses of "materialism, fanaticism, and ignorance" that plagued the public schools, Evans registered his shock at the "public delirium of belief in the efficacy of universal school attendance." He suggested that laws mandating school attendance served to ensure the moral corruption of the nation's youth.

Others on the far right echoed the fears of Welch and Evans about the perilous state of education in America. Throughout the 1950s and 1960s, many conservatives cautioned that the nation's public schools had fallen victim to a secular humanist conspiracy, a plot hatched by liberals whose machinations threatened not only the nation's churches but also the very foundations of its government. The institutionalization of secular humanism in the public schools was especially galling to religious conservatives. Two fundamentalist Christians declared that humanism was essentially a faith "at war with Christianity, and the battleground in that war is the public school classroom." It incensed these critics that children were being conscripted into this conflict by compulsory school attendance laws. By forcing youngsters to forsake their Christian faith for the values of humanism, such measures were primarily responsible for "a social contagion, a moral and spiritual plague, rampant in American society."

The ranks of the conservatives who mounted strident attacks on the operation of public schools included attorney William Ball, who would represent the New Glarus Amish and shepherd the *Yoder* case all the way to the U.S. Supreme Court. Throughout the 1960s, Ball argued vehemently that the institutionalization of the doctrines of secular humanism in the public schools violated the establishment and free exercise clauses of the First Amendment. Ball was especially passionate in arguing that the teaching of secular humanism in the public schools violated the religious liberty of students and their parents. He maintained that there was "a constitutionally protected freedom in the pupil from imposition by government of ideology which conflicts with his conscience (or in the case of a child, the conscience of his parents). Certainly the area of forbidden imposition is far broader than theistic religion." In Ball's opinion, if the tenets of Christianity were prohibited in the schools, so too were those of secular humanism. Thus, students could reasonably contend that their right to free exercise of religion was compromised each day they attended public schools and were forced to absorb what Ball lamented as "'legal' religion in the schools."

Like many who shared his ideology, Ball loathed compulsory school attendance laws. To him, they were a deplorable mechanism for foisting secular humanism on children. In a speech delivered at Oral Roberts University, he described compulsory education as "an unhallowed establishment of religion supported by taxes extracted from the pockets of all citizens and supported by the criminal sanctions of the truancy laws." This system was contemptible to Ball, and in his mind it "raised a challenge to religious liberty, the rights of taxpayers, to parental freedom—and to the Christian lawyer—which should not go without response." Ball himself would answer that challenge by devoting an enormous amount of time and effort to defending the New Glarus Amish.

Ball was not the only conservative outraged by the New Glarus school attendance dispute. Throughout the late 1960s and early 1970s, lawmaker Kenneth Merkel, a member of the John Birch Society, championed the Amish cause in Wisconsin's legislature. Like Ball, Merkel believed that the mistreatment of the New Glarus Amish represented another example of the state attempting to exert too much control over individuals and thereby circumscribing some of their fundamental freedoms. Merkel resolved to end this oppression by changing public policy. Appalled by the events in New Glarus, he introduced several bills designed to preserve the religious liberty and parental rights of the Amish. His proposals — which usually failed to garner much support among his colleagues in the legislature — included measures that would exempt the Amish from physical education requirements and the state's compulsory school attendance law.

The Amish share with political conservatives an abiding wariness of the coercive powers of the state. The roots of this fear among the Amish stretch back almost half a millennium. After their dramatic break with the Catholic Church in the sixteenth century, the Anabaptists endured brutal state-sponsored persecution throughout Europe. Civil authorities drowned or beheaded some victims; they burned others at the stake. Such oppression had a lasting impact on the Amish. From it arose an enduring reluctance among members of the faith to interact with government or participate in the affairs of state.

The Amish do not routinely challenge the actions of governmental authorities. The idea of *Gelassenheit* undergirds their interactions with the state. According to scholar Donald Kraybill, the term "means submission — yielding to a higher authority. It entails self-surrender, resignation to God's will, yielding to others, self-denial, contentment, and a quiet spirit." As Kraybill has noted, the Amish adherence to this principle leads them to a position of subjection rather than one of active citizenship. Members of the faith thus quietly accede to most manifestations of state authority. They pay taxes and adhere to most secular laws. Yet the Amish generally avoid doing much more to participate in the "worldly" realm of civic affairs. An Amishman would never run for public office, for instance, or serve on a jury.

In several notable instances, however, the Amish have adopted a more assertive posture in their dealings with the state. Before the *Yoder* case reached the courts, members of Amish communities in several states—including Iowa, Kansas, Ohio, and Pennsylvania—stubbornly challenged the efforts of state authorities who attempted to force them to comply with compulsory school attendance laws and related measures. Raising many of the same basic questions regarding the religious liberty of the Amish, the rights of parents, and the state's interest in mandating education, these controversies foreshadowed the drama that unfolded in New Glarus in the late 1960s. They also established some of the legal precedents with which the attorneys in the *Yoder* case would have to grapple.

The most prominent conflict between the Amish and school authorities occurred in the 1960s in Buchanan County in northeast Iowa, where a particularly conservative group of Old Order Amish had lived and worshipped since 1914. In the fall of 1965, after several years of escalating tensions between the Amish and authorities in the communities of Hazleton and Olewein, local authorities stepped up prosecutions of Amish parents who sent their children to the one-room schoolhouses operated by their faith. Because the schools did not employ state-certified teachers, officials charged, the parents who enrolled their children in them were subject to sanctions under the provisions of the state school code.

Many Amish parents in the area defied the state. They obstinately refused to send their children to public schools or pay fines after the local justice of the peace found them guilty of violating the law. To maintain pressure on them, authorities announced that the penalties would be levied each day the parents failed to comply with the school code and that their property would be sold at auction if they were unable to settle their debts.

County attorney Harlan Lemon respected the Amish and their beliefs, and he had no desire to see them driven away from the Hazleton area by the threat of constant prosecutions. Yet he also believed that the state had a duty to fairly enforce its school code and thus ensure that all children—whatever the religious beliefs of their parents—

received adequate schooling from qualified teachers. "The question," he said at one point in the dispute, "is: 'Do these parents have the right to withhold just a basic education from their children under the guise of religious freedom?'" Arthur Sensor, the local superintendent of schools, shared Lemon's worries. Although he too respected the Amish, he was reluctant to make an exception to the school code for them. "My feeling is that the law is for all the people of Iowa," he said. "It ought to be enforced, not winked at."

After meeting in the fall of 1966 with a group of Amishmen who seemed open to compromise, local authorities dispatched a school bus to pick up Amish youngsters and transport them to public schools. This effort proved to be a debacle. Some Amish children hid when the bus stopped at their farms; others simply departed for one of their faith's one-room schoolhouses. The empty vehicle eventually made its way to one of the Amish schools, as did the sheriff, the county attorney, a throng of reporters and photographers, and several worried Amish parents. Following the authorities' orders, a group of Amish children glumly filed out of the school. Before they reached the waiting bus, however, an Amish spectator called out "Run!" in German. Many of the youngsters fled, some charging into nearby fields and galloping all the way back to their families' farms. A few children who were either too slow or too timid to flee were detained by authorities and eventually transported by bus to a public school in Hazleton.

Thanks in part to a dramatic *Des Moines Register* photograph that depicted Amish children fleeing into the fields to escape authorities, the strife in Hazleton was front-page news not only in Iowa but across the country. At least initially, the adverse publicity did nothing to weaken the resolve of authorities in Buchanan County, and they continued to pursue Amish children in the area. A few days after their disastrous first attempt to collect Amish youngsters, truant officer Owen Snively and superintendent Sensor boarded a school bus and once again made the rounds of local Amish farms. As had been the case earlier, most of the Amish children were nowhere in sight.

When Snively and Sensor reached the Charity Flats Amish school, they were met by the county sheriff, one of his deputies, and county attorney Lemon. A knot of Amishmen attempted to block their passage into the building, but the sheriff moved them aside. Inside the school, the local authorities encountered a group of sixteen Amish schoolchildren who wept and loudly sang "Jesus Loves Me." Also on hand were a horde of newspeople, several agitated Amish parents (many of whom were sobbing themselves), and Amish leader Dan Borntreger. While Snively and Lemon attempted to persuade the cowering children to accompany them to the regular public school, Borntreger intoned passages from the Scriptures.

It was Snively who caused the greatest disturbance of the morning. Prodded by Lemon, the truant officer placed his hands on the shoulders of an Amish girl and attempted to gently guide her toward the door. The girl screamed and pulled away. Snively then made another try, this time grasping the youngster by the arm, but he failed once more; she let out another cry and scampered toward a group of her classmates. This encounter seemed to convince the truant officer that his efforts were futile, and he and his colleagues eventually left the school without any students.

A second day of frustration and embarrassment prompted the county attorney, sheriff, and school superintendent to fly to Des Moines, the state capital. The Buchanan County contingent met with Governor Harold Hughes, and he prevailed on them to temporarily suspend their efforts to enforce the school laws against the Amish. Shortly after the three-week moratorium was announced, Hughes flew to Buchanan County to meet with local authorities and leaders of the Amish community. The governor eventually pieced together a settlement acceptable to both sides. Under the terms of the pact, which would remain in effect for the remainder of that school year and all of the following one, the Amish would lease the two one-room schoolhouses to the school district for one dollar a year. The school board would provide certified teachers for the schools, but funds for the teachers' salaries would have to come from the state or outside sources. Perhaps most significantly for the Amish, the school board signed a formal statement pledging that "adjustments will be made in the curriculum offered and in the teaching aids and methods used in those two schools, consistent with Iowa law, to avoid conflict with Amish religious beliefs."

Even this scheme had its shortcomings, but it at least laid the groundwork for an enduring solution to the vexing problem of Amish education in Iowa. Governor Hughes established a committee of prominent Iowans to examine the issue and make policy recommendations to the legislature. Endorsing a proposal favored by the American Civil Liberties Union, the committee urged that the state school superintendent be granted the authority to "exempt from the school standards those members or representatives of a local congregation of a recognized church or religious denomination established for 10 years or more within the state of Iowa prior to July 1, 1967, which professes principles or tenets that differ substantially from the objectives, goals or philosophy of education embodied in the state-standard law." The state legislature eventually passed a bill codifying the committee's plan.

Only 150 miles separated Hazleton and New Glarus, and the Amish who lived in the latter community closely followed the Buchanan County controversy. In fact, many of them, including Adin Yutzy, had experienced it firsthand and fled. These refugees arrived in Wisconsin having learned some harsh lessons. The prosecutions in Iowa highlighted for them the manifold dangers of bargaining with authorities over the education of Amish children. The calamity in Hazleton also demonstrated just how reluctant some public officials were to bend education laws to accommodate the religious beliefs of the Amish.

A dispute over schooling in Kansas attracted less notice among the New Glarus Amish, but it would have serious consequences for them as well. In 1965, state representative John B. Unruh sponsored a bill in the Kansas legislature to raise the state's compulsory school attendance age from fourteen to sixteen. There was little doubt that the bill was aimed at members of religious minority groups. Unruh later acknowledged that although he believed that the measure was "good for all the youth of Kansas," one of his primary goals was to provide an Amish or Mennonite youngster "the same opportunity to attend high school as his neighbor." In the fall of that year, a school superintendent in Reno County became convinced that Old Order families in his district were not complying with the new law, and he filed charges against one Amish father, LeRoy Garber, for failing to enroll his fifteen-year-old daughter in an accredited school. Sharon Garber had been taking correspondence courses through the Chicago-based American School, but she was not enrolled in an accredited Kansas high school.

Garber responded to the charges by enrolling his daughter in Harmony, a school in the town of Yoder, Kansas, operated by a group of Old Order Amish. Modeled on the vocational schools established a decade earlier by the Amish in Pennsylvania, Harmony had been founded in the fall of 1965 in direct response to the new state compulsory education requirement. Despite the fact that Sharon Garber was enrolled in Harmony and continued to take correspondence courses, authorities in Reno County pressed on with the prosecution of her father. After LeRoy Garber was found guilty and fined five dollars, he appealed to the Kansas Supreme Court, claiming that application of the compulsory school attendance law violated his religious freedom. That court handed down a ruling in Garber's case in November 1966, just as the crisis in Iowa was reaching its boiling point.

In its opinion in *State v. Garber*, the Kansas Supreme Court first dealt with Garber's claim that his daughter's matriculation at Harmony and her enrollment in correspondence courses satisfied the state's compulsory attendance requirement. The court found that Sharon Garber's participation in these two "essentially home instruction systems" violated the state law, for neither school was a "private, denominational or parochial school within the meaning of [the Kansas] truancy act." Next, the court assessed Garber's argument that his religious liberty had been violated by enforcement of the education law, and again it dismissed his contention as groundless. After reviewing the U.S. Supreme Court's rulings in cases involving the First Amendment freedoms of members of other religious minority groups, including the Mormons and Jehovah's Witnesses, the court concluded that "[t]here is no infringement upon the right to worship or to believe insofar as either [Garber] or his daughter is concerned. Their freedoms to worship and to believe remain absolute and are not affected by our compulsory school attendance law."

The *Garber* ruling drew heavy fire from scholars such as Robert Casad, a University of Kansas law professor. It astonished Casad that the supreme court had applied what was known as the "secular regulation" rule, under which, as he described it, "the state had no power to regulate a person's right to believe as he chose [but] could impose reasonable restrictions on the right to *act* upon those beliefs." The U.S. Supreme Court had long since forsaken this line of reasoning, Casad wrote, and several of its recent opinions had established robust protections for religious liberty. Chief among these newer rulings was

Sherbert v. Verner, a case involving a Seventh-Day Adventist who had been denied unemployment benefits by the state of South Carolina because she refused to work on Saturday, her faith's Sabbath. In an opinion written by Justice William Brennan, the Supreme Court held that the woman's right to free exercise of religion had been violated by application of the state unemployment compensation law, because South Carolina had failed to demonstrate a "compelling state interest" in enforcing the measure at issue in her case. Casad argued that the standard outlined in *Sherbert*, one that provided sturdy protections for religious liberty, had been completely ignored. "There is nothing in the *Garber* opinion to indicate that the court was even aware of the *Sherbert* decision," he wrote of the Kansas ruling.

Like the Hazleton imbroglio, the *Garber* case provided cold comfort for the New Glarus Amish. It showed the lengths to which some state authorities would go to assert control over the schooling of Amish children. More significantly, the case provided an unfavorable judicial precedent. Although it was not controlling in Wisconsin courts, the Kansas Supreme Court's poorly reasoned opinion in *Garber* could provide direction and guidance for judges evaluating the constitutional arguments put forth by attorneys representing the New Glarus Amish.

CHAPTER 4

The National Committee for Amish Religious Freedom Enters the Fray

In the fall of 1968, reports of the travails of the New Glarus Amish reached the National Committee for Amish Religious Freedom (NCARF). After he received a copy of a newspaper article describing the school attendance case, William Lindholm, the Lutheran minister who served as the organization's leader, wrote to the Amish defendants and indicated that the committee's resources would be made available to them if they chose to contest the charges in court. Like all of the NCARF's members, he felt that it was unconscionable for the state to penalize a people who were doing nothing more harmful than simply trying to live in accordance with their religious beliefs.

Lindholm had become sensitized to the plight of the Amish when he served as a minister in East Tawas, Michigan. In the fall of 1966, Lindholm and his wife often listened to WHO in Des Moines, a powerful radio station that carried frequent reports on the controversy between the Amish and school authorities in the Hazleton area. The radio dispatches stunned them. "Do you know what is happening in Iowa?" his wife asked one day in November. "Today the sheriff chased a whole bunch of Amish kids from a schoolhouse into a cornfield!" As it happened, Lindholm was the nephew of Iowa public school superintendent Paul Johnston, one of the state authorities embroiled in the dispute over Amish schooling. Although he sympathized with his uncle, Lindholm was aghast at how the authorities were treating the Amish in Buchanan County.

The Amish suffered from poor public relations during the debacle in Iowa, and Lindholm felt that they desperately needed help on that front. Throughout the dispute, the Amish were harmed by inaccurate or incomplete press reports regarding their beliefs and practices. If he could counter this kind of misinformation, Lindholm sensed, the Amish — who recoiled at the notion of conducting such a campaign themselves — might benefit immeasurably. "I believed that if someone told the Amish side of the story before the public became utterly misinformed and polarized, it would greatly aid the Amish cause," he later wrote. "If the public understood that the Amish were not acting out of ignorance, but with wisdom to preserve their religious society, the Amish cause would prevail." With that goal in mind, Lindholm began exploring the possibility of forming a committee of concerned clergy, academics, and public figures who would serve as an advocacy group for the reticent Amish.

In 1967, Lindholm's budding efforts on behalf of the Amish received a boost when he traveled to Chicago and attended a conference on state regulation of nonpublic schools. Donald Erickson, a University of Chicago education professor who had closely examined the Amish schooling controversy in Iowa, organized the meeting. The strife in Buchanan County distressed Erickson, in part because he believed that in regulating nonpublic schools, the states should "encourage the pursuit of pluralistic goals," not circumscribe parental rights and stifle religious liberty. He hoped that by focusing attention on the problem of heavy-handed state regulation, the conference might prevent future clashes between minority groups and state authorities.

With disturbing images of the dispute in Iowa still fresh in their minds, few speakers at the conference had positive things to say about state oversight of nonpublic schools. States claimed that their educational regulations served the best interests of children, but conferees such as Anne Strickland of the American Civil Liberties Union scoffed at that contention. In a discussion session, Strickland asserted that "the Amish parent claims the right to educate his child under the Free Exercise Clause of the First Amendment. This claim has priority over the question of what is educationally best for the child." At another point in the conference, Strickland acknowledged that "a state could legitimately regulate nonpublic schools . . . to seek minimum standards of competence in the interests of the state and the interests of the child." Although she did not dispute a state's right to regulate private and parochial schools, Strickland argued forcefully that such powers of oversight should be limited. Expressing a point of view shared by many champions of nonpublic schools, including the Amish and their defenders, she maintained that "the state's legitimate interests in regulating nonpublic schools [should be] subjected to substantially more rigid tests when a claim of religious liberty is made against the state's regulations." In these instances, she suggested, the state's regulatory efforts would fail to pass such a test because they so clearly compromised the freedoms guaranteed by the First Amendment.

During the conference, Lindholm organized a dinner and invited anyone interested in the Amish schooling issue to attend. His summons drew a number of clergy, attorneys, and scholars. Representatives from Amish communities in Ohio, Iowa, and Canada joined them. After discussing their goals and outlining possible strategies for attaining them, the non-Amish participants at the dinner formed the National Committee for Amish Religious Freedom and elected Lindholm as their chairman. Lindholm later wrote that the members of the new organization immediately committed themselves to zealously "defending the Amish by telling their story and providing legal defense." Lindholm worked diligently to recruit members for the nascent committee, and he quickly assembled an impressive roster of academics, religious leaders, and civil libertarians. Among them were Dean Kelly of the National Council of Churches and John Hostetler, a Temple University professor widely regarded as the leading scholarly authority on the Amish.

The NCARF stated that its mission was to help "extend freedom of religion to those who have organized their lives around other values — perhaps just as valid — but different than those of the rushing mainstream." A large part of its work lay in educating the public about what the Amish believed and why their suppression at the hands of public authorities was so unconscionable. The organization explained in one brochure that the Amish were reluctant to expose their children to dangers posed by the public schools because doing so "violates their morals, their religious convictions, and if their children embrace the 'worldly' values the Amish way of life will be destroyed." That same document also warned that efforts such as those undertaken by officials in Iowa to compel Amish children to attend public schools threatened both parental rights and educational diversity. Stressing the former danger, the NCARF cautioned that maladroit attempts by states to regulate Amish education interfered with "the liberty of the Amish parents to direct the upbringing of their children according to their religious conscience, a practice that does not threaten the public peace and order."

For its first major campaign, the NCARF helped LeRoy Garber

appeal his conviction under Kansas's revised school attendance law. Its goal was straightforward: according to one fund-raising piece, the NCARF hoped "to make it possible to request a full scale legal review of Amish religious rights before the United States Supreme Court." Lindholm's work on behalf of Garber received the endorsement of a group of prominent Roman Catholic legal scholars, including William Ball. An attorney from Harrisburg, Pennsylvania, Ball was a well-known advocate of public funding of private and parochial schools, and he had attended the conference at which the NCARF had been formed. At Lindholm's request, Ball reviewed the *Garber* case and came to the conclusion that the Supreme Court would not hear the appeal. Ball believed that the weakness of the case lay in the thin trial record. Most of the facts had been stipulated, and Garber's attorneys hadn't provided much evidence regarding the beliefs of the Amish or the state's apparent lack of compelling interest in enforcing the attendance law. For the Amish to have a chance, Ball felt, such facts would have to be laid out clearly — and exhaustively — in the trial record.

As it happened, Ball's fears about the *Garber* appeal were realized when the U.S. Supreme Court denied certiorari in October 1967, leaving the Kansas ruling in place. If the NCARF wanted the high court to hand down an opinion on the applicability of compulsory school attendance laws to the Amish, it would have to find another case — presumably one with a more extensive trial record. Given the Amish's long-standing aversion to the courts, this wouldn't be an easy task.

As legal scholar Charles Epp has observed, "cases do not arrive in supreme courts as if by magic." In many instances, landmark cases are guided through the courts by interest groups that seek to influence a particular area of public policy. By using "test cases" to conduct sustained and well-planned campaigns in the courts, these organizations have precipitated change in fields ranging from the environment to civil rights.

The efforts of interest groups have resulted in hundreds of rulings in courts of all levels, including the U.S. Supreme Court. In the landmark case *Muller v. Oregon* (1908), a state law that limited women's workdays to ten hours was defended by future Supreme Court justice Louis Brandeis and his colleagues at the National Consumers League

(NCL). (The NCL was particularly qualified to defend the law at issue in *Muller* because the group had lobbied extensively for its passage.) The National Association for the Advancement of Colored People (NAACP) waged a lengthy crusade in the courts to end segregation in public schools and higher education. Its tireless work culminated in the Supreme Court's landmark opinion *Brown v. Board of Education* (1954), in which the justices formally repudiated the doctrine of "separate but equal."

Interest groups have several decided advantages over individual litigants. Backed by large rosters of donors, organizations such as the American Civil Liberties Union (ACLU) can muster the financial resources necessary to sustain a case over the course of several years. They can underwrite the work of investigators, fund the travel expenses of expert witnesses, or pay for the photocopying of lengthy depositions and trial transcripts. These organizations also possess legal expertise. Many interest groups employ attorneys who are standouts in their fields. "Simply stated," scholars Lee Epstein and C. K. Rowland noted, "many interest groups are known for their ability to select and cultivate outstanding legal talent." Most individual litigants don't have deep pockets or a team of expert lawyers at their disposal.

Interest groups commonly join litigation that is already in the courts. Organizations often identify promising criminal or civil cases and then offer their services to litigants whose claims seem to jibe with the group's goals. Ideally, these partnerships benefit both the individual litigants and the interest groups that decide to champion their rights in court. While the group gains an opportunity to promote its agenda through the courts, the individual receives expert legal help at no cost. Sometimes, however, conflicts emerge when litigants feel that the outside organizations are neglecting their narrow interests and instead focusing on promoting the group's broader goals.

Such tensions would build as the *Yoder* case made its way through the courts. Over time, it would become apparent that the Amish were reluctant partners with the NCARF and never shared the organization's zeal for pursuing a test case. They lacked enthusiasm for the litigation at least in part because the Amish are famously reluctant to "go to law" to resolve disputes. As one observer of the faith put it, they are, unlike most Americans, "unalterably opposed to instituting suits at law." This disinclination is rooted in large part in their adherence to the ethical principles detailed in the Sermon on the Mount. There, as he counsels meekness and nonresistance, Christ admonishes: "If any man sue you at law, and take away thy coat, let him have thy cloak also." To the Amish, being sued or prosecuted is not quite the same as suing, for defendants in legal cases typically have not chosen to invoke the law; in most instances, they have been dragged into the courts by other people. "Nevertheless, the Amish believe that they should avoid such involvement as much as possible," according to one study of the faith. "Normally, if the judgment of the court is against the defendant, he should obey the law as interpreted by the court."

But as the NCARF's William Lindholm recognized when he began looking into the New Glarus school attendance case late in 1968, strictures against "going to law" have not stopped a few Amish from relying on the courts to resolve disputes. "In practice," scholar John Hostetler wrote, "some Amish have made use of the law . . . , depending on the circumstances and their conscience." Indeed, prior to the New Glarus case, Amish had participated in litigation over compulsory school attendance laws not only in Kansas (the *Garber* case) but also in Pennsylvania, Ohio, and Indiana. Not all members of the faith had approved of these dealings with the courts, but some justified them on the grounds that the Amish typically had been defendants in criminal actions rather than plaintiffs in civil matters. They hadn't exactly gone to law; in a sense, the law had come to them.

When the NCARF considered the possibility of intervening in the school attendance case in New Glarus, "it was told that the Amish would never allow court action on their behalf," Lindholm later wrote. In keeping with the tenets of their faith, many Amish had simply "turned the other cheek and took their punishment," as Lindholm put it, after they were charged with crimes. In fact, the New Glarus defendants initially declined the NCARF's offer of help, but in doing so, they appeared to leave open the possibility that they might accept legal assistance at a later date. "We want to thank you for offering your assistance in case of need," the Amish school board replied to Lindholm in November 1968. "So far we have had no serious troubles, although a few threats as to what would happen if we don't have our children above eighth grade attending school, but so far nothing has happened, and we hope nothing will happen, but if we should need help we are glad to know that you are willing to help us."

In responding to Lindholm, the Amish apparently did not mention that their religious beliefs might complicate any attempt to wage a fight in the courts against the compulsory school attendance law. Their reservations on that score were abundantly clear, however, when the three defendants were ordered to appear in Green County Court in December 1968 and respond to the formal charges that had been leveled against them by Louis Koenig, the district attorney. When the Amishmen appeared before Judge Roger Elmer, defendant Wallace Miller said that they would not be represented by counsel because "our religion doesn't permit us to hire a lawyer." He went on to contend that the defendants viewed their prosecution under the state compulsory attendance law as an unconstitutional infringement on their religious freedom. "I don't think we are guilty," Miller said, yet he repeatedly resisted attempts by both Elmer and Koenig to have the Amishmen enter a plea to that effect.

At the hearing, it was obvious that the Amish fathers were torn between their firm conviction that the charges against them were groundless and their equally strong determination not to hire a lawyer to represent them in court to prove the validity of that sentiment. In comments before Elmer and in interviews after the hearing had ended, Miller, Yoder, and Yutzy indicated that they might explore three options as they dealt with the charges. In addition to attempting to work out a compromise with the Department of Public Instruction and seeking legislation that would exempt Amish children from the law altogether, they would contact the NCARF to determine if they might be able to contest the charges in court. Yoder and Yutzy both indicated that in deciding which course of action to take, the defendants would be obliged to follow the wishes of their church community. "We represent the whole colony," Yutzy said. "They will help us decide what we are going to do."

At the hearing, the district attorney seemed open to the idea of reaching a compromise with the Amish that would eliminate their need to hire an attorney. Apparently wary of engaging in a protracted court battle with the Amish, Koenig said that he "would be prone to dismiss the charges" against the three fathers if they agreed to comply thereafter with the state compulsory attendance law — an unlikely possibility at best — or if they could, as one newspaper account put it, "make some arrangement with school officials for a workable vocational plan." Given that such plans were in operation in other states, including Pennsylvania, the latter part of Koenig's suggestion offered a glimmer of hope that the dispute in Green County could be resolved without intervention by the courts.

Aware that they might be in for a long battle, the Amish in New Glarus contacted the NCARF immediately after the inconclusive hearing before Judge Elmer. Their message reflected the ambivalence that had been so apparent when the three fathers appeared in court. Writing for the defendants, Wallace Miller seemed both surprised and dismayed that the problem hadn't simply blown over. "Now it looks like they are going to make a court case out of it," he wrote to Lindholm on December 18, 1968. Miller went on to explain that Judge Elmer had responded to the defendants' somewhat confused behavior at the hearing by adjourning the proceedings until January 7. Without specifically asking it to provide a legal defense, Miller left the door open for the NCARF to take part in resolving the mounting crisis. "Now we leave it up to you whether you want to help us," Miller wrote. "We would appreciate it if we could talk with someone of the committee before January 7th if possible."

At this point, any doubts regarding the state's intention to prosecute probably were erased by a letter sent by Max Ashwill, an attorney for the Department of Public Instruction, to Roman Miller, the head of the Amish school board in New Glarus. Ashwill expressed concern that Amish families in the New Glarus area were attempting to use a substandard vocational educational program as "a guise or façade to escape the compulsory attendance requirements" of state law. The state would not be fooled by this ruse, Ashwill assured Miller, and the Amish could expect to be prosecuted if their children were not enrolled in an accredited school until they reached the age of sixteen.

With Ashwill reiterating the state's intention to go forward with the prosecutions, Lindholm wasted little time after receiving Miller's guarded but clear plea for support. He drove from his home in Michigan to New Glarus and undertook the delicate task of convincing the Amish fathers to allow the NCARF to defend them. In individual visits to each defendant's farm, he did his best to assuage their fears about allowing themselves to be represented by counsel. "I explained that they were charged as criminals in the legal complaint," Lindholm recalled. "The committee's attorney would simply tell the judge what the Amish believed, and ask the judge to rule that their actions were protected by the Constitution's guarantee of religious freedom." Specifically addressing one of the chief Amish reservations about using the services of lawyers, he maintained that allowing the NCARF to intervene on their behalf in the present circumstances "would not be 'suing anyone' or 'taking anyone to law,'" because they would not be initiating the legal proceedings. Moreover, the committee would not ask them to contribute any financial support for their defense, Lindholm said.

As he spoke with the Amish in New Glarus, Lindholm also noted the potentially wide-ranging significance of their case. "I explained that a case like theirs had never been won before," he recalled, "and if legal efforts were successful, it would help many other religious believers in the United States who highly acclaim the principle of religious freedom." Lindholm knew that the case would have broad importance only if it was heard by appellate courts, and he shrewdly prepared the defendants for the possibility that the legal battle waged on their behalf might be a lengthy one. Referring to a passage from the Book of Acts, he mentioned that when Saint Paul was unjustly charged, he not only defended himself but also appealed his case to Rome in an effort to secure protections for the rights of all Christians. If they permitted the NCARF to argue their case before an appellate court, Lindholm suggested, the New Glarus defendants would be following in Paul's noble footsteps.

Lindholm's persistence eventually paid off. In time, he was able to overcome the misgivings of the Amish fathers and persuade them to accept legal representation by the NCARF. "I asked them, 'If we take your case, would you not object?'" he recalled. "Finally they said, 'OK.'" Before the rescheduled hearing took place before Judge Elmer in early January 1969, the defendants signed a formal "Understanding and Agreement" effectively authorizing the committee to argue their case in court. According to that document, the Amish stipulated that they would not raise objections to the efforts of "these good neighbors who want to intervene to help." The agreement also contained language meant to mollify those who might suspect that the Amish fathers were somehow motivated by self-interest in accepting the NCARF's aid. It claimed that the defendants were "not concerned so much about themselves as they are in allowing the committee to defend the principle of religious freedom for others."

The agreement elated Lindholm, but others were less enthusiastic about the prospect of the NCARF intervening on behalf of the New Glarus defendants. As Jonas Yoder later acknowledged, their decision to allow the committee to defend them in court "wasn't approved by all our people all over the country" because some believed that it amounted to "going to law" and thus violated the teachings of their faith. Dan Borntreger, a prominent Amishman from Iowa whose daughters lived in Wisconsin, voiced strong objections to the arrangement. Writing to the NCARF, Borntreger did not claim that the use of lawyers violated the tenets of his faith but rather expressed fear that actively battling the compulsory school attendance law might backfire. "I have talked to Bishops and church members," he wrote, "and we don't feel it would help to take the New Glarus school case to court at this time. . . . Remember if you lose, things will be worse." Borntreger's admonition seemed to indicate that there might be widespread opposition among the Amish to the NCARF's taking a role in the New Glarus case, and it was not taken lightly by Lindholm. He wondered if it might mean that the Amish "were . . . now telling the committee to stop the legal defense."

In the end, Lindholm came to believe that he had received all the authorization he needed from the defendants themselves, and he pressed forward. With the January 7 hearing fast approaching, he knew that his first task was finding an attorney who would represent the Amish fathers. After returning to Michigan from New Glarus, Lindholm telephoned Pennsylvania attorney William Ball. Lindholm knew that Ball had harbored doubts about the chances of successfully appealing the conviction of LeRoy Garber to the U.S. Supreme Court, but he hoped that the attorney might conclude that the New Glarus case — the three separate prosecutions were known collectively as *State of Wisconsin v. Yoder* — held more promise.

"We've got a case," Lindholm said, explaining that the Amish had agreed to allow the NCARF to represent them. "Do you think you can handle it?" Never one to back down from a challenge, Ball told him, "I would like to think that I can."

Over the course of his long and distinguished career, William Ball argued cases in nearly two dozen states and served as lead counsel in ten cases heard by the U.S. Supreme Court. Ball did not make much money from these tireless efforts — if he was lucky, he managed to cover his expenses — but they did earn him a formidable reputation. When Ball died early in 1999, Stephen Krason, president of the Catholic Society of Social Scientists, said that the attorney's track record made him "the preeminent practicing Catholic constitutional lawyer in the country of the last 30 years." Another observer went a step further, claiming that Ball "would be accurately described as the premier constitutional litigator of this century in matters of church and state."

After graduating from the University of Notre Dame College of Law in 1948, Ball worked in the legal departments of two large corporations. His deliverance from the drudgery of corporate law came in 1955, when he was invited to join the faculty of the fledgling Villanova University School of Law in Philadelphia. He taught there until 1960, when he left to help launch the Pennsylvania Catholic Conference, an organization founded jointly by the state's dioceses to "basically look out for legislative matters that would affect the church statewide in Pennsylvania," according to Ball's former student Joe Skelly. This was no small task, for the Catholic Church was involved in enterprises ranging from schools and hospitals to cemeteries. As the conference's executive director and general counsel, Ball monitored state government and worked, through lobbying and litigation, to protect the church's interests in those areas. Business was so brisk that Ball eventually recruited Skelly to serve as assistant counsel.

During his tenure with the state Catholic conference, Ball built a national reputation for his dogged advocacy of plans designed to furnish state funding for private and parochial schools. After the Kennedy administration made clear its opposition to such programs, Ball authored the National Catholic Welfare Conference's contentious response. Throughout the 1960s, he wrote numerous articles about the subject in publications such as *Commonweal* and *The Catholic World.* Many of these articles were meant to demonstrate that, as he wrote in one, "there is an impressive and authoritative body of interpretation of the First Amendment which . . . admits aid to church-related education."

Ball felt so strongly about this issue that he devoted a great deal of time to crafting applicable legislation and then defending it in court. As his colleague Skelly put it, Ball was "one of the prime authors" of a Pennsylvania measure designed to funnel public funds to private and parochial schools. (It authorized the state to "purchase" from nonpublic schools various "secular educational services," such as instructional materials and teachers' salaries.) When a constitutional challenge to the law reached the U.S. Supreme Court in a case called *Lemon v. Kurtzman* (1971), Ball vigorously argued the state's case. He believed that "the precedents were on our side," but the high court thought otherwise: it held that the school funding scheme violated the First Amendment's establishment clause.

Ball's well-known interest in promoting and defending funding plans for nonpublic schools left some skeptical observers wondering about his motives in becoming involved in the New Glarus case. After the U.S. Supreme Court handed down its landmark decision in *Yoder* in 1972, the magazine *Christianity Today* undertook the most searching examination of these issues. In a hard-hitting editorial headlined "Using the Amish?" it addressed a number of basic questions regarding the genesis of the defense of the Amish fathers, as well as the agendas of those who championed their cause. Its harsh conclusions cast serious doubt on Ball's intentions.

Is the Wisconsin school attendance case "simply a battle for religious freedom for the Amish?" the *Christianity Today* editorial asked. "Or is it also an instance of strange bedfellows making politics?" The editorial, noting the aversion of the Amish to "going to law," observed that they generally "think it wrong to press any kind of litigation." The New Glarus fathers' apparent breach of this principle could be explained only by the troubling intervention of the National Committee for Amish Religious Freedom. The case might have ended without much fanfare had the NCARF not offered to direct and fund the defense. The journal claimed that the Amish "are embarrassed and offended by these 'favors'" and argued that "this kind of intervention violates their religious scruples."

The editors of *Christianity Today* thought they knew why NCARF members had taken so keen an interest in such a minor legal dispute. Their editorial suggested that a "sudden supposedly humanitarian concern [was] being imposed upon the Amish against their will" because outside groups saw in the case an opportunity "to enhance the stature of non-public education in a way that makes it seem deserving of government financial support." To help substantiate this accusation, the editorial noted that the Amish were being represented in court by William Ball, "who for years has been the leading lawyer in the Catholic bid for public money for parochial schools."

The unsparing *Christianity Today* editorial drew protests from two prominent members of the NCARF, Franklin Littell and William Lindholm. In a curt letter to the journal, Littell stated that he was "very disappointed" by the article's accusatory tone, particularly as it related to the attorney who was representing the Amish. "Your reference to Bill Ball is unworthy of a Christian journal," he wrote. "I have known and worked with him for years, and I don't know a finer layman nor one more devoted to fairness to persons of different conscience and church." Littell ascribed the tenor of the "Using the Amish?" editorial to "the old Protestant bigotry" that had plagued Catholics for generations. (*Christianity Today* was an evangelical Christian publication.) For his part, Lindholm took issue with the suggestion that supporters of the Amish in *Yoder* were somehow engaged in "a maneuver to undermine the public schools" simply because Ball was "a noted Catholic."

The vehemence of these protests did not stop the Catholic journal *Commonweal* from following *Christianity Today*'s lead and exploring the possibility that some of those who supported the Amish in *Yoder* were essentially opportunists. In an article examining "the bad press that Catholics have received for their support of the Amish," writer Jim Castelli asked rhetorically, "How pure were Catholic motives in supporting the Amish school case?" While Castelli was careful not to openly question the motives of those who directed the defense of the Amish, he did point out that there were several "potential benefits to be gained by Catholics" by an Amish victory in the New Glarus case. For instance, if the Supreme Court upheld "the right of the Amish parents to keep their children out of school for religious beliefs, even though their religion does not offer an alternative education, it may serve as a precedent in some future case where Catholics will seek government aid for alternate schools which stem from *their* religious beliefs."

Although neither *Christianity Today* nor *Commonweal* did so, critics of Ball's involvement in the New Glarus case could have found ammunition in some of his own voluminous published work. Writing in the journal *Catholic Lawyer* in 1970, Ball discussed the issue of public funding for private and parochial schools, which he called "the most difficult and most extensive of all law-religion problems in the nation." Ball suggested that advocates of funding schemes needed to explore fresh approaches if they hoped to prevail in the courts. Although the First Amendment's establishment clause stood as a potential stumbling block, the free exercise clause held promise. Ball argued that "a new look has to be taken at the free exercise clause . . . when we come to discuss the constitutionality of programs to aid education in religiously affiliated schools."

Ball argued that advocates of funding plans might successfully defend them by grounding their arguments in the Constitution's protection of religious liberty. The free exercise rights of deeply religious families were violated, Ball asserted in his *Catholic Lawyer* article, when they were given no alternative but to use their tax dollars to support the teaching of the "legal religion" of secular humanism in public schools. Schemes designed to funnel tax dollars to private and parochial schools were constitutionally defensible, Ball argued, in part because they alleviated this burden on religious families. No longer would they be forced to pay for schooling that essentially required them to forsake their religious faith.

Ball's exploration of this novel argument continued:

> It is very clear that people exercise religious liberty by sending their children to religiously affiliated schools. If that is an exercise of religious liberty, then the state may not, either directly or *indirectly*, interfere with that exercise of religious liberty. The manipulation of the taxing and spending powers to deny to any person or parent a free educational choice based on religious conscience — where the education sought meets reasonable state requirements — is not only a denial of the free exercise of religion and of the equal protection of the laws but indeed may be viewed as a taking of property, through taxation, without due process of law.

After confessing that "these constitutional positions are now in the exploratory stage," Ball asserted that "it is not unlikely that they will be advanced as elements in the defense of some of the current litigations." He then launched into a detailed discussion of the New Glarus school attendance case.

It was difficult to question the sincerity of Ball's commitment to the Amish. When he discussed his reasons for becoming involved in *Wisconsin v. Yoder*, he emphasized his hope that "these good people will be protected in [the] exercise of religious liberty." Nonetheless, the line of argument developed in Ball's essay in *Catholic Lawyer* suggested that, just as his critics charged, he discerned a potential link between the Wisconsin case and efforts to secure public funding for private and parochial schools.

Some insightful speculation regarding Ball's motives in so aggressively pursuing the New Glarus case has been offered by Donald Kraybill, a leading scholarly authority on the Amish, and Tom Eckerle, a Wisconsin attorney who worked closely with Ball in the early stages of the litigation. Kraybill, the author of several well-regarded books on the Amish, has observed several instances in which members of the faith were represented in the courts by outsiders. In his view, the *Yoder* case was typical of these interactions. According to Kraybill:

> If a case emerges, or a conflict emerges, then you get a cadre of sympathetic outsiders that in a sense pick up the case. And they almost get ahead of the Amish. Particularly if they see that there are church and state or First Amendment issues at stake, they want to push it as far as they can from a philosophical-legal perspective, despite the reluctance of the Amish even to go along. And I think that's what happened in *Wisconsin v. Yoder*, in many ways. You had Bill Ball and [Temple University professor] John Hostetler and some other scholars who really wanted to take this thing forward. Their motivations were twofold. One was to truly help and assist and protect the Amish. But, secondly, they hoped to make a contribution toward legal understandings and legal precedents in terms of church and state and First Amendment issues.

Kraybill believed "without a doubt" that Ball and his colleagues in the NCARF "saw both of those purposes" when they became involved in the New Glarus case.

Tom Eckerle had a great deal of respect for Ball, believing him to be a superb attorney and a compassionate man. He never doubted that his courtly senior colleague was sincerely committed to aiding the Amish by shielding their religious liberty from encroachment by the state. Yet, over time, Eckerle came to understand that Ball probably intended to serve a variety of interests — not solely those of the Amish — when he rushed to the defense of Wallace Miller, Jonas Yoder, and Adin Yutzy. Eckerle further suspected that Ball hoped all along to advance those interests in the most sweeping and dramatic manner possible — by taking the *Yoder* case all the way to the U.S. Supreme Court.

To Eckerle, it was hardly coincidental that Ball and other champions of nonpublic schools played such a central role in *Yoder*. After all, in the late 1960s, these advocates were looking for cases that would further their agenda. "When the right case came, they were going to run with it," Eckerle said, "and they were going to take it as far as they had to go." It was apparent to Eckerle that Ball, hoping to make the most of the opportunity provided by the Amish case, always had his eye on the justices of the U.S. Supreme Court, whose rulings apply nationally. "Ball was very aware that this wasn't likely to end in Monroe, Wisconsin," he recalled, referring to the site of the *Yoder* trial. "He was very capable and knew exactly where he was going with it. . . . He knew, he knew. Absolutely."

Over time, Eckerle's perspective on the case changed. A confessed bleeding-heart liberal, he initially believed that the Amish "were the underdogs, so of course they were on the right side." Eckerle's feelings about the litigation began to shift when he became aware that the NCARF had received a contribution from Bill Dyke, Madison's conservative mayor. Being on the same side of the compulsory attendance issue as Dyke and Kenneth Merkel, the John Birch Society member who had championed the Amish cause in the state legislature, made Eckerle pause. "It was like a lightbulb went off in my head," he said of learning that Dyke had given money to the NCARF. "I thought, 'My God, if *he*'s for them, it must be that this wasn't the liberal cause I thought it was.'"

Without too much coaxing from the NCARF's William Lindholm, William Ball agreed late in 1968 to defend Wallace Miller, Jonas Yoder, and Adin Yutzy. For Ball, the timing was perfect. Having recently scaled back his duties at the state Catholic conference to open a law practice with Joe Skelly, he had plenty of time to devote to the case.

In January 1969, after the defendants were granted another continuance by Judge Roger Elmer in Green County Court, Ball wrote on their behalf to William C. Kahl, the Wisconsin superintendent of public instruction. Despite his ambitions to press the cause of the Amish to the nation's highest court, Ball dutifully proposed to Kahl a means for settling the case. Reviewing the circumstances of the New Glarus prosecutions, Ball noted that the Amish fathers had run afoul of Wisconsin's compulsory attendance law because they "consider it required by their religion that their children should not attend school beyond eighth grade, but rather that they should, in the very sensitive years of early adolescence, be integrated into the church-community Amish culture." After establishing that crucial background, Ball implored the superintendent to take action that would resolve the New Glarus dispute and preserve the religious liberty of the Amish.

Ball asked "whether some administrative accommodation cannot be worked out by your Department whereby Amish children will not be required to attend school after eighth grade." He envisioned the state establishing an exemption procedure in "which proper application is made by the parent and procedures to establish that the claim is bona fide have been followed." The formulation of such a policy would benefit Amish throughout Wisconsin, and it could be particularly helpful to the fathers in New Glarus who had been charged with violating the compulsory school attendance law. Ball hoped that if the state reached an accord with the Amish, "it might be possible to get the present criminal charges dismissed" and thus "avoid what would probably become a religious liberty test case."

Ball closed his letter to Kahl by expressing his hope "that a plan can be worked out" that would both safeguard the religious liberty of the Amish and honor the state's general right to enforce appropriate laws. He claimed that the Amish and the NCARF were doing everything in their power to avoid a battle in the courts against the state. Ball assured Kahl that "no one is seeking to make a test case of the present prosecution." Yet he also hinted that the NCARF would go to court on behalf of the Amish if no alternative presented itself. Ball noted that the "very peaceable defendants in question" would not back down and surrender their "well established claim of religious liberty" if they failed to reach a compromise with the state. Alluding to the possibility of a contentious trial and subsequent appeals process, Ball informed the superintendent that the Amish fathers in New Glarus would rather have the dispute over the compulsory school attendance law resolved by the courts than give up and "compromise their beliefs."

Kahl's response disappointed Ball. The superintendent indicated that he had no intention of exempting the Amish from the provisions of the state school code. In his reply to the NCARF attorney, Kahl maintained that the Wisconsin statutes governing education limited his authority to act in the manner Ball had suggested. In Wisconsin, the superintendent noted, "certain instruction may be approved as substantially equivalent to that offered in the schools of the area and substituted for school attendance." Kahl could exercise his discretion only if it were a case of judging the appropriateness of this "substantially equivalent" schooling. "In other cases the determination is left to the local truant officer." In developing this point, Kahl did not explicitly reject Ball's suggestion that he give his imprimatur to a vocational educational plan that would exempt the Amish from compulsory school attendance. However, his discussion of the standard of substantial equivalence implied his doubt that the kind of vocational program advocated by the NCARF attorney would be deemed an appropriate substitute for education in a public high school.

Kahl next derogated Ball's request that he issue a blanket ruling that would permit qualified Amish students to claim a "legal excuse" from mandatory school attendance. This would be impossible, the superintendent claimed, because "the compulsory attendance statute does not provide for the State Superintendent's ruling or determination as to what legal excuse should be." Individual school districts did in fact have the discretion to provide the kind of release proposed by Ball, but Kahl's office in Madison took pains to remind them that the power to grant "any excuse . . . should be exercised with due regard for the compulsory attendance requirement mandate of the statute." Kahl asserted that when members of individual school boards in Wisconsin considered plans such as the one advanced by the NCARF, they would be constrained not only by the compulsory school attendance law but also by a section of the Wisconsin code that prescribed penalties for "any member of a school board who votes to exclude from any public school any child on account of his religion, nationality or color." Kahl himself would be subject to penalties, he argued, if he attempted to "excuse on religious grounds" Amish students.

After receiving Kahl's bleak letter, Ball forged ahead in preparing the case for trial. Aware that he was at a geographical disadvantage in representing the Amish fathers, the Pennsylvania lawyer searched for a Wisconsin attorney to help him handle the case. He contacted Don Rush, counsel for the Wisconsin Catholic Conference, and Rush in turn phoned Tom Eckerle. A self-described "liberal Catholic" who had graduated from the University of Wisconsin Law School, Eckerle had worked for the U.S. attorney in Madison for several years before losing his position with the election of Richard Nixon in 1968. When Rush reached him, Eckerle had been in private practice only a few days, and he had yet to generate much legal work to occupy his time. After hearing a thumbnail sketch of the case, he quickly agreed to help.

From the outset, William Ball had an almost visceral response to the New Glarus case. The prosecutions of Miller, Yoder, and Yutzy genuinely horrified him, and he leaped to their defense. Eckerle approached the school attendance dispute somewhat differently. "I didn't have a clue what was going on," he recalled. "I knew that these were good Amish farmers who were being picked on, but that's about all I knew. I was looking for clients and hoping to pay my bills." For him, the case was a job, not a cause.

Eckerle had to act quickly. Rush informed him that the defendants were soon due to reappear before Judge Elmer in county court. Eckerle sped from Madison to Monroe, the Green County seat, and immediately went to work. Speaking for the Amish in Elmer's courtroom, Eckerle announced that "they would fight the constitutionality of the Wisconsin law requiring all students to attend school through age sixteen on grounds of religious freedom," as one observer put it. He also explained to the court that the Amish in New Glarus had already established a Pennsylvania-style vocational education program, even though state and local authorities had indicated that such a move probably would not moot the charges against the three men.

As the hearing was in progress, Eckerle made another attempt to reach a compromise with the state. The Madison attorney met with representatives of the Amish community and New Glarus school superintendent Kenneth Glewen during an hour-long recess in the proceedings. Nothing came of this last-ditch conference, however, and both sides resigned themselves to having the courts resolve their dispute. Clearly exasperated, Green County district attorney Louis Koenig groused that the county "was doing all [it] can" to accommodate the Amish. "We have to wait for a decision in the matter," he said, referring to the prospect of a trial. "We can't force them to go to school."

In addition to bringing Eckerle on board, Ball prepared for the trial by consulting with John Hostetler, a Temple University anthropology professor who was a leading authority on the Amish. Hostetler tutored the NCARF attorney, explaining the heritage of the Amish, their beliefs and practices, and the structure of their society. Ball was fascinated to learn from Hostetler how the Amish doctrine of nonresistance had left them open to intense religious persecution in Europe. The attorney later wrote of coming to understand that because of such oppression, the Amish "had developed a profound sense of wariness of those in seats of worldly power — the men of learning and science at whose hands they had suffered and with which they identified worldliness." Hostetler also took his pupil on a tour of some of the Amish communities in Lancaster County, Pennsylvania. There Ball became acquainted with Amish people who were, as he later recalled with fondness, "mild mannered, invariably good-humored, and kindly."

Having prepared himself under Hostetler's tutelage (and secured the scholar's commitment to testify on behalf of the Amish), Ball journeyed to Wisconsin to meet with his clients and discuss with them his strategy for the trial. As he drove out to Jonas Yoder's farm on a cold, rainy morning in April 1969, Ball knew that his task would be a delicate one. The Amish, he understood, "wanted as little to do with 'lawyering' as possible," and they probably wouldn't want to spend a great deal of time strategizing. Indeed, the pretrial meeting, held in Yoder's kitchen, was fleeting. "Without emotion, or even comment," Yoder informed Ball that the Amishmen would plead not guilty and take the witness stand to answer whatever questions might be put to them. Ball asked Yoder if one of his daughters might be available to provide testimony at the trial, and he indicated that fifteen-year-old Frieda would oblige. Ball spoke briefly with the "rosy-cheeked, good-natured, quiet" young woman before heading back out into the rain.

Later that day, a disconcerted Ball telephoned his partner Joe Skelly and described his meeting with Yoder. His voiced tinged with disappointment, Ball reported that his conference with the lead defendant had not gone smoothly. "He can't understand me well," he despaired to Skelly. "We're having a terrible time communicating." On the eve of the trial, Ball worried that Yoder, though sincere in his beliefs and innocent of the charges leveled against him, might not make an effective witness. Yoder's somewhat limited communication skills were "a point of real concern with [Ball]," Skelly later said, and he became concerned that they might impede his presentation of the case. Although he would have preferred to elicit testimony from Yoder, Ball decided not to call him as a witness the following day.

CHAPTER 5

Judicial Precedent and *Yoder*

In addition to lining up witnesses to testify, defense attorney William Ball prepared for the trial in *Wisconsin v. Yoder* by carefully scrutinizing judicial precedent. Of particular interest to him was the U.S. Supreme Court's last significant decision in a religious liberty case, *Sherbert v. Verner*, handed down in 1963. Written by Justice William Brennan, the majority opinion in *Sherbert* would provide, Ball later wrote, "the basic constitutional theory on which our Amish case would have to rest." Prior to the trial, Ball also reviewed several landmark Supreme Court decisions relating to the rights of parents. Justice James McReynolds's majority opinion in *Pierce v. Society of Sisters* (1925), long a favorite of Ball's, stood out as the most important of these. It too would serve as a cornerstone of his defense of the Amish.

Ball owed much of his eventual success in the New Glarus school attendance case to his foresight in developing sound constitutional claims for the Amish. Primarily concerned with prevailing in the appellate courts, he didn't fret too much about actually winning the case at trial. Ball instead resolved to use the trial to build an exhaustive record that would support constitutional claims grounded in such precedents as *Sherbert* and *Pierce*. Already a veteran of several lengthy, high-profile cases, he understood that arguments backed up by a persuasive record stood the best chance of withstanding the scrutiny of the appellate courts.

While the NCARF attorney doggedly laid the groundwork for a potential appeal, the lawyers representing the state of Wisconsin in *Yoder* pursued a more short-term goal: prevailing at trial. Unlike their adversary, they adopted a narrow approach to the case, focusing mainly on the facts of the school attendance dispute and intentionally downplaying the kinds of broader legal issues that Ball continually stressed. This strategy had several obvious benefits. For instance, by focusing their attention on the relatively straightforward matter of proving that the defendants had violated a valid law, prosecutors avoided the arduous task of researching mountains of judicial precedent and then relating their findings to the case at hand. (This job usually fell to the attorneys in the state attorney general's office who handled cases at the appellate level, not trial lawyers.) But this approach also had an enormous drawback: it deprived the state of a crucial opportunity to expose several apparent weaknesses in Ball's case.

Ball argued throughout *Yoder* that his clients' conduct should be protected by the clause of the First Amendment that shields the "free exercise" of religion. But his claims on behalf of the Amish were not so easily reconciled with the First Amendment clause that prohibits the establishment of religion by the state. The state might be seen as privileging members of a single religious faith if it exempted only them from the provisions of the school attendance statute. The U.S. Supreme Court's establishment clause jurisprudence was notoriously murky, but it appeared to bar such action. Ball's eagerness to invoke the protections of parents' rights furnished in precedents such as *Pierce* was problematic as well, because some of those opinions also contained fairly explicit language acknowledging the state's right to enforce school attendance statutes.

The state of Wisconsin's lawyers eventually pursued these lines of argument, but they did so in later phases of the case, long after the trial had concluded. As a result, they were burdened by a painfully thin evidentiary base when appellate courts heard *Yoder*. It appeared all the more slender when compared with the reams of trial testimony that Ball furnished to support his arguments.

"The bedrock test of a government's commitment to protecting the free exercise of religion," legal scholar Jesse Choper wrote, "arises when general government regulations, enacted for secular purposes, conflict with an individual's religious beliefs." Before the Amish school attendance case reached the courts, many such conflicts had involved adherents of other unconventional faiths, among them Mormons, Jehovah's Witnesses, and Seventh-Day Adventists. Refusing to yield to the constraints placed on their religious practice by generally applicable laws, litigants from these faiths prompted the U.S. Supreme

Court to hand down a succession of landmark religious liberty opinions. As Ball prepared to navigate *Yoder* through the courts, the Supreme Court's rulings in these cases provided a kind of jurisprudential road map, showing which routes of argument were safe and which held the most peril.

Reynolds v. United States (1879), in which Mormon George Reynolds challenged the constitutionality of a federal statute banning polygamy, gave the Supreme Court its first real opportunity to define the parameters of the First Amendment's free exercise clause. The longest and most significant part of Chief Justice Morrison Waite's opinion for the Court addressed Reynolds's claim that the federal anti-polygamy law compromised his religious liberty. Waite began his discussion of this issue by stressing that Congress lacked the authority to pass any law that would abrogate the religious liberty of individuals living in territories such as Utah. "The first amendment to the Constitution expressly forbids such legislation," he wrote. "Religious freedom is guaranteed everywhere throughout the United States, so far as congressional interference is concerned." Waite simply did not believe, however, that polygamy was a bona fide religious practice and thus beyond the reach of the regulatory authority of Congress. It was, after all, an especially "odious" custom, and "it may safely be said there never has been a time in any State of the Union when polygamy has not been an offence against society, cognizable by the civil courts and punishable with more or less severity." Moreover, marriage, for all its religious trappings, was at bottom "a civil contract," and as such it was "usually regulated by law." Surely this "most important feature of social life" was subject to some degree of control by the state, which maintained order at least in part by regulating a host of "social relations and social obligations and duties."

Waite went on to make a crucial distinction that would influence free exercise jurisprudence for decades to come. "Laws are made for the government of actions," he wrote, "and while they cannot interfere with mere religious belief and opinions, they may with practices." Reynolds, in short, was free to *believe* anything he wished, but his *conduct* remained very much subject to regulation by the state, particularly when it threatened to undermine a civil institution (marriage) that was critical to "the organization of society." That this repulsive conduct might have been inspired by a religious belief did not mean that the First Amendment protected it. "Can a man excuse his practices to the contrary [of established law] because of his religious belief?" Waite asked. "To permit this would be to make the professed doctrines of religious belief superior to the law of the land, and in effect to permit every citizen to become a law unto himself. Government could exist only in name under such circumstances."

Reynolds's most significant — and durable — legacy was the distinction between belief and conduct articulated by Chief Justice Waite. Reaffirmed by the U.S. Supreme Court in two subsequent cases involving the Mormons and polygamy, it essentially removed religious conduct from the purview of the First Amendment. In many ways straitjacketed by the *Reynolds* precedent, litigants pursuing safeguards for religious conduct were forced to seek shelter under other constitutional protections.

The Jehovah's Witnesses were particularly successful in evading the constraints of *Reynolds* and gaining judicial protections for their religious conduct. Persecuted throughout the United States during the World War II era because of their obstreperous proselytizing activities and refusal to salute the American flag (they considered the ceremony idolatrous), the Jehovah's Witnesses repeatedly sought judicial safeguarding of their imperiled civil rights. Between 1938 and 1946, their stubborn efforts resulted in nearly two dozen Supreme Court opinions and hundreds of rulings in lower state and federal courts. This unprecedented torrent of litigation had such an impact on constitutional jurisprudence that Justice Harlan Fiske Stone remarked, "I think the Jehovah's Witnesses ought to have an endowment in view of the aid which they give in solving the legal problems of civil liberties."

When Stone and his colleagues shielded the religious conduct of the Jehovah's Witnesses, they typically cited the First Amendment protections afforded to speech, press, and assembly rights. In *Cantwell v. Connecticut* (1940), however, the Supreme Court more directly addressed a religious liberty claim brought by a Witness.

The appellants in *Cantwell* challenged a Connecticut statute that required religious proselytizers to obtain a municipal permit before they canvassed in public. Their attorney, Hayden Covington, hoped that their claim would prompt the Supreme Court to expand judicial protections of religious liberty. In two previous cases involving Witness appellants — *Lovell v. Griffin* (1938) and *Schneider v. New Jersey* (1939) — the Court had continued its piecemeal incorporation of First Amendment freedoms into the due process clause of the Fourteenth Amendment. The First Amendment applied only to actions by the federal government, but the absorption of some of its protections into the Fourteenth Amendment meant that they now applied to actions by the states as well. Those cases, however, had involved free speech and free press issues; the right to free exercise of religion had not yet been incorporated. Covington urged the Court to use *Cantwell* to continue the process of incorporation and bar states from abridging an individual's religious liberty.

Justice Owen Roberts's majority opinion in *Cantwell v. Connecticut* by no means indicated that the Supreme Court was totally abandoning its reasoning in *Reynolds*. Roberts echoed Chief Justice Waite's opinion in the Mormon polygamy case by writing that the free exercise clause encompassed "two concepts — freedom to believe and freedom to act. The first is absolute, but in the nature of things, the second cannot be." In short, the state might exercise control over some forms of conduct even though they were motivated by an individual's religious beliefs. In the context of the Witnesses' proselytizing, this regulation might involve the nondiscriminatory regulation of the time, place, and manner of their public solicitation.

Cantwell differed from *Reynolds* in the level of scrutiny applied to the actions taken by the state to limit religious conduct. In the Jehovah's Witness case, the Supreme Court examined the state's regulation with heightened scrutiny. Using this more rigorous standard, the Court determined that application of the permit requirements to the Witnesses' religious conduct represented an unconstitutional infringement on their religious liberty. Justice Roberts wrote that although the Connecticut permit law at issue was neutral on its face, it was so broadly drawn that public officials had wide latitude to take actions infringing on religious liberty. He reasoned that a more narrowly drawn law would not have placed "a forbidden burden upon the exercise of liberty protected by the Constitution."

Cantwell was a watershed for religious liberty. In addition to incorporating the free exercise clause into the Fourteenth Amendment, the Supreme Court for the first time recognized constitutional protections for religious conduct. But *Cantwell* did not signal that the justices were enthusiastic about claims made strictly under the free exercise clause. In subsequent Jehovah's Witness cases, the Court seemed willing to strike down generally applicable laws only if they were challenged as infringements of multiple First Amendment freedoms. The Court's analysis in these cases typically focused on press and speech issues; religious liberty seemed to take a backseat. Indeed, strict religious liberty claims uniformly failed.

In *Braunfeld v. Brown* (1961), the Supreme Court began to fashion a new approach to such claims. This case involved a challenge by a group of Orthodox Jewish merchants to a Pennsylvania statute that prohibited certain businesses from operating on Sundays. The merchants, whose faith proscribed business transactions on Saturdays, asserted that enforcement of the state blue law unfairly disadvantaged them by effectively forcing them to observe another Sabbath day. Their claim failed: the Supreme Court held that the indirect burden placed on the merchants' religious liberty resulted from their own actions rather than the state's. As it ruled against the appellants in *Braunfeld*, the Court began to flesh out a balancing test for evaluating legislation that regulated religious conduct. The justices held that a state's interests in enforcing a generally applicable law should be weighed against the potential impact of granting an exemption to such a statute. "If the state regulates conduct by enacting a general law within its conduct," Chief Justice Earl Warren wrote, "the purpose and effect of which is to advance the state's secular goals, the statute is valid despite its indirect burden on religious observance unless the state may accomplish its purpose by means which do not impose such a burden." In other words, the state had to demonstrate that its interests could not be served by a less restrictive action.

In *Braunfeld*, the Supreme Court recognized that judicial accommodation of religious beliefs could raise potential establishment clause issues. In his opinion for the Court's plurality, Chief Justice Warren observed that a state might violate the establishment clause if it exempted religious objectors from generally applicable laws. Exempting the Orthodox Jewish merchants from the blue law, he noted, "might well provide these people with an economic advantage over their competitors who must remain closed on [Sunday]." It also might precipitate a deluge of religious exemption claims from unscrupulous merchants who sought to evade the strictures of the Sunday-closing law. "This might make necessary a state-conducted inquiry into the sincerity of the individual's religious beliefs," Warren wrote, "a practice which a state might believe would itself run afoul of the spirit of constitutionally protected religious guarantees."

The Supreme Court built on *Braunfeld* in *Sherbert v. Verner* (1963), a decision that "completely reformulated free exercise doctrine," in the words of legal scholar Carolyn Long. Justice William Brennan's majority opinion in *Sherbert* introduced a new balancing test to evaluate religious liberty claims. The three-tiered *Sherbert* standard subjected government actions to a higher level of scrutiny than had been applied in previous cases centering on the free exercise of religion.

Brennan began the majority opinion in *Sherbert* — in which a Seventh-Day Adventist named Adell Sherbert challenged South Carolina's denial of unemployment benefits because she refused to work on Saturday, her faith's Sabbath — by restating a few of the central tenets of free exercise jurisprudence. He noted that while "the door of the Free Exercise Clause stands tightly closed against any governmental regulation of religious beliefs as such," an individual's conduct could be regulated if it "posed some substantial threat to public safety, peace or order."

Having acknowledged those rough parameters, Brennan addressed the main constitutional issues presented by Sherbert's claim. First was the question of whether the Seventh-Day Adventist's right to the free exercise of religion had been violated by the state's decision to disqualify her from receiving unemployment benefits. Brennan's opinion for the Court held that such an infringement had in fact taken place. The state of South Carolina, he wrote, had compelled Sherbert "to choose between following the precepts of her religion and forfeiting benefits, on the one hand, and abandoning one of the precepts of her religion in order to accept work, on the other hand. Governmental imposition of such a choice puts the same kind of burden upon the free exercise of religion as would a fine imposed against [her] for her Saturday worship."

After answering the first question of the *Sherbert* test — did the government's action burden the claimant's religious liberty? — Brennan moved on to assess the state's interest in applying the regulation at issue. Known as the "compelling state interest" test, this second prong of the *Sherbert* standard considered whether the state's uniform application of the regulation served to protect it from "the gravest abuses, endangering paramount interests," as the Court had put it in another case. Brennan asserted that the relatively innocuous circumstances of *Sherbert* did not present such a dire threat to the state's interests. "No such abuse or danger," he wrote, "has been advanced in the present case."

Under the third and final question of the *Sherbert* standard, the Court asked whether an exemption to the generally applicable regulation would undermine the state's compelling interest. South Carolina had attempted to address this question by painting a bleak picture of what might happen if the state set an example by providing Sherbert with benefits. It asserted, as Brennan put it, that "unscrupulous claimants feigning religious objections to Saturday work" might exploit the unemployment compensation system or disrupt work schedules of factories. Brennan dismissed this line of reasoning by pointing out that "there is no proof whatever to warrant such fears of malingering or deceit."

Using this new framework for analyzing religious liberty claims, the U.S. Supreme Court ruled in favor of Sherbert. In doing so, the justices broke new ground by explicitly applying a higher level of scrutiny to a regulation that, despite its surface neutrality, encumbered an individual's religious belief or practice. The rigorous *Sherbert* standard placed a heavy burden on states, requiring them to justify the need to enforce such laws when the particular application of a statute appeared to imperil religious liberty.

No one appreciated this more than William Ball. As soon as the NCARF attorney became involved in the New Glarus case, he recognized that his best hope for prevailing lay in asking the courts to subject Wisconsin's actions to the heightened scrutiny mandated by *Sherbert*. Convinced that the state's case was likely to crumble under such a searching inquiry, he planned to argue that the prosecutions of the New Glarus Amish failed under all three prongs of the nascent *Sherbert* standard.

Although Ball's claims on behalf of the Amish seemed to square with the Supreme Court's religious liberty jurisprudence, they were more difficult to harmonize with judicial precedent regarding the First

Amendment's other religion provision, the establishment clause. His dilemma demonstrated just how tangled the Supreme Court's approach to these two areas had become.

The First Amendment's religion clauses are ostensibly separate, and it is convenient to analyze the Supreme Court's religion jurisprudence along similarly distinct lines. On the one hand are the Court's decisions in cases such as *Sherbert*, in which state action appears to inhibit an individual's right to the free exercise of religion; on the other hand are its decisions in cases in which the state appears to be promulgating laws "respecting an establishment of religion." But, as Carolyn Long noted, the dividing line between the religion clauses is fuzzy at best. "The two religion clauses appear separate but they actually overlap," Long wrote, "and there is often tension between the two, although each works to protect religious freedom." The Supreme Court's religion jurisprudence reflects the sometimes ambiguous distinction between the religion clauses. It has developed along two ostensibly separate lines that often intersect and conflict with each other.

No single approach has dominated the Supreme Court's interpretation of the establishment clause. In its first significant decision dealing with that provision, *Everson v. Board of Education* (1947), the Court held that government and religious bodies should be strictly separated. Justice Hugo Black's majority opinion in *Everson* referred to Thomas Jefferson's famous declaration that there should be a figurative wall dividing church and state. But *Everson* showed just how difficult it is to apply such broad concepts to specific practical contexts. Although all the justices endorsed Black's call for strict separation, only a bare majority agreed with his conclusion that the program at issue, which used public funds to reimburse parents for the costs of transporting their children to religious schools, was in fact constitutional.

In two cases involving so-called released-time programs, the task of strictly separating church and state in the context of public education continued to vex the Supreme Court. In *Illinois ex rel. McCollum v. Board of Education* (1947), the Court struck down an Illinois public school board's plan that permitted clergy of various faiths to provide religious instruction to students on school grounds during regular school hours. Writing for the majority, Justice Black argued that even though students were not required to participate in it, the released-time program furnished impermissible public aid to religion. But, much to Black's consternation, the Court appeared to back away from *McCollum* in *Zorach v. Clauson* (1952), its next decision on a released-time program. Because the program at issue in *Zorach* provided religious instruction off school grounds, the Court held that it did not violate the strictures of the establishment clause. Justice William Douglas's opinion in *Zorach* downplayed the notion of strict separation and instead stressed the importance of accommodating religion, another important theme in the Court's establishment clause jurisprudence.

In *Abington School District v. Schempp* (1963), the Supreme Court formulated a two-pronged test for evaluating statutes that appeared to violate the establishment clause. The law at issue, the Court held, must have a secular legislative purpose, and its main effect could neither advance nor inhibit religion. Viewed within this framework, *Schempp*, which involved a law mandating Bible readings in public schools, was a relatively easy call for the justices: they held that the statute violated the strictures of the establishment clause. (They had reached a similar conclusion a year earlier in *Engel v. Vitale* [1962], another school prayer case.)

The Supreme Court attempted to further refine its establishment clause jurisprudence in *Lemon v. Kurtzman*, another case in which attorney William Ball played a prominent role. (It reached the Supreme Court in 1971, just before *Yoder*.) In *Lemon*, Ball defended a Pennsylvania law that authorized the state to purchase "secular educational services" from nonpublic schools. In striking down the plan, the justices synthesized the "cumulative criteria developed by the Court over many years" in such cases as *Schempp* and *Board of Education v. Allen* (1968). They completed this thorny task by adding a third prong to the test first articulated in *Schempp*. Under this third standard, a statute did not conform with the establishment clause if it fostered excessive entanglement between the state and religion.

Few scholars, attorneys, or jurists who reviewed these establishment clause decisions found them consistent or easy to discern. The Supreme Court seemed to struggle to develop a bright-line standard that would reconcile the notions of strict separation, neutrality, and accommodation. With new tests being announced by the high court at almost every turn, it became difficult to predict how the justices would evaluate a particular state action under the establishment clause. What's more, decisions that bolstered the establishment clause sometimes seemed to undermine the protections of the free exercise clause. Not only did the Supreme Court have difficulty harmonizing various strains within its establishment clause jurisprudence; it also struggled with the larger task of reconciling the First Amendment's two religion clauses.

But even in the muddle of the Supreme Court's jurisprudence in this area, it appeared that the exemption sought by the Amish in *Yoder* was open to challenge under the evolving set of standards that came to be known as "the *Lemon* test." For instance, it would be difficult for Ball to argue that there was a truly secular purpose behind exempting members of a single religious faith from the provisions of Wisconsin's school attendance law. Such an action certainly would seem to have the nonsecular goal of safeguarding the Amish alone and not adherents of other faiths. And wouldn't the exemption entangle the state and the Amish? Wouldn't state officials be required to conduct an investigation into the beliefs and practices of the Amish to determine whether their claims were bona fide? In *Braunfeld*, hadn't the Court cautioned that such an inquiry might "run afoul of the spirit of constitutionally protected religious guarantees"?

Such questions were a potential minefield for Ball, and he planned to tread lightly around them at the trial in *Yoder*. His primary focus would be on free exercise and parental rights issues. Although he crafted the bulk of his case around the *Sherbert* precedent, Ball also felt strongly that the state's action against the New Glarus Amish was vulnerable to a parental rights claim. At least on the surface, judicial precedent in this realm seemed to bolster the Amish case as well.

The U.S. Supreme Court has long acknowledged the right of parents to direct the upbringing of their children. In an opinion handed down by the Supreme Court in the spring of 2000, Justice Sandra Day O'Connor noted that "the interest of parents in the care, custody, and control of their children . . . is perhaps the oldest of the fundamental liberty interests recognized by this Court." Among the Supreme Court's earliest opinions dealing with these matters was *Meyer v. Nebraska* (1923), a case in which a teacher named Robert Meyer challenged a Nebraska law banning instruction in foreign languages.

In his majority opinion in *Meyer*, Justice James McReynolds acknowledged the state's power to regulate education and act within its well-established authority to ensure that the welfare of minors was safeguarded. The law at issue in the case, however, only served to protect youngsters from knowledge of a foreign language, "and experience shows that this is not injurious to the health, morals or understanding of the ordinary child." Consequently, the "statute as applied is arbitrary and without reasonable relation to any end within the competency of the state."

The heart of McReynolds's opinion dealt with Meyer's claim that the state statute infringed on his right to pursue his profession as a teacher. McReynolds grounded his response to this contention in the due process clause of the Fourteenth Amendment. He acknowledged that although the Supreme Court had yet to provide a precise definition of the "liberty" guaranteed by the Fourteenth Amendment, it undoubtedly included "the right of individual to contract, to engage in any of the common occupations of life, to acquire useful knowledge, to marry, to establish a home and bring up children, to worship God according to the dictates of his own conscience, and generally to enjoy those privileges long recognized at common law as essential to the orderly pursuit of happiness by free men."

Although the narrow issue in *Meyer* was a teacher's right to pursue his profession, this broad application of the notion of "substantive due process" also afforded protection to parents' interests in directing the upbringing of their children. It included an acknowledgment that parents possessed the right "to control the education of their own."

The notion of substantive due process was grounded in the idea that individuals have inalienable liberties that merit protection from unreasonable state action. According to this controversial doctrine, these fundamental rights are worthy of safeguarding even though they might not be explicitly mentioned in the Constitution or particular statutes. In the early part of the twentieth century, a conservative Supreme Court majority invoked due process to justify the notion of "freedom of contract" and strike down a variety of Progressive reforms that regulated workers' wages and hours. The doctrine of substantive due process also came into play in cases such as *Meyer* and *Pierce v. Society of Sisters*, when the Court held that it shielded the right of parents to direct the upbringing of their children without undue interference by the state.

Pierce involved a challenge to an Oregon law that mandated attendance in public schools (and effectively banned enrollment at parochial institutions). In his opinion for the Supreme Court, Justice James McReynolds did not deny that the state possessed a general right to compel school attendance. But to McReynolds, it was "entirely plain" that the Oregon law represented an overextension of the state's legitimate authority to govern education. Hearkening back to the Court's substantive due process holding in *Meyer*, McReynolds wrote that the Oregon law was unconstitutional because it "unreasonably interferes with the liberty of parents and guardians to direct the upbringing and education of children under their control." In the most famous passage of his *Pierce* opinion, McReynolds reiterated the Court's commitment to protecting the right of parents to control the upbringing of their sons and daughters: "The child is not the mere creature of the state; those who nurture him and direct his destiny have the right, coupled with the high duty, to recognize and prepare him for additional obligations."

McReynolds's words in *Pierce* resonated with attorney William Ball. In his book *Mere Creatures of the State?* (the title was borrowed, of course, from McReynolds's opinion), Ball insisted that the U.S. Supreme Court's ruling in the Oregon case "flatly contradicted blank-check public regulatory power over private education." The decision was sound constitutionally, and it also squared "with the teachings of Catholics, Evangelicals, and Orthodox Jews on education and parental rights and in defense of religious schools and parental rights and duties." For those reasons, *Pierce* was a touchstone for Ball, and it troubled him to see "the rights which it defined . . . come under attack," as had happened in the decades after the opinion was handed down. The rights of parents and children who used private and parochial schools were imperiled because "precisely the situation envisioned by the Court, and scathingly rejected by it in *Pierce*, has come into existence, with enormous power claimed by the state over the education of the young." For Ball, the *Yoder* case mattered so much because it provided a chance to stem this tide and help preserve "the freedom of religious education from rampant state power."

But ironically, the attorneys representing the state of Wisconsin in *Yoder* also could take some hope from the U.S. Supreme Court's ruling in *Pierce*. Ball believed that *Pierce* amounted to nothing less than a charter for parents' rights, but portions of it acknowledged the government's right to regulate education through the enforcement of reasonable laws. In one passage of the *Pierce* opinion, McReynolds noted that the case raised "no question . . . concerning the power of the state reasonably to regulate all schools." Nor was there any question that the state could "require that all children of proper age attend some school." McReynolds's majority opinion in *Meyer v. Nebraska* included similar language: it recognized "the power of the state to compel attendance at some school and to make reasonable regulations for all schools."

Although Ball stressed their importance as shields for the rights of parents, there was little doubt that *Meyer* and *Pierce* also provided some support for the proposition that states did not trample on individual rights when they enforced basic laws to regulate education. Indeed, both opinions went so far as to suggest that operating schools and providing sufficient oversight for them were essential functions of the states. As judicial precedent, they were double-edged swords for the Amish.

Like *Meyer* and *Pierce* before it, the high court's landmark opinion in *Brown v. Board of Education* (1954) lent weight to the argument that it was constitutionally permissible for states to enforce measures such as compulsory school attendance laws. "Today, education is perhaps the most important function of state and local governments," the Court concluded unanimously in *Brown*. "Compulsory school attendance laws and great expenditures for education both demonstrate our recognition of the importance of education to our democratic society." The state could point to this passage if Ball referred to the *Sherbert* precedent and asserted that the state lacked a sufficiently compelling interest in enforcing the Wisconsin law mandating school attendance.

And the state of Wisconsin could reach beyond the *Brown*, *Pierce*, and *Meyer* precedents when it defended the enforcement of the compulsory school attendance statute. The U.S. Supreme Court's opinion in *Prince v. Massachusetts* (1944), for instance, seemed to support a claim that the doctrine of *parens patriae* (the notion that the state has a role as the guardian of juveniles and others who are under legal disability) permitted it to compel school attendance. *Prince* involved a challenge to the enforcement of a child labor law by a Jehovah's Witness who maintained that it infringed on her religious liberty. (She had been charged under the law after her niece sold religious tracts in public.)

The Supreme Court denied her claim, with Justice Frank Murphy writing for the majority that there were limits to the protections afforded by the Constitution to parental rights and religious liberty. The family, Murphy wrote, "is not beyond regulation in the public interest, as against a claim of religious liberty. . . . And neither rights of religion nor rights of parenthood are beyond limitation."

Prince also addressed the potential conflict between parents' rights and school attendance laws. "Acting to guard the general interest in the youth's well being," Murphy wrote, "the state as parens patriae may restrict the parent's control by requiring school attendance, regulating or prohibiting the child's labor, and in many other ways." As it had in *Meyer* and *Pierce*, the Supreme Court in *Prince* specifically noted that states possessed the right to enforce school attendance laws.

Judicial precedent thus provided no easy answers for the attorneys involved in *Yoder*. Although the Supreme Court's free exercise jurisprudence seemed to bolster the claims of the Amish, its decisions in establishment clause cases appeared to support the state's actions. Precedent in the field of parents' rights was similarly ambiguous. Heading into the trial, it was difficult to determine whether either the Amish or the state of Wisconsin really had the law on its side.

CHAPTER 6

The Trial of Wallace Miller, Jonas Yoder, and Adin Yutzy

On the morning of April 2, 1969, spectators streamed into the Green County Courthouse in Monroe, Wisconsin, for the trial of Wallace Miller, Jonas Yoder, and Adin Yutzy. Alert to the potential significance of the case, newspaper reporters arrived from as far away as Milwaukee. They filed into the second-floor courtroom with a solemn contingent of Amish. These "strangely garbed, bearded dissidents," as one observer called them, watched the trial in silence from the back of the courtroom.

There would be no jury. Attorney William Ball claimed that public animus toward the Amish made it impossible for his clients to get a fair hearing before a panel of jurors. "Local press stories unfavorable to the Amish and Amish lack of association with the general population of Green County," he explained, "made me feel that my clients might do as well, or better, without a jury." Ball took his chances with Judge Roger Elmer, who was "studious-seeming, equable, interested."

The proceedings began with a couple of routine technical matters, among them a defense motion to excuse defendant Adin Yutzy from attending the proceedings. Yutzy had moved to Missouri not long after authorities charged him with violating Wisconsin's compulsory school attendance law. According to defense attorney Tom Eckerle, Yutzy had indicated that "it would be a considerable hardship to return today for the trial" and asked to be excused from attending. After securing the approval of the prosecution team — Green County district attorney Louis Koenig and deputy state attorney general Robert Martinson — the judge granted the defense's motion.

After Judge Elmer excused Yutzy, Ball took over from Eckerle. His first order of business was to make a motion to dismiss the complaints against the defendants. Ball asserted that although Wisconsin's compulsory school attendance law was not unconstitutional per se, its application to the Amish defendants deprived them and their children of rights that were protected by both the federal and state constitutions. Ball maintained that the measure was "unconstitutional as it applies to these defendants due to the fact of their religious beliefs and practices. We believe this is a fact." No single claim was more central to the defense's case, and over the next several years, Ball would reiterate it numerous times in briefs, oral arguments, interviews, and published writings.

Deputy attorney general Martinson, whose presence at the trial signaled the state's keen interest in fending off a challenge to its school attendance statute, responded to Ball's motion with a two-pronged attack. He began by noting that the Wisconsin Supreme Court in *State v. Freudenberg* had ruled that the state's compulsory school attendance law was constitutional. Next, he referred to the defense's Achilles' heel, the Kansas Supreme Court's ruling in *State v. Garber.* In that case, Martinson said, "almost the same claim" had been made by the Amish defendants — namely, "that the compulsory school attendance law is in violation of the Constitution of the United States as to the religious freedom." The Kansas court, however, had rejected that claim and upheld LeRoy Garber's conviction, and the U.S. Supreme Court had refused to hear his appeal, effectively giving the lower court ruling its imprimatur. Although the Kansas ruling was not binding in Wisconsin courts, Martinson believed that Judge Elmer should reach a similar conclusion, for "the religious beliefs of the defendants has nothing to do with the case here."

Ball abhorred the comparison to *Garber,* and he did what he could to undercut Martinson's contentions. Making a final effort for his motion to dismiss the charges, he scoffed at the idea that the Wisconsin court should follow the shaky precedent established by *Garber.* The Kansas case, he insisted, was not directly analogous to the Green County prosecutions. What's more, even if *Garber* was comparable, "it was badly decided" and thus not worthy of Elmer's attention. In the end, his arguments failed to sway the judge; Elmer denied the motion to dismiss and instructed the state to begin its case.

After sparring with Ball over the motion to dismiss, Martinson did not make an opening statement to the court. Instead, he plunged directly into the state's case by calling Kenneth Glewen, the superintendent of the New Glarus school district, to the stand. Martinson led

Glewen through a largely perfunctory review of his sixteen-year career as an educator in various small communities in Iowa and Wisconsin. Then, prompted by the deputy attorney general, Glewen described in some detail his interactions with the Yoder and Miller families during the late summer and fall of 1968. When the school year had begun that August, Glewen testified, he had learned that numerous Amish children in the New Glarus area had failed to report to school. Investigating the situation, he had discerned that the Amish "would be building their own school in the very near future, and they intended to get at it and get it built so students could attend," he told the court. When the Amish school was up and running, Glewen had compared its attendance rolls with a list of absentees from the public high school and determined that seven youngsters who had yet to reach their sixteenth birthdays, including the Yoder, Miller, and Yutzy children, had not enrolled in either school. They had been truant.

Glewen had directly informed most of the Amish parents involved that they were violating the state's compulsory attendance law by not enrolling their children in school. To underline the seriousness of the problem posed by the children's truancy, he also had sent the parents warning letters via certified mail. Glewen testified that he had taken up the attendance issue with several members of the local Amish school board, including Wallace Miller, one of the defendants. As Glewen recalled on the stand, Miller had told him that "he was right in not sending his child to school because it was against their belief, and he felt that the First Amendment to the Constitution of the United States gave them this freedom to practice their religion, and in this case felt this was part of his religion that his child should not attend school beyond eighth grade." This contention had not made much of an impression on the school administrator, and he had initiated the charges against the Amish fathers.

It didn't take Ball long to start hammering away at Glewen. During his cross-examination, he asked the school administrator about the opening of the Amish school in the fall of 1968 and its impact on the local public school system. A reluctant Glewen acknowledged that his school district had lost about three dozen Amish students and that their defection had cost the district approximately $18,000 in state aid. Glewen sheepishly conceded that he had endeavored to mitigate this blow to the school district's finances by attempting to persuade some of the Amish parents to "hold off" on transferring their children out of public school "until the third Friday of September, when we count our school population." Because state aid was allotted on a per-pupil basis, this bit of chicanery would have prevented the school district from losing the $18,000. The Amish, however, had balked at Glewen's scheme, and it had come to nothing.

Martinson called Fola Thacker, the clerk of the New Glarus school board, as the prosecution's next witness. Thacker testified only briefly, and her sole contribution was to confirm that none of the children had been granted an exemption from attending school by the school board. Minnie Weaver followed Thacker on the stand. Led by Martinson, she told the court that she had been the teacher at the Pleasant View Amish school during the fall of 1968. She explained that classes had been in session for more than six hours a day, five days a week; that she had instructed pupils in "arithmetic, English, spelling, reading, geography, [and] social studies"; and that a total of twenty-three Amish students had been enrolled in the school in grades one through eight. Martinson did not specifically ask Weaver if the Yoder, Miller, and Yutzy children had attended the school that fall. Instead, he used her testimony to establish that the Pleasant View school had not accommodated any older Amish students.

The state rested after Weaver's testimony. Doing his best to dodge the broad constitutional issues raised by the state's decision to enforce the compulsory attendance law against the Amish, Martinson had put on a bare-bones case, with only Glewen offering much substantive testimony. This strategy allowed the state to frame the case as a relatively straightforward matter: the courts in Wisconsin had long accepted the constitutionality of the state's school code, and the Amish defendants clearly had violated that statute by failing to send their children to accredited schools after they reached age fourteen. If the law was valid and the Amish had breached it, the state's argument went, they must be guilty as charged.

Ball's trial strategy was evident from the moment he began the defense's case. In his opening statement, he stressed that application of the state compulsory attendance law to the Amish "will jeopardize their freedom of religion," because forcing them to attend a public high school "removes them from the religious environment which is the core of their religion" and "subjects them to influences which run [counter] to their religious belief." Ball intended to develop his arguments on this score as exhaustively as possible. The NCARF attorney believed that the Amish had failed in *Garber* at least in part because most of the facts had been stipulated at trial. Thanks to the inadequate trial record, the appellate courts had failed to fathom how oppressive compulsory school attendance laws were to the Amish. Already looking ahead to the appeal of the *Yoder* case, Ball was determined not to repeat that mistake.

After his opening statement, Ball called Glewen back to the stand. As he put it midway through his questioning, Ball hoped to determine what sort of values were being taught in the public schools and how they might conflict with the beliefs of the Amish. Glewen stated that although the theory of evolution was routinely taught, the schools did not tout the Ten Commandments "as a norm or standard to be followed," as Ball put it. Prompted by the defense attorney, Glewen also noted that the schools did not provide "moral training" in either formal or informal settings. When Martinson objected to this line of questioning, Ball shot back that he was merely trying to demonstrate that the Amish were "extremely God-centered," and for them "to be placed in an atmosphere which is not God-centered [creates] a problem in conflict with their basic religious beliefs."

Temple University professor John Hostetler was Ball's next witness. After running through his expert's extraordinary qualifications and soliciting a brief history of the Amish faith, Ball asked Hostetler to summarize a few of the characteristics that made the Amish belief system so unique and all-encompassing. This he did by emphasizing four separate points: the requirement that a church community be "separate from the world"; the use of adult baptism to signal an "ethical obligation to God and man"; "the maintenance of community rules that are binding on the members" of the faith; and the cultivation of an "affinity to nature — to soil, the simple life, the moderate life best expressed in the rural society." For the case at hand, the stress on separation was clearly the most important principle, and Ball immediately asked Hostetler to elaborate on it. "The concept of separation is part of the process of the saved community," he explained. "You need the assistance of the saved brotherhood in order to get to the final destination, which in the church and religion is heaven." But to reach that ultimate goal, he continued, "one cannot walk with the unbeliever, one cannot be a part of the unbelieving world, have the same values."

Hostetler's discussion of separation led to an exploration of Amish attitudes toward education. The Amish, he said, "have great concern about the values that are taught to their children," and they, like members of most religious groups, were greatly concerned with teaching their youngsters "the ultimate meaning of their faith." In the course of imparting this knowledge, most Amish parents conveyed a number of basic teachings to their children, Hostetler testified. He said that the Amish "have very strong teachings in regard to obedience to parents, strong teachings [regarding the] value of physical work in the community, the dignity of work, the importance of work." Hostetler, recognizing that such teachings were not central to public school curricula, added that "the goals of the Amish culture with reference to children do contrast sharply with the values that are promoted in the non-Amish society," particularly in the public schools.

Hostetler was quick to point out that the Amish were not opposed to all forms of formal schooling. As he put it in a summary of a federally funded study of Amish education, "Children are urged not to be idle but to learn to read and write so that they may acquire a knowledge of the Scriptures." Learning the basic elements of arithmetic was important as well, for those skills could prove useful around the home or farm. But while the Amish recognized that primary schooling could provide their children with some useful literacy skills, they viewed high school as part and parcel of a "plainly corrupt" world that was to be avoided at all costs, Hostetler testified. "In the Amish view, the high school is higher learning," he said. "It is an effort toward wisdom which is wisdom not responsible to the community. . . . It militates against the obedience to the community and religion." Part of what made high school so threatening to the Amish was that they viewed it "as deterrent to a way of salvation, as an introduction of topics that are competing against the value system, against the religion in their own society."

Hostetler also commented on the immense dangers that compulsory education laws posed to the Amish. He followed up his comments on the goals of Amish education by stating flatly, "And I think that if the Amish youth are required to attend the value system of the high school as we know it today, the church-community cannot last long. It will be destroyed." A number of Amish who had been victims of "some similar kinds of persecution" had recently immigrated to Central America, and Hostetler suggested that Amish families in Green County might follow suit if their children were compelled by law to attend high school. He added that should the Amish be "forced to attend school against the religion of the church-community, and to remain in the school teaching values contrary to their belief, great psychological harm can be done to their children."

Martinson felt that there were several weak spots in Hostetler's testimony, and he probed most of them in a lengthy and tense cross-examination that marked one of the high points of the trial. Attempting to chip away the defendants' justifications for breaking the state compulsory attendance law, the deputy attorney general forced Hostetler to concede that the Amish routinely interacted with their neighbors and thus did not completely separate themselves from the world at large. "There is a preferred pattern of isolation, but they do not want total isolation [from] the world," Hostetler said. "They want to be in the world but not of the world, not in its spirit." Once he had established that the Amish principle of separation was not an absolute, Martinson suggested that the eighth-grade cutoff for school attendance was more or less arbitrary. After all, he noted, none of the defendants had been able to point to "anything in the Amish religion specifically saying, such a rule or illustration, that no child of the Amish faith could properly attend high school." Hostetler maintained his composure and patiently explained that the principles governing a particular Amish community—its *Ordnung*—were established by "oral consensus" and not a written code.

Not satisfied with these small victories, the deputy attorney general pressed on with his cross-examination, asserting that Hostetler advocated allowing members of minority groups to "set up their own rules as to whether they shall or shall not be educated." Hostetler responded, "I think we need to know a great deal about how to teach the culturally different child . . . and I think it is dangerous to put all children through the same type of value orientation." Martinson replied that high schools hardly imposed a uniform curriculum; elective courses were readily available, "so the children won't all have to take the same" classes. Hostetler didn't see how that was relevant to the case at hand. For the Amish, he noted, "it doesn't matter what courses they take" in high school, for they are still being exposed to an overall environment that fosters worldliness and threatens to undermine their faith.

Hostetler's refusal to give ground frustrated Martinson, and he tried a different tactic by asking what appeared to be a straightforward question: "The principal purpose to attend school is to get an education, is it not, isn't that the primary purpose?" He apparently was trying to corner Hostetler: once the witness agreed to the seemingly obvious proposition that parents sent their children to school to provide them with an education, Martinson would be able to argue that no one in a modern society could reasonably believe that children could be harmed by learning. But Hostetler refused to fall into the trap. In response to Martinson's question, he testified that he believed "there is a great deal of difference what education means, education for what." To Martinson, the answer was obvious: "To put it bluntly, education so the child can make his or her place in the world."

Here Hostetler hesitated, and the courtroom fell silent. After a pause, the witness finally said, "It depends on which world."

Shortly after this moment of "intense drama," as Ball later called it, Martinson concluded his cross-examination and yielded to Ball, who realized that Hostetler had drawn a profound distinction between temporal and spiritual worlds. The defense attorney immediately returned to Hostetler's comments on the purpose of education. "Coming back to your remark of two worlds," Ball said, "were you suggesting that Amish education has as its basic goal the achieving of heaven?" Hostetler said that he meant exactly that, and a few moments later he agreed when Ball suggested that "an education which did not direct itself to that solution or ultimate goal would not be education to the Amish." In short, Hostetler argued that attending a public high school and being continuously exposed to what Martinson had described as its "worldly influence" would provide the wrong kind of instruction for Amish students who hoped to prepare themselves for heaven.

In retrospect, it is difficult to overstate the importance of Hostetler's testimony. His examination of the beliefs of the Amish and their bearing on the dispute would serve as the backbone of the exhaustive trial record that Ball built to support his arguments on behalf of Miller,

Yoder, and Yutzy. As *Yoder* made its way through the appellate courts, his conclusions would be cited repeatedly — and favorably — by the judges who were attempting to resolve the case.

Reuben Hershberger, the next witness called to the stand by Ball, made some of the same points stressed by Hostetler, though he did so from a far different perspective. An Amishman who lived on a farm in Belleville, Wisconsin, Hershberger testified that sending youngsters to school beyond eighth grade "is against our religion." When Ball asked him to elaborate, Hershberger struggled to match Hostetler's scholarly examination of Amish beliefs. "It was explained very much this forenoon," he said. "It is — well, as I said, I can't explain things like some people can, but see the way things are going, and that for the religious problems we have, we see that we can handle our religion better, our religious battle better, if [children] do not attend school." Perhaps because he understood that they might be uncomfortable testifying, Ball kept his direct examination of Amish witnesses, including Hershberger, relatively brief. Martinson took longer to question Hershberger on cross-examination, and in doing so he gave the Amishman a chance to speak more eloquently about his faith. When Martinson asked him about the eighth-grade limit for schooling, Hershberger provided a revealing, homespun answer. "Well, when the children get to that age," he said, "we feel that someone else has to take hold . . . and you got to get that religion in them. Just like when you plant a tree — you got to plant it straight or it always will be crooked."

Hershberger's testimony provided the most unsettling moment of the trial for the defense. When Ball asked him an apparently routine question about whether the absent Adin Yutzy "was a member in good standing" of the Amish faith and thus held the same beliefs regarding education as his codefendants, Hershberger caught attorneys Ball and Eckerle by surprise. "He was no member within our church," Hershberger said. Ball dropped the matter, then came back to it a few moments later, asking again if Yutzy was "an Amishman in good standing." Again, Hershberger said he wasn't.

Although the exact circumstances of his decision are unclear, Yutzy apparently had drifted away from the Old Order Amish in New Glarus sometime in the late 1960s. Before he left for Missouri, he had affiliated himself with a Conservative Amish Mennonite Church in Muscoda, Wisconsin. His minister there was named Roy Headings.

Ball was taken aback by Hershberger's pronouncements about Yutzy because he hadn't spoken extensively with the witness before the trial. "You should always know what your witness is going to say," Eckerle later commented. "That was one of Ball's few mistakes." Hershberger's testimony about Yutzy "just blew us out of the water" because it undercut a pillar of the defense's case — the notion that the defendants were bound together by a uniform set of beliefs, which included a prohibition of formal schooling beyond the age of fourteen. Disastrously for the defense, it was now unclear whether Miller, Yoder, and Yutzy actually shared the same faith. The state easily could pounce on that uncertainty to bolster its claim that application of the compulsory school attendance law did not violate the defendants' religious liberty.

Prosecutor Martinson inexplicably missed the import of Hershberger's comments regarding Yutzy, and they were not mentioned again during the remainder of the trial. After dodging the proverbial bullet, Ball gave Eckerle the task of repairing any damage done to the trial record by Hershberger's testimony. After the trial, the Madison attorney scrambled to contact Yutzy and have him submit to the court a statement regarding his religious faith. In that document he wrote: "The reason we kept [our son] out of school was because it went against our religious beliefs to send him to a school where some of the teachings and surroundings were contrary to our beliefs. . . . I feel we kept our son home from school for the same reason the other two families at New Glarus did." Vernon Yutzy agreed with his parents that it would be wrong for him to attend high school. "Vernon also did not want to go for [the] reason that he felt the evil influence outweighed the good," Yutzy wrote.

The two other members of the Amish community who testified at the trial were more directly involved in the case than Hershberger was, and their testimony benefited the defense. Ball initially had not intended to call any of the Amish children as witnesses. However, William Lindholm of the National Committee for Amish Religious Freedom "absolutely insisted" on it, because "they were the ones that were being affected" by the prosecution. During a trial strategy session, Lindholm bluntly told Ball, "I want the Amish students on [the stand]." The defense attorney eventually relented and agreed to call Frieda Yoder to testify.

Obviously cowed by the proceedings, the fifteen-year-old gave one-word answers to fifteen of the sixteen questions put to her by Ball and Martinson. Nonetheless, she managed to make an important contribution to the defendants' case by agreeing with Ball's assessment that attending high school would be "against your religious belief." When Martinson, trying to handle the cross-examination as sensitively as possible, gently asked her if that was indeed true, she stood her ground.

Wallace Miller was the only Amish defendant to testify, and Ball, having already established through the testimony of Hostetler and Frieda Yoder that Amish beliefs prohibited high school attendance, took a slightly different approach in questioning him. Throughout his involvement in the case, the defense attorney had urged local and state officials to work out a compromise with the Amish by allowing them to operate vocational schools for high school–age students, as Pennsylvania had done. By the time of the trial, the Amish in New Glarus were running such a program, and Ball hoped to use Miller's testimony to establish that it was a viable alternative to a traditional high school. Miller first described the vocational aspects of the program, testifying that the students, including his own daughter Barbara and Frieda Yoder, "cook, bake, sew, . . . help with the chores, anything to do around the farm" and "keep a diary of what they are doing." He then explained that the students "go to the schoolhouse three hours a week" to complement their vocational training. As part of this more formal schooling, the youngsters took "German, some spelling, and writing, and it connects up with our religion," Miller said.

Ball's exploration of the vocational school alternative had one glaring weakness: for all its advantages, the plan described by Miller during his direct examination was a relatively new one, and it had not been in operation in New Glarus when Miller, Yoder, and Yutzy were charged. Martinson immediately pounced on this during his cross-examination of Miller. When questioned by the deputy attorney general, Miller conceded that his daughter had not been enrolled in any school, vocational or otherwise, when he had been charged under the state compulsory attendance law in the fall of 1968. Judge Elmer briefly questioned witnesses throughout the trial, and he underscored Martinson's point by asking if the vocational program had actually been in operation "at the time of the complaint, in October of 1968, or since that?" Miller confessed, "Since that."

Ball also summoned two men who had served as public officials in Green County — a former sheriff and the director of the county's social services agency. Both men testified that the Amish generally were solid citizens who caused little trouble. Their testimony supported Ball's contention that "the fact that the Amish children do not attend public or private full-time high schools has no effect in adding to the social burdens carried by the taxpayers of Green County."

The testimony of University of Chicago professor Donald Erickson constituted the final major part of the trial of the three Amish fathers. Erickson believed that limiting the freedom of the Amish to control the education of their children was shortsighted and fundamentally counterproductive. On the stand, he argued that a state-mandated alteration of Amish educational practices was particularly misguided because they were already doing a marvelous job of preparing their children for fruitful lives as adults. The Amish, by providing vocational education for adolescents, stressed "learning by doing," and their youngsters thus were educated in "an ideal system," Erickson said. Far from being harmed by participating in such a system, Amish youth like Frieda Yoder and Barbara Miller were in "a very fortunate position."

Ball initially had planned to call a third expert witness, Franklin Littell, to buttress the testimony offered by Erickson and Hostetler. The president of Iowa Wesleyan College, Littell was active in the NCARF and, like Ball and Erickson, had attended the nonpublic schools conference at the University of Chicago in 1967. But Littell could not reach Monroe on the day of the trial; he had been delayed by a prolonged meeting at the Chicago Theological Seminary. If the defense wanted to call Littell as a witness, it would have to ask for a continuance and conclude the trial the following day.

Ball faced a tough choice. As William Lindholm later explained, the defense attorney believed as the trial wound down that the state had made a feeble case for conviction. Martinson's only important witness had been Kenneth Glewen, the New Glarus school superintendent, and Ball's cross-examination suggested that Glewen had initiated the charges against Miller, Yoder, and Yutzy because the defection of the Amish schoolchildren had cost the school district thousands of dollars in state aid. Martinson had not countered Hostetler and Erickson with experts of his own, but Ball feared that he might "bring in heavyweights," as Lindholm put it, if the trial were continued until the next day. Apprehensive that a delay might actually hurt the defendants, Ball "felt that while he was ahead of the game, he would just stop right then and there and not have Littell testify the next day," Lindholm recalled. He decided not to ask for a continuance.

Judge Elmer did not rule immediately after the trial concluded. Instead, he invited both sides to submit briefs addressing the central issues of the case and to present oral arguments two months later, on June 13, 1969. The state's brief, submitted by Green County district attorney Louis Koenig, was short and straightforward. "Although one's freedom *to believe* is absolute under the United States Constitution," Koenig wrote, developing an argument that the state would cling to throughout the case, "the freedom *to act* pursuant to those beliefs cannot, in the nature of things, be absolute; one's conduct remains subject to regulation for the good or protection of society." Viewed within that framework, Koenig asserted, the state's decision to enforce the compulsory school attendance law against the Amish clearly was constitutional, for it had done nothing to infringe on the defendants' unquestioned right to adhere to their faith. Koenig noted that in *Garber*, a case strikingly similar to the Green County prosecutions, the Kansas Supreme Court had confronted the same issues and had ruled against the Amish. As for the testimony of Hostetler and Erickson regarding the defendants' reasons for abjuring high school, it was "irrelevant and immaterial," according to Koenig, because the compulsory school attendance law provided no exemptions on religious grounds.

Ball's brief was six times longer than the state's, and it focused on what he termed "the primary issue presented in this case: that of religious liberty." The state contended throughout the case that no constitutional issues were truly at stake, but Ball insisted that the prosecutions presented a clear threat to the First Amendment freedoms of the Amish. Although Ball conceded that Wisconsin's compulsory school attendance law was valid on its face, he maintained that, as applied to the Amish in this case, the measure "deprive[d] them of their right to rear their children according to the requirements of the Old Order Amish religion." Moreover, application of the state attendance law deprived the defendants' children of their own religious liberty, and the fathers had standing to object to that unconstitutional state action.

Ball vehemently disagreed with the state's reliance on *Garber*: "This case," he claimed in his brief, "is directly controlled by the principles laid down by the Supreme Court of the United States in *Sherbert v. Verner*." If Judge Elmer applied the three-pronged *Sherbert* test to the New Glarus case, Ball argued, he would have to find in favor of the defendants, for the state had clearly failed to prove its "compelling interest" in enforcing the school attendance law against them.

Wisconsin v. Yoder proved to be the most prominent case in Judge Roger Elmer's career on the bench. That he took his task seriously was apparent from the beginning of his opinion, which he handed down four months after the trial. "The State should know no heresy," Elmer wrote. "It should condone no new Salem Witch trials." After presiding over the trial and wading through the briefs submitted by both sides, Elmer had little doubt that the Amish were "sincere in their religious convictions" and blessed with "exceptional morality." He also understood their belief "that any education of a secular nature, past eighth grade, absolutely obstructs their compliance with the commands of God and destroys their communal family life." But even though Elmer acknowledged this tenet of the Amish faith, he confessed that he was bothered by its potentially damaging implications for the "appreciable number of Amish-reared youth [who] may decide to subsequently adopt a different faith, join a different church, or leave the Amish community to become a part of a different culture." Once they ventured outside the close-knit Amish community, those who had abandoned the faith might be at a distinct disadvantage because they had not been allowed to obtain a traditional high school education. Their critical thinking skills might not be sharp; they might lack the ability to solve complex problems in the workplace.

From the moment he became involved in *Yoder*, defense attorney William Ball attempted to frame the New Glarus prosecutions in terms of religious liberty and its protection under the First Amendment. In his view, the case presented significant constitutional issues, and in both his brief and at trial he had asked Elmer to confront them directly. But Elmer was only a trial judge, and he clearly felt uncomfortable ruling on the constitutionality of the state compulsory attendance law as it was applied to the Amish, for such judgments were usually made at the appellate level. Citing a state supreme court opinion, he noted in his *Yoder* ruling that "it is an established and longstanding rule of our law that the exercise of the power to declare legislation unconstitutional by trial courts . . . 'should be carefully limited and avoided if possible.'" That same ruling, *State v. Stehlek*, had cautioned "that unless it appears clearly beyond a reasonable doubt that the statute is unconstitutional, it is considered better practice for the court to assume the statute is constitutional, until the contrary is decided by the court of appellate jurisdiction." By invoking that standard in his opinion, Elmer signaled that he would prefer to let the appellate courts grapple with the weighty constitutional issues presented by the case.

And that, in the end, is precisely what Elmer did. Had the compulsory school attendance law "effected and concerned only adult members of the Old Order Amish," he might have agreed with Ball's arguments and found that its application to the Amish was indeed unconstitutional. "However, in view of the innate conflict with the rights of the Amish youth whose attendance it does require, as well as the basic interest and duty of the state in regard to the education of its children, [the court] does not find the statute unconstitutional in its application to [the] defendants." Although he understood that enforcement of the compulsory school attendance law in some ways interfered with the Amish fathers' "freedom . . . to act in accordance with their sincere religious belief," Elmer found that it was "a reasonable and constitutional exercise of the governmental function of the State." Elmer found Miller, Yoder, and Yutzy guilty and ordered each man to pay a five dollar fine.

Elmer had a great deal of respect for the Amish, and anyone who read his opinion closely understood that he had not arrived at his conclusions easily. Even as he found the three Amishmen guilty, the judge went out of his way to praise them. "No one involved in this proceeding has questioned the sincerity of the Defendants in their conviction that they were violating no constitutional law," Elmer wrote.

"No one has questioned the exceptional morality of these Defendants as Amish people, their history in relation to their admirable record of lawful conduct in areas other than school laws." He ruled in favor of the prosecution "regretfully" and felt that he could impose only a "symbolic penalty" — a small fine — against the defendants.

In terms of both its tenor and its substance, Elmer's ruling in *Yoder* was admirable. Although he was mindful of the limits of his authority as a trial judge, Elmer did not hesitate to examine the broad legal issues raised by the prosecution of the New Glarus Amish — no small feat, given the paucity of the case put on by the state. If his analysis of these matters broke little new legal ground, it at least furnished a thoughtful assessment of the compelling arguments offered by both sides of the case.

William Ball reacted calmly to his defeat. He told reporters that he wasn't at all surprised by the unfavorable verdict, because it "is most unusual for a local trial judge to declare a state statute unconstitutional." The attorneys representing the Amish had been primed all along for a long battle in the courts, and they announced that they would appeal Judge Elmer's ruling. For a brief time, the mechanics of appealing a misdemeanor conviction confounded the Amish defense team. After digging a bit, the attorneys determined that a county court verdict in a misdemeanor case could not be appealed directly to the Wisconsin Supreme Court. The case instead went to the Green County Circuit Court for a trial de novo (a form of appeal in which the appeals court holds a trial as if no prior trial had been held). Judge Arthur Luebke heard the case in October 1969.

The proceeding before Luebke was a trial de novo in name only. Both sides essentially agreed to stipulate to the evidence previously presented and have Luebke address the constitutional claim raised by the defense. Tom Eckerle appeared for the Amish, and district attorney Louis Koenig and Max Ashwill of the Department of Public Instruction represented the state. There was a thorough exploration of Amish beliefs and practices, as well as a discussion of the state's lax regulation of private and parochial schools. During this portion of the arguments, Ashwill addressed the possibility that the entire compulsory attendance controversy might be moot if the Amish agreed to operate suitable vocational schools for high school–age youngsters. He suggested that for such schools to pass muster with the state, students would have to spend a significant amount of time doing genuine academic work—presumably, more than the three hours a week required under the program in New Glarus. For his part, Koenig was incredulous that a gifted Amish boy could be "denied the privilege of developing his talents" because his faith supposedly prohibited high school attendance. "This is denying something to the general welfare of all mankind, by not letting him become a doctor, a scientist, etc.," he said. "Wouldn't an Amish father be proud of his child to have such an education?"

When it came time for him to craft an opinion in the case, Luebke's carelessness rankled the defense lawyers. Ball and Eckerle believed that the judge's slipshod drafting threatened to scuttle their plans to appeal the case to the state supreme court. In the drafts of his opinion, Luebke "kept forgetting to say that it was a trial de novo," Eckerle recalled. "We really didn't have a basis to appeal because he was phrasing it all wrong." Eckerle was so concerned that he finally took charge of the matter, providing Luebke with the appropriate language for the opinion. The crisis passed once the judge agreed to insert Eckerle's wording.

The opinion came down several weeks after the trial de novo. Like Elmer before him, Luebke acknowledged in his ruling that the Old Order Amish were "a sect admired and respected by all who know them for their integrity, rugged self-reliance, high moral character, and ability to support and care for their brothers." Also like Elmer, he recognized that enforcement of Wisconsin's compulsory school attendance law interfered with Amish families' right "to act in accordance with their sincere religious beliefs." Luebke nonetheless affirmed the guilty verdicts, calling the enforcement of the attendance statute "a reasonable and constitutional exercise of the governmental function of the state."

Luebke supported his decision to affirm the convictions by briefly developing three arguments. First, he noted that the Amish were not in fact being compelled to jeopardize the future of their faith by sending their children into the secular and worldly environment fostered by the public high schools. Like members of numerous other faiths who had found the public schools "unsatisfactory," the Amish were "legally free to create their own parochial high schools," and doing so would allow them to comply with state education laws while still maintaining the integrity of their communities. Second, it had been established at trial that many people who were born into Amish families eventually left the church instead of submitting to baptism in adulthood. To Luebke, it seemed obvious that these people might be woefully unprepared for life outside the faith if they were "deprived of a reasonable degree of education" in adolescence. The state, he wrote, "owes a duty to a child to insure and protect his basic rights," and it would be failing to provide that guardianship if it allowed him to be poorly educated. Finally, Luebke was concerned by the eighth-grade cutoff for schooling. "Although there was testimony introduced that the Old Order Amish believe that any education beyond 8th grade is and must be of a corrupting nature and contrary to the will of God," he wrote, "there was actually no documentary evidence introduced to explain how and when this practice became an article of faith, and whether this is really doctrine or merely a generally recognized practice."

With his workmanlike opinion, Luebke punctured several holes in the defense's case. Perhaps most notably, he refuted Ball's claim that the Amish desire for separation and the state's desire to enforce the school code were essentially irreconcilable. Luebke pointed out that if the Amish operated their own parochial high schools, they might be able to maintain their treasured isolation — and with it their religious liberty — while still complying with the law. Remarkably, many of the circuit court judge's colleagues on the bench somehow failed to grasp this fairly obvious point as *Yoder* made its way through the courts. Among them were a majority of the justices sitting on the Wisconsin Supreme Court, which heard the case next.

CHAPTER 7

Yoder in the Wisconsin Supreme Court

Not long after he learned of Judge Luebke's ruling in *Yoder*, attorney William Ball resolved to keep the New Glarus case alive. To do so, he appealed to the Wisconsin Supreme Court, which sat in Madison, the state capital. The court could have exercised its discretionary power and refused to hear the appeal if it believed that the legal issues lacked statewide significance. The justices found, however, that the Amish challenge to the state's compulsory school attendance law involved matters of potentially broad importance, and they agreed to hear the case in the court's August 1970 term.

In addition to submitting his own lengthy brief, Ball arranged for the submission of an amicus curiae brief to support the defendants in *Yoder*. Working under Ball's direction, attorney Tom Eckerle contacted Jim Greenwald, a Madison-area lawyer, and coordinated the drafting of a brief meant to be submitted jointly by the state Catholic conference and several other organized religious groups. The formation of this ecumenical coalition and the drafting of the brief were far from spontaneous. "We kind of created the amicus, to some extent," Eckerle later said. "Clearly, we were involved in [drafting the brief], and Jim signed it."

The amicus curiae brief began by reporting that all the groups involved in its submission were "of the view that a grave threat to the religious liberty of the Old Order Amish sect is threatened by the prosecution in this case." After establishing that opposition to the *Yoder* prosecutions cut across denominational lines, Greenwald touched on several cases not stressed by Ball, most notably one from California, *People v. Woody* (1964). He pointed out that in *Woody*, a case involving the prosecution of Native Americans who had used peyote as part of a religious ceremony, the California Supreme Court had relied on the "compelling state interest" standard in holding that the prosecution was unconstitutional. He went on to argue that *Yoder* was analogous in that "it is manifest that the state of Wisconsin proved no compelling state interest justifying denial of the religious liberty of the Appellants."

Greenwald's reference to a case involving peyote caused an uproar among the religious groups slated to submit the amicus curiae brief. According to Eckerle, "all the organized groups ran like hell" when they learned of the brief's reliance on *People v. Woody*. "The Catholic conference wouldn't touch it." After some last-minute scrambling, Ball and Eckerle eventually found three individual religious leaders who were willing to put their names on the document: the Reverend Willis Merriman of the Wisconsin Council of Churches, rabbi Manfred Swarensky, and Monsignor Andrew Breines, pastor of Saint Thomas Aquinas Church in Madison.

In addition to arguing that the state's action against the Amish was unconstitutional, the amicus curiae brief emphasized the devastating effect on the Amish community if the three defendants' convictions were allowed to stand. The brief maintained that if the Wisconsin Supreme Court upheld the lower court rulings it "would at once sound the death knell to the Old Order Amish way of life in Wisconsin, or else force its believers to move to another state in pursuit of religious liberty and of peace." The case wasn't merely about safeguarding the religious liberty of three men; it was also about preventing an entire culture from being wiped out in Wisconsin.

William Ball made much the same claim when the Wisconsin Supreme Court heard oral arguments in *Yoder* on December 1, 1970. As always, he described the case in stark terms. "The destruction of a way of life is involved here," Ball told the court. If these "God-fearing people" were compelled "to allow their children to be indoctrinated into an alien environment of a culture which values competition, acquisition, materialism, and technology," their entire faith would be so jeopardized that they might have no choice but to flee the state. As he urged the court to overturn the convictions and protect the religious liberty of the Amish, Ball vigorously argued that the state had no business interfering with their way of life, even if it did so in the name of providing education. "Society has no right to conscript the services of a youth into the ranks of the educated," he said. "There is no right to force anyone into a pursuit of technology. Neither does the state have a right to force everyone into a common mold, even if the common mold is one of opportunity. The products of the Amish education are superb; they are excellent citizens."

Ball's opposite number that day was John W. Calhoun, an assistant attorney general for the state of Wisconsin. It fell to Calhoun to flesh out the sketchy arguments that had carried the state's case through the two lower courts. This was, as Calhoun himself realized, no small task. The state had not put on an exhaustive case at trial, and it had failed to fully develop a coherent theory to address the numerous constitutional issues presented by the school attendance dispute. To make matters even worse for the state, Ball had done a masterful job of presenting evidence at trial and then framing constitutional claims on appeal. If the state hoped to prevail before Wisconsin's highest court, Calhoun would have to catch up to Ball and bolster a heretofore weak case.

Although Calhoun admired the Amish way of life, he supported the prosecutions under the school attendance statute because he appreciated the law's long-standing importance. "We spent 100 years in this country getting kids into school," he said at one point during the case. "Now are we going to let them run free?" Calhoun also believed that it was important for Amish youngsters, who were reared in extraordinarily insular communities, to be given as many educational and social choices as possible in their formative years. "These Amish kids have no other options than to stay and join the order; it's hard for them to get into the mainstream without a high school education."

In his oral argument before the Wisconsin Supreme Court, Calhoun was careful not to denigrate the Amish or their way of life. He indicated that the state had "the greatest admiration for the farming abilities of the Amish people, and for their conduct as good citizens." He acknowledged at another point in the argument, "I think the Amish way of life is fine." But Calhoun believed that Ball was missing the point of the case when he emphasized the laudable nature of Amish society or the purported threat that the state's action posed to their religious liberty. As Calhoun saw it, the state's action in enforcing the compulsory school attendance law regulated not the beliefs of the Amish but only their behavior. Making a distinction that was central to the prosecution's case, Calhoun told the court, "The right to think is unrestricted, but the right to act is not."

As he attempted to justify the state's prosecution of the Amish fathers in New Glarus, Calhoun invoked the First Amendment's establishment clause. If the state granted exemptions to the compulsory school attendance law based on religious beliefs, he said during oral argument, it would in effect put itself in the business of establishing religion. According to Calhoun, the state had a duty to remain strictly neutral in religious matters, and that entailed enforcing generally applicable laws without regard to a citizen's faith. Exempting the Amish from the compulsory school attendance law would privilege their faith, he said, because members of "every other religion" would still have to comply with it.

Chief Justice E. Harold Hallows led the court's assault on Calhoun's assertions. Before joining the court in 1958, Hallows had taught law for more than two decades at Marquette University's law school, and he occasionally grilled the attorneys who appeared before him as if they were students who had failed to prepare adequately for class. He immediately zeroed in on the weak points of Calhoun's argument and peppered him with questions. Scoffing at the state's contention that exempting the Amish from the compulsory attendance law would violate the First Amendment's establishment clause, he asked Calhoun, "How do you establish a state religion by recognizing an individual's personal belief?" He also pointed out that other statutes (such as selective service laws) provided religious exemptions without violating the establishment clause.

Justice Horace Wilkie asked an even more pointed question. Throughout the case, Ball made much of the origin of the prosecutions, highlighting the fact that New Glarus school superintendent Kenneth Glewen had decided to press charges against the Amish fathers only after he had determined that the local school district would lose some $18,000 in state aid because of the opening of Amish schools in the area. Addressing the issue of the school district's motives, Wilkie asked Calhoun, "What effect will this have on state aid to education at the high school involved?" The assistant attorney general's heart must have sunk when he heard the question, for it seemed to indicate that one of Ball's main claims — that school authorities were trampling on religious freedom simply to protect their pocketbooks — had resonated with the court. He did the best he could, responding that the issue of state aid simply wasn't relevant.

After reviewing the briefs and hearing the oral arguments, the justices of the Wisconsin Supreme Court discussed the *Yoder* case during one of their regular conference sessions. When the members of the court exchanged their views on the case, it became clear that only one justice, Nathan Heffernan, favored upholding the lower court rulings in *Yoder*. Chief Justice Hallows and Justices Connor Hansen, Horace Wilkie, Bruce Beilfuss, Leo Hanley, and Robert W. Hansen all indicated that they favored reversing the convictions of the Amish fathers. The task of writing the court's opinion fell to Hallows, who had assumed the chief justice's duties in 1968.

Determined to get a thorough picture of the appeal, Hallows assigned law clerk John Hein, a recent graduate of New York University's law school, to draft a memorandum detailing the facts and all the relevant constitutional issues. In an eighteen-page assessment of the case, Hein concluded that the court was obliged to follow the multipronged test established by the U.S. Supreme Court in *Sherbert v. Verner* and resolve the case in favor of the Amish appellants.

In his opinion in *Wisconsin v. Yoder*, the chief justice took his cue from Hein and attorney Ball. "The determination of whether a law infringing religious liberty is justified," Hallows wrote, "requires the weighing of the burden on the free exercise of one's religion and the importance of the state's interest asserted in justification of the substantial infringement." There was little doubt in Hallows's mind that the enforcement of the state compulsory school attendance law compromised the religious liberty of the Amish. Echoing the findings of the two lower courts, he concluded that the measure clearly "infringes upon the free exercise of religion by the appellants within the scope of the protection of the First Amendment." In its attempt to defend enforcement of the law, the state had asserted that the regulation of school attendance in no way burdened the Amish method of worship but rather restricted, as Hallows described it, "merely a practice or a way of life." The chief justice dismissed this claim by reviewing some of the beliefs and practices of the Amish and concluding that they believed "how long a child should attend a formal school is a religious question."

The effects of this infringement on Amish families were likely to be profound, Hallows wrote. If the state compelled Amish children to attend high school, "they would experience a useless anguish of living in two worlds," and their exposure to alien values might very well prompt them to question and abandon their faith. As he discussed the possible impact of application of the compulsory attendance law to the Amish, Hallows also restated a claim that was made repeatedly throughout the course of the *Yoder* case by defenders of the Amish. The chief justice noted that many Amish had come to Wisconsin after clashing with school authorities in neighboring Iowa. Such migrations were not uncommon. "The impact on the Amish of compulsory education laws is so severe that in other states where they were required to send their children to public schools," he wrote, "they sold their farms and sought religious freedom elsewhere." If every state chose to enforce compulsory attendance laws against them, these victims of intolerance could run out of options, and "the impact may result in the extermination of their religious community."

After making this grim forecast, Hallows examined the state's interest in enforcing the school attendance statute. The chief justice's clerk had written in his memorandum that the state's interest was valid and deserved careful consideration, but Hallows came to a far different conclusion. He derided the state's contention that its interest lay in helping to ensure that those Amish who eventually left the faith would be prepared to function as productive members of modern society. It was folly to use "speculation [that] some Amish children may after adulthood leave their religion" to justify an action that not only compromised the free exercise rights of Amish families but also threatened the very existence of their entire community. "To force a worldly education on all Amish children, the majority of whom do not want or need it," Hallows wrote, "in order to confer a dubious benefit on the few who might later reject their religion is not a compelling interest."

Hallows next turned to the potential impact of exempting the Amish from the compulsory school attendance law. "Granting an exemption from compulsory education to the Amish," he wrote, "will do no more to the ultimate goal of education than to dent the symmetry of the design of enforcement." Furthermore, accommodating the Amish posed no real threat to the First Amendment's establishment clause, as the state had claimed. Calling the state's argument on this point misconceived, Hallows noted that the state could maintain its neutrality in terms of establishment while still making "special provisions for religious interests in order to relieve them from both direct and indirect burdens placed on the free exercise of religion by increased governmental regulations."

The Wisconsin Supreme Court was not the first court to address these prickly issues. Hallows acknowledged three previous cases from other states involving compulsory education and the Amish: *State v. Hershberger* (Ohio), *Commonwealth v. Beiler* (Pennsylvania), and the much-maligned *State v. Garber* (Kansas). The Amish had lost each of these cases, but the chief justice insisted that the decisions were "not controlling or persuasive." Hallows's assessment of *Garber* was particularly harsh. He derided the opinion's "mechanical separation of religious conduct from religious belief" and the "narrowness of [its] concept of the scope of protection afforded by the Free Exercise Clause." A faulty opinion to begin with, the *Garber* ruling "lost luster" after legislators in Kansas amended that state's compulsory school attendance law to provide exemptions for members of religious groups such as the Amish. To Hallows, the enactment of these provisions demonstrated "the fact that the important goals of education can be attained by alternative forms of regulation without infringing First Amendment rights."

The conclusion of Hallows's opinion in *Yoder* was straightforward. "We conclude that although education is a subject within the constitutional power of the state to regulate, there is not such a compelling state interest in two years high school compulsory education as will justify the burden it places upon the appellants' free exercise of their religion," he wrote. "Therefore, the Wisconsin Compulsory School Attendance Law . . . is unconstitutional as applied to these Amish appellants, and the convictions must be reversed."

As he overturned the lower court rulings, Hallows made a small concession to those who feared that providing an exemption to the Amish might undermine the efficacy of the school attendance law. He ruled that the court "reserve[d] the right to reexamine the question" of exemptions if at some point in the future it became clear that the effectiveness of the measure was being "seriously jeopardized."

Hallows's opinion in *Yoder* was forcefully worded but not always tightly reasoned. The chief justice accepted many of Ball's arguments at face value and thereby failed to raise some obvious questions about the claims of the Amish. Perhaps most notably, Hallows agreed that the Amish would be forced to endure a potentially cataclysmic exposure to alien values if they were compelled to comply with the provisions of the school attendance law. Had the chief justice analyzed this claim more thoroughly, he might have concluded that the attendance statute did not pose such a dire threat to the religious liberty of the Amish. Hallows apparently failed to recognize that the Amish might be able to maintain their separation from the world at large and still comply with the attendance statute if they merely opened their own parochial high schools.

In the late 1960s and early 1970s, the members of the Wisconsin Supreme Court were in the habit of rendering decisions relatively quickly. On average, about a month would elapse between oral arguments and the publication of the court's opinion in a given case. One member of the court later said that its rapid turnaround on cases made it one of the fastest courts in the country in terms of dispensing justice. But when they were confronted with a particularly difficult or noteworthy case, it was generally understood that members of the court might take somewhat longer to forge a decision. Among other things, the justices might use the additional time to further discuss the case among themselves or comment more extensively on circulated drafts of majority opinions and dissents.

With all the trappings of a major case, *Yoder* certainly appeared to be a candidate for unhurried consideration by the court. However, to the amazement of some justices, Hallows rendered his decision in the case with the court's usual dispatch. The court heard oral arguments on December 1, and Hallows received a memorandum on the case from his clerk ten days later, on December 11. The chief justice apparently wrote and revised his opinion for the court over the next few weeks — which included the Christmas and New Year's holidays — and completed it during the first week of January. On January 7, 1971, he informed his fellow justices that he hoped to announce the court's decision early the following morning.

The other members of the court were stunned by Hallows's urgency. (The chief justice's attempt to present them with a fait accompli so nettled his fellow justices that they later came up with a joking name for his tactic — "Amishing" — and instituted new procedural rules to prevent it from happening again.) Because of the holidays and the usual crush of the court's business, the text of the chief justice's opinion had not even been circulated to all the other members of the court. Justice Nathan Heffernan later said that he hadn't seen the majority opinion until the day before it was to be handed down, and it seems likely that the other members of the court had been in a similar position. Having intended all along to dissent, Heffernan was particularly disturbed by the chief justice's rush to hand down the majority opinion. He now had less than a day to write an opinion of his own.

Nathan Heffernan enjoyed crafting opinions for the Wisconsin Supreme Court and thus marking the parameters of state law. But Heffernan had a belletristic streak, and he never quite reconciled himself to making the stylistic compromises inherent in piecing together a majority opinion. "When you write a majority opinion," he once said, "you have to express the views and preferences and doubts of all those judges, not just your own; consequently, the prose is apt to have all the faults of committee prose." Although Heffernan made no secret that he reveled in the relative freedom of dissenting, particularly when in doing so he stood up for individual rights, he was by no means a profligate dissenter. When considering whether he should strike out on his own and break with the court's majority, he often thought of the words of U.S. Supreme Court Justice Oliver Wendell Holmes, Jr.: "You only dissent when the blood rushes to your head."

Wisconsin v. Yoder clearly got Heffernan's blood moving. He was especially nettled by Chief Justice Harold Hallows's "sleight of hand" in his handling of the majority opinion. Several years after he had retired from the court, Heffernan recalled that he and a few fellow justices had been suspicious of Hallows's motives in producing the majority opinion in *Yoder* so hastily and then giving them virtually no time to review the decision before it was announced to the public. Heffernan later speculated that the chief justice might have been attempting to use the New Glarus case to lay the groundwork for a subsequent opinion regarding state aid to parochial education. Heffernan suspected that Hallows, an advocate of public funding for religious institutions, knew that the court would eventually be called on to assess the constitutionality of a Wisconsin program that provided public aid for the dental school at Marquette, the Catholic university where the chief justice had studied and taught. *Yoder* afforded a chance for the court to deal with some related issues, including the boundaries of the First Amendment's establishment clause. Heffernan surmised that Hallows handled the Amish case so unusually because the chief justice was determined to make the most of this opportunity.

Heffernan's claim on this score is difficult to prove yet hard to ignore. No conclusive documentary evidence has been uncovered to show that Hallows intentionally crafted his opinion in *Yoder* to help "bolster what was in the pipeline," as Heffernan later described it, regarding public funding for the dental school at Marquette. By the same token, it's worth noting that Marquette, hoping to erase its dental school's sizable deficit, announced its plan to ask the Wisconsin legislature for a $1.2 million annual appropriation in December 1970 — the very time that the Wisconsin Supreme Court was reaching its decision in the Amish case. What's more, after the legislature approved public funding for the dental school, a legal challenge did indeed reach the state supreme court, and Hallows vigorously supported the financing scheme. (He did so in dissent; the court ruled in *State ex rel. Warren v. Nusbaum* that the funding program violated both the establishment clause and the free exercise clause of the First Amendment.)

Hallows's purported motives were only part of what prompted Heffernan to dissent in *Yoder*. He was by no means an authority on the Amish, but he possessed at least a passing knowledge of their beliefs and culture before the case arrived at the Wisconsin Supreme Court. Going into *Yoder*, what Heffernan knew about the Amish approach to education troubled him, and the record of the case did nothing to ease his misgivings. The justice and his wife were longtime members of the Madison Literary Club, and one of their fellow members worked as a librarian in New Glarus. This acquaintance was familiar with the Amish who lived in Green County, and she told Heffernan "how tragic she thought it was that the children who wanted to be in school were not permitted by their parents to attend," he recalled. Her lament, he said, "made an impression on me from the beginning," sensitizing him to the plight of curious Amish youngsters who bridled under the rigid strictures of their faith. The children also had rights, and in Heffernan's mind, it would be tragic if they were sacrificed in the name of preserving their parents' First Amendment freedoms.

One aspect of the *Yoder* case especially bothered Heffernan: although their rights were at stake, the Amish youngsters were not represented by counsel. In the late 1960s and early 1970s, the Wisconsin

Supreme Court had issued a series of rulings dealing with this issue in the context of divorce cases. Summarizing the court's holdings, Heffernan wrote in a later opinion that, as "necessary, and indeed indispensable, parties" to divorce proceedings, children "must be represented in their own capacity as parties" by guardians ad litem. *Yoder* was not a divorce case, of course, but Heffernan considered the Amish children "indispensable parties" who merited representation by an attorney who would look after their interests. That they hadn't been so represented — in fact, the issue apparently never had been considered by either side in the case — vexed Heffernan, for it appeared as though no one had seriously considered their rights. In framing the case's main issues, the defense had spoken in relatively general terms about the paramount importance of preserving the First Amendment freedoms of all the Amish, but to Heffernan, this was a shaky assumption. After all, the court's ruling was sure to have the greatest and most lasting impact on Amish children, not their parents.

With these concerns in the forefront of his mind, Heffernan resolved to complete a dissent in time to meet Hallows's surprise deadline of January 8. He believed that the chief justice's ruling for the court was "an illiberal opinion which cemented parental tyranny over children," and he simply could not allow it to become law without voicing his strenuous objections. Having devoted relatively little attention to the case over the preceding month, and having only received Hallows's majority opinion on January 7, he essentially had to write the dissent overnight. To make matters worse, he was obliged to attend a meeting on the University of Wisconsin campus that night. With Hallows's deadline only hours away, Heffernan returned to his home in Madison at approximately 10 P.M. and began writing. He would later call the dissent he drafted in those trying circumstances "one of the opinions I am proudest of."

The first words of Heffernan's dissent in *Yoder* established its frank tone. Hallows's opinion for the court, he wrote, "reaches an erroneous conclusion based upon questionable reasoning and a misstatement of the facts." Heffernan began highlighting these flaws by noting that the Wisconsin compulsory school attendance law did not compel the Amish to send their children to public high schools until age sixteen. The law did in fact mandate school attendance until that age, but students were free to attend private high schools where, presumably, they might avoid the pitfalls of worldliness. Hallows's opinion thus "rest[ed] in part upon the misconception that the defendants' only alternative to criminality" was to dispatch their children to a public school and thus compromise their religious beliefs. "Such is not the case," Heffernan wrote. "The law makes no such requirement."

After this initial blast, Heffernan turned to his primary concern—protecting the rights of Amish children. Among the numerous faults of Hallows's opinion was that "it completely ignores the personal liberty of the Amish children to avail themselves of educational opportunities beyond eighth grade," he wrote. Furthermore, although the court's ruling safeguards the First Amendment freedoms of their parents, "the freedom of these young people to make a religious choice is completely ignored." Here, for Heffernan, lay the central irony of the court's ruling in *Yoder*: In holding that the Wisconsin compulsory school attendance law could not be constitutionally applied to the Amish, Hallows's opinion "purport[ed] to strike a blow for religious liberty," but in fact it did "little for religion and impinge[d] upon personal liberty" by subordinating the freedoms of Amish children to the rights of their parents.

As he stressed the importance of shielding the rights of Amish children, Heffernan worried over the fate of Amish youngsters who eventually left the faith. Countering a claim made by the defense in *Yoder*, he asserted that numerous Amish abandoned their rigid faith "and are thereafter forced to make their way in the world." If they were barred by their parents from receiving proper training in the schools and thus reached adulthood lacking an "education that equips them for modern life," these youngsters could face enormous difficulties. The court's ruling in *Yoder*, he argued, effectively left "these young people . . . abandoned without the intellectual tools to survive should they elect to leave the Amish way of life."

That this abandonment—which relegated Amish youngsters "to a life of ignorance"—was allowed to take place "without a hearing" made it all the more intolerable to Heffernan. In a footnote to his dissent, he noted that "no guardian ad litem was appointed to represent the children's interests." Heffernan did not deny that the prosecutions at issue in *Yoder* threatened to compromise the Amish parents' right to free exercise of religion. However, he asserted that the children's "interest is of equal importance"; their lives, after all, would be most directly affected, in both the short and long terms, by the court's decision on the applicability of the state compulsory school attendance law. Given the youngsters' obvious stake in the outcome of the case, "reason dictates that representation by a guardian ad litem was a *sine qua non* of the majority's result," but the Amish youngsters had not been represented by separate counsel at any point in the proceedings.

The cornerstone of both William Ball's arguments for the defense and Harold Hallows's opinion for the court had been the contention that the state had not demonstrated a sufficiently compelling interest in enforcing the mandatory attendance statute. Heffernan balked at this claim. "Education has been a prime and compelling interest of this state from the very beginning," he wrote, and the state legislature had enacted the school attendance law to promote that long-standing interest. In making this point, Heffernan referred to the U.S. Supreme Court's landmark ruling in *Brown v. Board of Education*, handed down in 1954. In that opinion, the Court had observed that "education is perhaps the most important function of state and local governments. Compulsory school attendance laws and the great expenditures for education both demonstrate our recognition of the importance of education to our democratic society." *Brown* and *Yoder* were not completely analogous cases, but Heffernan shrewdly used the former opinion—surely the most significant that the U.S. Supreme Court ever had issued in a case relating to education—to bolster his dissent.

Although Heffernan clearly believed that the state had a compelling interest in enforcing the compulsory attendance law, it was obvious from his dissent that he disapproved of the state's heavy-handed approach to the prosecution of the Amish fathers. He was especially critical of superintendent Kenneth Glewen, who had initiated the prosecutions back in the fall of 1968. The evidence in the case strongly suggested, he wrote, "that the purpose of this prosecution was not to further the compelling interest of the state in education, but rather the reprehensible objective . . . to force the Amish into the school only for the purpose of qualifying for augmented state aids." The origins of the case had been ignoble, and Heffernan wanted to make sure that his dissent was not misinterpreted as an endorsement of the state's abhorrent tactics.

In one stern passage, he maintained that the problems posed by the clash between the Amish and the state "ought not to be solved by fining [the Amish] or sending them to jail if they choose not to conform to the usual mores of the state." According to Heffernan, the state had blundered in handling the issue because education officials had failed "to deal realistically or imaginatively with a difficult problem." Several other states had successfully worked out compromises with the Amish over the enforcement of school laws, although "usually only after Gestapo tactics by school authorities outraged the non-Amish community into reaching reasonable alternatives." Acknowledging Amish resistance to exposing adolescents to the worldliness of public high schools, Pennsylvania, for instance, had permitted Amish youngsters to attend vocational schools operated by their faith. Heffernan contended that the implementation of a similar plan in Wisconsin would safeguard the religious liberty of the Amish without sacrificing the state's clear interest in fostering education. What's more, such a scheme "would better enable those who fall away from the [Amish] community to adjust to the outside world and to continue their education if they so desire."

As he finished his dissent, Heffernan restated his claim that, contrary to the assertions of Ball and Hallows, "the state's compelling interest in education has been abundantly demonstrated" and thus could not be dismissed out of hand. Honoring that interest, and realizing that the establishment of vocational schools was a viable option for the Amish, he wrote that he would affirm the convictions of Miller, Yoder, and Yutzy. There was, however, a caveat to Heffernan's conclusion: he would stay execution of the sentences until the Amish in the New Glarus area had been given the opportunity to set up vocational schools similar to those already operating in Pennsylvania. When those schools became operational, Heffernan wrote, the complaints against the three Amish fathers should be dismissed.

Heffernan's dissent might have been the most sensible of all the judicial opinions written in *Yoder*. Although he wrote in haste, Heffernan rigorously examined both the state's arguments and the claims of the Amish. This evenhanded analysis revealed some glaring weaknesses in Ball's case and highlighted some of the undeniable strengths of Calhoun's. Heffernan also considered how the rights of Amish children were affected by the application of the school attendance statute. In exploring this issue, he challenged the main premise of Ball's case — that *Yoder* turned on the question of how the state's actions impacted the religious liberty of Amish parents. Heffernan made the compelling argument that the rights of Amish children deserved careful consideration as well.

Heffernan toiled until the early-morning hours and scratched out his dissent in longhand on a yellow legal pad. His first audience approved of his work: Heffernan's wife, whom he had roused from sleep, read and praised the opinion. After sleeping for a few hours, Heffernan drove to his chambers in the state capitol and gave his secretary the dissent to type. He was adamant that his colleagues on the court be given a chance to at least glance at his dissent before it was formally handed down, and he was able to prevail upon the chief justice to put off announcing the *Yoder* opinions until later that afternoon. The delay gave the beleaguered Heffernan time to circulate his dissent.

The circulation of Heffernan's mordant dissent prompted another round of hasty opinion-writing. After reading Heffernan's effort, Justice Connor Hansen produced a short concurring opinion. In his concurrence, Hansen wrote that he agreed with the result reached by Hallows; he too believed that the convictions of the Amish fathers should be reversed, in part because "there has been an inadequate showing that the state's interest in establishing and maintaining an educational system overrides the defendants' right to the free exercise of religion." Yet Hansen wrote that he endorsed the court's opinion in *Yoder* "only to the extent that children of members of the Old Order Amish religion or Conservative Amish Mennonite Church, living as members of the Amish community, should not be required to attend a school which meets the requirements of state law beyond the eighth grade." Hansen's caveat suggested that he was concerned that the *Yoder* ruling might lead to the granting of numerous exemptions to the state's school laws. He further maintained that the Amish should remain exempt from the compulsory attendance law "unless and until further experience indicates that so invoking the First Amendment poses a serious threat to the effective functioning of an educational system within the state." His concurrence was filled with guarded language, and Hansen appeared to be saying that he might view the issues presented in *Yoder* differently if the court's ruling proved to be too disruptive. Four members of the Wisconsin Supreme

Court — Horace Wilkie, Bruce Beilfuss, Leo Hanley, and Robert Hansen — joined Connor Hansen's concurrence.

———

Because of miscommunication between the National Committee for Amish Religious Freedom and the Amish, Jonas Yoder initially believed that the Wisconsin Supreme Court had ruled against him and his fellow defendants. When William Lindholm first learned that the court's opinion had been handed down, he mistakenly surmised that the majority had upheld the constitutionality of the application of the compulsory school attendance law to the Amish. (It seems that Lindholm jumped to the conclusion that the Amish had lost when he learned that Heffernan, widely known for his liberal sympathies, had dissented.) He promptly telephoned Yoder in New Glarus with the bad — but erroneous — news. Yoder was devastated by Lindholm's message, and he wondered whether he and his family would be able to remain in Wisconsin with their faith in so much jeopardy. "I felt I would have to move, I would have to sell out and leave Wisconsin," he said. But as Yoder pondered his fate, Lindholm called again and gleefully told him that there had been a mistake; the court had actually overturned the convictions of the three Amish fathers. "It was wonderful," Yoder recalled of hearing that he and his coreligionists had prevailed.

Attorney William Ball echoed Yoder's jubilant comments. It turned out that Ball had also heard an inaccurate report of the court's ruling in *Yoder*. He was already contemplating the issues he might raise on appeal to the U.S. Supreme Court when he learned that the court's ruling in fact favored the Amish and not the state. He couldn't have been happier to hear that the convictions had been overturned. Hallows's opinion for the court was nothing less than a "landmark decision in favor of religious liberty," Ball said, and it was sure to be "widely respected throughout the country, where there are numerous religious groups which do not have great economic, political or numerical strength." He went on to praise the court for its courage in not endorsing the state's dubious claims and thus not "ducking" the weighty First Amendment issues at stake in the case. The court had confronted these matters head-on, and in Ball's mind, it had done a superlative job of resolving them.

One of Wisconsin's largest newspapers greeted the Wisconsin Supreme Court opinion in *Yoder* with similar approval. In Madison, the *Wisconsin State Journal* termed it a "landmark decision" that might sensitize the public to "those groups that are 'different' from ours." On the whole, however, most newspapers in Wisconsin were not overly impressed by the *Yoder* ruling. Especially strident criticism came from the *Capital Times*, Madison's other daily newspaper. In an editorial headlined "Amish School Decision Unwise," the paper expressed bafflement that the justices who voted to overturn the convictions in *Yoder* could "ignore the legal mischief their Amish school decision is apt to bring not only to Wisconsin's educational system, but to the individuals involved — in this instance the Amish themselves." Thanks to the court's misguided ruling, "Wisconsin's young Amish may be tragically denied a suitable education," the newspaper argued.

William Kahl, the state school superintendent, also criticized the ruling in *Yoder*. In a public statement, Kahl asserted that the state supreme court's "plethoric opinion" in the New Glarus case threatened to cripple Wisconsin's compulsory school attendance law. Thanks to *Yoder*, he said, "It is impossible to tell at this time whether this law will long endure as a viable instrument for the administration of public school systems." A definitive answer to that question might be provided by the U.S. Supreme Court, and Kahl stated his hope that Robert Warren, the state attorney general, would appeal the *Yoder* case to that tribunal.

CHAPTER 8

Arguing *Yoder* in the U.S. Supreme Court

Less than a week after the Wisconsin Supreme Court handed down its opinion in *Yoder*, assistant attorney general John Calhoun prepared a five-page confidential memorandum on the decision for attorney general Robert Warren and William Kahl, the state school superintendent. In it he offered a harshly critical assessment of Chief Justice Hallows's opinion for the court and Justice Connor Hansen's concurrence.

After acknowledging that the "long range effect of this decision is difficult to estimate," Calhoun asserted that the "judicial experiment" of Hallows's ruling, by opening the door to challenges to the state school code, might generate an inordinate amount of litigation and possibly "create chaos out of order in the area of secondary education." The concurrence was scarcely better: Calhoun argued that Hansen had "taken it upon himself to write a new compulsory attendance law which would require Amish children to attend school only to eighth grade."

If there was a glimmer of hope for the state, it lay in the fact that both Hallows and Hansen had equivocated in their opinions. Both men had openly "express[ed] doubt as to the effect of their action." As Calhoun reported in his memorandum, "it is highly irregular for the Court to hedge a decision in the manner in which it [was] done here." Perhaps the court's own hesitancy was a sign that its majority opinion might not withstand a strong challenge.

Calhoun believed that the state now had two options. It could petition for rehearing with the Wisconsin Supreme Court, or it could petition to the U.S. Supreme Court for a writ of certiorari. Although he sympathized with the Amish, Calhoun genuinely believed that Hallows's opinion in *Yoder* was so ill conceived that it threatened to plunge the state's public education system into turmoil. The state had an obligation to attempt to remove such a potential hazard, and it could do so only by eliminating *Yoder*. Though it seemed unlikely that the Wisconsin Supreme Court would grant a motion for rehearing, Calhoun was more hopeful about the state's chances with the U.S. Supreme Court.

In defending the Amish fathers, William Ball had gotten plenty of mileage out of the U.S. Supreme Court's opinion in *Sherbert v. Verner*, and that ruling loomed as a major obstacle for the state on appeal. In addressing the challenge of getting past *Sherbert*, Calhoun was quick to point out that fidelity to that opinion had not stopped the Supreme Court from denying certiorari to the Amish defendant in *State v. Garber*, a case bearing more than a passing resemblance to *Yoder*. He reasoned that if the Court had allowed *Garber* to stand, it might choose to reverse a Wisconsin ruling that had been decided the opposite way. With this in mind, he recommended that the state appeal the *Yoder* decision to the high court.

Not everyone in the attorney general's office agreed with Calhoun's advice. A number of attorneys in the office wrote their own memoranda on the case after the Wisconsin Supreme Court handed down its decision. Veteran attorney Betty Brown (who later served as the state's solicitor general and argued several cases before the U.S. Supreme Court) encouraged Warren to drop the case. "I told them, 'Don't do it,'" she later said of her advice regarding the *Yoder* appeal. "I thought they were going to lose." To Brown, an appeal seemed pointless because the law simply wasn't on the state's side.

Brown's arguments ultimately fell on deaf ears. On March 30, 1971, attorney general Warren followed Calhoun's suggestion and formally petitioned the U.S. Supreme Court for a writ of certiorari in *Yoder*. Ball was incredulous at Warren's decision to press on with the case. "We greeted [news of the petition] with absolute disbelief," Ball later wrote. "We could not imagine why the state wanted to pursue this baseless prosecution any further, having received so decisive an answer by the Wisconsin Supreme Court." Searching for an explanation, he could only speculate that the "prosecutorial appetite" of the state had not been fully sated by the state courts' handling of the case. Like Ball, attorney Tom Eckerle was dumbfounded by the state's decision to appeal. "I don't know what they were thinking about on appeal," he later said. "I think they thought we had a conservative U.S. Supreme Court, and they were going to win."

Many Wisconsin residents shared the defense attorneys' misgivings about the state's move to appeal *Yoder*. Several critics reproached Warren for keeping the prosecution alive, and he was forced to defend his handling of the case. Clearly bothered by having his judgment questioned, Warren announced that his decision to appeal "was not meant to in any way reflect on the Amish people or their way of life," which he characterized as "exemplary." The determination that an appeal was in order thus "was not an easy one on my part," Warren noted, but he felt compelled to file for the writ of certiorari because he and other state officials were worried by the *Yoder* decision's "potential effect on public education in Wisconsin."

The sharpest criticism of Warren came from Wisconsin's legislature. In June 1971, state assemblymen Fred Kessler and Kenneth Merkel (who had previously championed the Amish cause in the legislature) introduced a resolution "requesting the attorney general not to appeal the recent state supreme court opinion which refused to compel Amish residents to comply with the state's compulsory school attendance law." When the resolution came up for discussion, Kessler passionately defended the Amish and castigated the attorney general for continuing to pursue a case against them. Assistant attorney general John Calhoun testified against the measure, telling a group of skeptical lawmakers that the decision to appeal was "not taken lightly" by his office, but the state assembly ignored his objections. In a stinging rebuke to Warren, it approved Kessler's resolution by a vote of seventy-six to eighteen. This was a purely symbolic gesture, however, as the legislature had no authority to compel Warren to drop the case. It went forward without the lawmakers' support.

Few Wisconsinites ever accused Robert Warren of lacking enthusiasm for fighting crime. During his tenure as the state's attorney general, which lasted from 1969 to 1974, Warren established a formidable reputation as a law-and-order conservative. The former district attorney and state legislator zealously advocated a host of measures designed to curb the lawlessness of everyone from political protesters to organized criminals. His efforts led to, among other things, passage of the state's first wiretap law and statutes granting the attorney general's office increased authority to combat the activities of drug dealers.

Warren made no secret of his contempt for the demonstrators who frequently clogged the streets of Madison, a hotbed of student radicalism in the late 1960s and early 1970s. A minister's son and World War II veteran (he had been wounded in combat in 1944), the attorney general was appalled by the throngs of unkempt radicals so brazenly criticizing their government. "I am dismayed," he said in 1968, when the antiwar movement reached its zenith, "by the growth of the phenomenon known as civil disobedience." The chaos wrought by political dissenters so rankled Warren that he called for the development of a statewide system to compile information on them and track their activities.

When he tried to discern a cause for the uncivilized behavior of America's youth, the attorney general pointed to "the permissive attitudes expressed by a wide variety of adult teachers, parents, political leaders and even clergy to several generations of young people." Warren — whose fondest memory of high school was winning an essay contest on the theme "What Uncle Sam Means to Me" — believed that there was no place for this kind of coddling in Wisconsin's schools. Speaking in 1971 at an educators' convention in Milwaukee, he noted that many pampered students were challenging the constitutionality of school disciplinary regulations, including dress codes and the right of school officials to search desks and lockers. With this assertion of their rights came a host of serious obligations, Warren cautioned. "Young people have sought after and have received a more mature legal status and must now be taught to assume the duties and responsibilities of that position," he said.

Warren's unmistakable fervor in such matters was tempered by an abiding sense of fairness. As he called for students to live up to the responsibilities of citizenship, the attorney general urged public authorities to set a proper example by treating youngsters equitably. "If we fail to demonstrate . . . fairness for both young and old, if our laws cannot accept our children, then those laws impugn our own wisdom," he said at the Milwaukee convention. "The law cannot apply itself. Only the wise and fair approach in administration of law will spare us bitterness in the present and regret in the future."

For Warren, this "wise and fair approach" meant compelling members of all groups to abide by Wisconsin's school laws, including its statute mandating school attendance. Warren did not believe that exempting a tiny and admirable sect such as the Amish from this measure was a trivial matter. He felt, in fact, that accommodating the Amish might have potentially disastrous implications for the governance of the state's schools. Although the state supreme court's ruling in *Yoder* was narrowly drawn, the attorney general thought that it threatened to open a Pandora's box of exemption claims. Citing the precedent established in the New Glarus case, members of other groups — fringe political organizations, say, or religious cults — might feel free to challenge the constitutionality of other school regulations. If that happened, Warren feared, the state could lose its ability to maintain order in the schools.

In terms of political ideology, Warren appeared to have little in common with John Calhoun, the attorney who bore primary responsibility for arguing the state's case in the appellate courts. Almost everyone who worked with Calhoun (known as "Bill" to friends and colleagues) understood that he was not nearly as conservative politically as his boss was. As one friend later put it, he "usually was on the liberal side of things." Indeed, some of Calhoun's positions were so far to the left that they must have made Warren's head spin. Calhoun once served on a commission charged with studying the state's approach to prosecuting drug-related offenses on college campuses. After several months of study, Calhoun and his fellow commissioners recommended a dramatic liberalization of the state's drug laws. Warren advocated precisely the opposite approach: he wanted to lock up as many drug offenders as possible.

That Calhoun and Warren held immensely different political views did not prevent from them agreeing that the state could put on a strong case when it asked the U.S. Supreme Court to hear *Yoder*. Both men believed that a substantial body of judicial precedent supported the state's claim that the prosecution of the New Glarus Amish was constitutional. In other jurisdictions, the Amish had raised similar religious liberty and parental rights claims in challenging compulsory school attendance laws, and they had lost virtually every significant case. What's more, the U.S. Supreme Court had on several notable occasions acknowledged that the state possessed the authority to compel school attendance. The high court had also handed down decisions regarding parental rights and the First Amendment's establishment clause that seemed to support the state's claims in *Yoder*.

Part of what disturbed Warren and Calhoun about the Wisconsin

Supreme Court's ruling in *Yoder* was that it marked the first time the Amish had prevailed in an appellate court in a constitutional challenge to a generally applicable law mandating school attendance. Prior to *Yoder*, the Amish had lost similar cases in Kansas, Pennsylvania, and Ohio. In every instance, the courts had upheld the state's authority to compel school attendance and dismissed Amish claims that their religious liberty and parental rights had been violated. There was scant precedent directly supporting the claim that the tenets of the Amish faith entitled its members to an exemption from school attendance laws.

The most prominent of these failures for the Amish had come in the prosecution of LeRoy Garber. Although its reasoning had been savaged by many supporters of the Amish, the Kansas Supreme Court's ruling in *Kansas v. Garber* had weathered a challenge when the U.S. Supreme Court refused to hear Garber's appeal. To the attorneys representing the state of Wisconsin in *Yoder*, the high court's inaction in that earlier case seemed to signal that it might be sympathetic to their claims.

In addition to *Garber*, the state could invoke the U.S. Supreme Court's rulings in *Meyer v. Nebraska* and *Pierce v. Society of Sisters*. Justice James McReynolds's majority opinions in both cases included passages acknowledging a state's right to regulate education and enforce school attendance laws. Similarly helpful were the high court's later opinions in *Brown v. Board of Education* and *Prince v. Massachusetts*. Taken together, these four opinions seemed to provide a solid foundation for the state's claims in *Yoder*.

The state's attorneys also received a boost from Wisconsin Supreme Court Justice Nathan Heffernan. In his powerful dissent in *Yoder*, Heffernan criticized the assumption that only the rights of the Amish parents were at stake in the New Glarus case. Heffernan maintained that the interests of Amish children in gaining an education merited more judicial protection than did their parents' right to control their upbringing or to practice religion freely. In making this point, he highlighted one of the central flaws of the entire notion of parental rights: protecting the rights of parents could entail subordinating the rights of their children.

The arguments set forth by Heffernan seemed to be among the strongest in the state's favor. Attorney William Ball had urged the courts to resolve the *Yoder* case by weighing the religious liberty and parental rights claims of the Amish parents against the state's interest in mandating schooling. By contesting the parental rights claims of the Amish, the state's attorneys could present the case in a much different framework. If it followed Heffernan's lead, the state could ask the Supreme Court to weigh the parents' religious liberty against the state's interests in safeguarding the welfare of children and protecting their right to an education. Recast in this manner, the case turned on shielding the rights of children from encroachment by their parents.

As they looked for soft spots in Ball's arguments, the attorneys for the state of Wisconsin also seized on the First Amendment's establishment clause. The claims of the Amish seemed vulnerable under the evolving set of criteria that would be codified as "the *Lemon* test" later in 1971 (after the state petitioned for a writ of certiorari in *Yoder* but before the case actually reached the Court). Although the Supreme Court's establishment clause jurisprudence was unsettled, the high court's holdings in this area appeared to offer some justification for Wisconsin's position in *Yoder.* Calhoun and Warren could argue, for instance, that the state was barred from exempting the Amish from the school attendance law because such an action lacked a secular purpose and had the effect of advancing religion. They also could refer to *Braunfeld v. Brown*, in which the Court briefly discussed how states might run afoul of the establishment clause if they exempted religious objectors from generally applicable laws.

When he petitioned the U.S. Supreme Court for a writ of certiorari in *Yoder*, Wisconsin attorney general Robert Warren raised a host of issues that he claimed made the case a matter "of national importance" and thus worthy of the justices' attention. In the state's brief, Warren asserted that the Wisconsin decision directly conflicted with established constitutional law, as well as with rulings in several jurisdictions regarding school attendance statutes. The attorney general went on to submit that "because of its breadth and uniqueness," the *Yoder* decision threatened to hamstring compulsory education laws throughout the country.

Warren also pointed out in his petition that exemptions such as the one carved out for the Amish in Chief Justice Harold Hallows's opinion for the Wisconsin Supreme Court "are within the prerogative of the legislature, not the judiciary, to establish." Indeed, the situation in Wisconsin was unique, in that in each of the other states "where Amish religious beliefs have been accommodated to the compulsory attendance laws, the result has come by action of the legislative branch of government," not the judiciary. At several points in the late 1960s, Warren observed, legislators in Wisconsin had considered amending the state's education laws to provide exemptions for the Amish, but their efforts had made little headway. To Warren, it seemed inappropriate for the courts to produce "a piece of judicial legislation" when the legislature already had determined that changes in the law were not necessary.

The petition for certiorari in *Yoder* was scrutinized carefully in Justice William O. Douglas's chambers. As was customary, a law clerk drafted a memorandum on the case and outlined for Douglas the principal constitutional issues the Court would confront. "There is absolutely no doubt about the burden the compulsory education law places on the Amish," the clerk wrote. "The majority [of the Wisconsin Supreme Court] felt that a compelling state interest would have to be necessary to justify the burden." That interest, however, had not been demonstrated, so the convictions of the Amish fathers had been reversed. In reaching this decision, the lower court had relied on the three-pronged test articulated by the Supreme Court in *Sherbert v. Verner.* The state was claiming that the test established in that earlier free exercise case should not apply to the facts of *Yoder* because "to do so establishes a religion," as the clerk put it. For their part, the Amish were still maintaining that enforcement of the compulsory school attendance law violated their right to the free exercise of religion, which was shielded by the First and Fourteenth Amendments.

According to the clerk's memorandum to Douglas, disputes over the kinds of constitutional issues raised by *Yoder* were cropping up in numerous states. "The Amish reside in nineteen states," the clerk wrote. "In nine [states] they have been subjected to prosecutions similar to this one, while administrative accommodations have been reached in others." As Douglas considered whether to vote to grant certiorari in *Yoder,* this was a crucial point, for the Court often declined to hear cases that might result in an opinion limited to a single jurisdiction. Indeed, this may have been the reason for the Court's denial of certiorari in the *Garber* case. Douglas's clerk reminded him that he had voted to hear *Garber* and urged him to reach a similar conclusion in "a case reaching the opposite result," *Wisconsin v. Yoder.*

On May 24, 1971, the U.S. Supreme Court granted certiorari in *Yoder.* Six justices — Douglas and his colleagues Hugo Black, Harry Blackmun, Byron White, John Marshall Harlan, and Potter Stewart — agreed that the Wisconsin case should be heard in the Court's next term. Their decision precipitated another flurry of activity among the attorneys involved in the case. In Madison, attorney general Warren and assistant attorney general Calhoun crafted yet another brief detailing the state's arguments. Meanwhile, Ball, working in Pennsylvania, restated his case for the Amish.

In their brief for the state, Warren and Calhoun maintained that the lower court ruling in *Yoder* was "contrary to all historical and legal precedent" because "all cases, state and federal, support compulsory school attendance laws and declare them to be constitutional." Warren and Calhoun expressed no animosity toward the Amish, whom they praised as a "pious, industrious and thrifty people." Their ire was directed instead at the Wisconsin Supreme Court, which had badly misinterpreted *Sherbert* and altogether ignored both "the right of the state to insulate a child from the disease of ignorance" and "the concomitant right of the child to know." These rights, they claimed, were too precious to be compromised in the name of preserving the religious liberty of the Amish.

The attorneys for the state drew a comparison between *Yoder* and a selective service case heard by the Supreme Court in its previous term. The justices had suggested in *Gilette v. United States* (1971) that conscientious objectors seeking exemptions from the military draft "must object to all wars and not merely a particular war," as Warren and Calhoun summarized in their brief. There existed "more than a superficial resemblance" between the draft case and *Yoder*, in that the defendants in both cases, contending that their religious liberty was in jeopardy, sought "selective exemptions" from generally applicable laws. "This court rejected the concept" in *Gilette*, according to Warren and Calhoun, and it should do so again in the Wisconsin case.

In its brief, the state also contended that the exemption granted to the Amish by the Wisconsin Supreme Court violated the First Amendment's establishment clause. As they explored this claim, Calhoun and Warren did not directly refer to the applicability of "the

Lemon test," which was brand new when *Yoder* reached the Supreme Court. Calhoun and Warren submitted their brief in the New Glarus case on July 15, 1971, less than a month after the Supreme Court had handed down its opinion in *Lemon.* Lacking time to tailor their arguments specifically to the *Lemon* standard, they relied on the "cumulative criteria" from which the test had been drawn. The end result was that they essentially invoked the *Lemon* framework without specifically citing its source.

If, as Warren and Calhoun reminded the Court, exemptions had to be "secular in purpose, even handed in operation and neutral in primary impact," the state supreme court's ruling in *Yoder* had to be overturned, for it privileged one religious group over all others. Furthermore, the lower court ruling ran counter to the Court's decision in *Walz v. Tax Commission* (1970), in which it had found a law unconstitutional under the establishment clause because it fostered "an excessive degree of government entanglement" with the operation of religious organizations. Putting Wisconsin school authorities in a position of "determining the status of Amish in their community as well as their particular beliefs," Warren and Calhoun wrote, would create the very kind of "excessive entanglement" prohibited by *Walz.*

Ball's brief for the Amish showcased the claims that had proved so successful in the Wisconsin Supreme Court. *Sherbert* was his lodestar, and he relied on it time and again as he worked his way through his argument. As he attacked the state's arguments, Ball also cited the Court's rulings in two previous cases dealing specifically with school laws, including *Pierce v. Society of Sisters.* Those decisions, he maintained, "lend heavy support to the position of the defendants. It is clear from these decisions that the rights of parents, especially where they are intimately bound up with religious freedom, outweigh any claim by the state where (as here) the state shows no 'reasonable relation' between its abridgement of parental liberty and any purpose within its competence."

As the *Yoder* case reached the highest court in the land, Ball was aided by five amicus curiae briefs submitted on behalf of a total of six religious organizations. The National Council of Churches of Christ, the Synagogue Council of America and the American Jewish Congress (which submitted a joint brief), the General Conference of Seventh-Day Adventists, the Mennonite Central Committee, and the

National Jewish Commission on Law and Public Affairs all urged the Supreme Court to uphold the Wisconsin Supreme Court's decision in *Yoder*. (No outside group, religious or otherwise, submitted a brief advocating reversal.) The Supreme Court's resolution of *Yoder* was sure to have an effect on the Amish themselves, but the groups submitting amicus curiae briefs believed that it was imperative for the members of the Court to realize that their decision could affect numerous religious minority groups. The amici curiae sided with the Amish in part because, as one of the briefs put it, they had "a strong interest in religious freedom and in a religiously and culturally pluralistic America."

A number of arguments found their way into nearly all the amicus curiae briefs. Reiterating a claim made throughout the case by the defenders of the Amish, most of the outside religious groups warned the Court that the survival of the Amish was at stake in *Yoder*. The Mennonite Central Committee's brief put this assertion in particularly strong terms: it predicted that reversing the state supreme court decision and forcing the Amish to send their children to secondary schools might very well lead to "the destruction of their religion and culture as it exists in America today." A reversal by the Court essentially would leave the Amish with "no choice but to cease being Amish, to be branded as criminals or lawbreakers, or to flee to freer jurisdictions, much as they fled Europe to come to the New World in pursuit of religious freedom." This, of course, was hardly a choice at all, and the Bill of Rights would suffer irreparable harm if the Amish were compelled to make it.

In some ways, the prosecutions at the heart of the *Yoder* case embodied the worst fears of advocates of nonpublic schools. Although many of these champions, including William Ball, pursued public funding for private and parochial schools, they staunchly (and perhaps paradoxically) opposed state regulation and control. Although the amicus curiae briefs in *Yoder* focused on the plight of the Amish in particular, they also touched on some of these broader issues concerning the state's relationship with nonpublic schools. For instance, the brief submitted by the National Council of Churches of Christ began with a discussion of the principles of a policy statement that its general board had drafted regarding public funding for private and parochial schools. The brief itself did not directly address the funding issue, but it did refer to the policy statement's affirmation of "the right of all parents, all citizens, and all churches to establish and maintain non-public schools whose ethos and curriculum differ from that of the community as a whole." The brief went on to stress the right of religious groups to provide "a fundamentally different *type* of education from that generally prevailing in a given state or locality" without excessive interference by the state.

The Supreme Court heard oral arguments in *Yoder* on December 8, 1971. Because his side had lost in the lower court, assistant attorney general John Calhoun addressed the Court first. Calhoun had to convince only four justices of the wisdom of his position. Because of failing health, Hugo Black and John Marshall Harlan had retired from the bench a few months earlier, and their successors, Lewis Powell and William Rehnquist, had yet to be sworn in. Calhoun thus addressed seven justices rather than the usual complement of nine: Chief Justice Warren Burger and associate justices Harry Blackmun, William Brennan, William Douglas, Thurgood Marshall, Potter Stewart, and Byron White. That the Court was not quite at full strength did not save Calhoun from a grilling during oral arguments. As the assistant attorney general was beginning to make headway on his main argument, Justice Blackmun interrupted by asking, "Mr. Calhoun, was there any element of retaliation in this case?"

Blackmun apparently knew from reading Ball's brief that Miller, Yoder, and Yutzy had been prosecuted for violating the state compulsory attendance law just weeks after the Amish made their costly pullout from the local public school system. Ball had argued throughout the case that the prosecutions had been mounted in retaliation for the withdrawal of the Amish children, and his claim clearly troubled Blackmun. As any quick-witted attorney would, Calhoun did his best to parry Blackmun's question and get his argument back on track. "There was absolutely no evidence of [retaliation]," he said. "And, in fact, this has been a rather intelligently and studiously tried case from the beginning." Indeed, Calhoun explained, the defense at trial had brought in expert witnesses to support its contention that complying with the compulsory attendance law would force the Amish to violate some of the central tenets of their faith. "There's been no rancor," he continued. "And it's been a most interesting case because it has been free of that type of thing."

That gloss failed to satisfy Blackmun, and he probed further, specifically raising the contention that the prosecutions had been "triggered by the loss of state aid" after the Amish left the New Glarus public schools. Here Calhoun gave ground, but not much. "Well, yes, there is a loss of state aid, but that is really insignificant to the issues involved," he said. "I don't think that that has really anything to do about this. The state aids are very small compared to the real needs of the school district." Calhoun maintained that the case had little to do with money or retaliation. Moving past Blackmun's suspicions regarding the origins of the case, he told the Court that *Yoder* revolved around a single issue. "The question," Calhoun said, "is whether or not the Court can say that the Amish parents have a constitutional right to conscientiously object to education, to sending their children to school."

No such right existed, Calhoun told the Supreme Court, even though the Amish might be sincere in their beliefs. In a series of cases dating back to *Reynolds v. United States* and *Cantwell v. Connecticut*, "this Court has pronounced time and again that the freedom to act may be restricted in interpretation of the First Amendment, but the freedom to believe may not," he said. The beliefs of Miller, Yoder, and Yutzy had not been compromised; the state had attempted to regulate only their actions, and it had every right to do so, given its "compelling interest in education." What's more, to ensure that this compelling interest was satisfied, compulsory school attendance laws had been in existence for years, Calhoun told the Court, and had always been "applied and enacted in a democratic fashion."

Calhoun understood that he needed to confront and somehow dismiss *Sherbert v. Verner* before Ball touted the precedent's relevance in his own oral argument. Calhoun took up this challenge midway through his presentation to the Court, claiming that the earlier case dealt with an "entirely different set of values" because it had centered on a "social institution" (a state unemployment compensation system) that was in no way comparable to the public schools. Far more apt comparisons to *Yoder*, Calhoun hinted, could be found in cases such as *Gilette* and *Walz*. As he interpreted *Gilette*, the Supreme Court had held that exemptions from generally applicable laws could be granted only for purely secular purposes. Moreover, *Walz* indicated that the granting of such exemptions could not involve, in the words of the opinion, "an excessive degree of governmental entanglement" with religion. If the Court agreed with Calhoun's interpretation of those two precedents, it would have no choice but to uphold the convictions of the Amish fathers. To acknowledge instead that "anyone who has a conscientious objection based on a sincere moral belief" possessed a constitutional right to object to education "would raise havoc with the educational system, not only in Wisconsin, but throughout the country," Calhoun warned.

After the assistant attorney general yielded the floor, William Ball wasted little time in casting the prosecution of the New Glarus Amish in the worst possible light. Returning to Justice Blackmun's blunt question to Calhoun regarding the element of retaliation, Ball addressed the question of how "this prosecution came to be triggered" by quoting the dissenting opinion written by Justice Nathan Heffernan of the Wisconsin Supreme Court. Even though Heffernan had been the only member of that court to vote to uphold the convictions of the Amish fathers, he had been appalled by the state's apparent motivation in prosecuting them. As Ball now reminded the Supreme Court, Heffernan had written in his dissent, "There is strong evidence that the purpose of this prosecution was not to further the compelling interest of the State in education, but rather the reprehensible objective, under the facts of this case, to force the Amish into school only for the purpose of qualifying for augmented State aid." Calhoun had asserted that Wisconsin's compulsory school attendance law was implemented "for the benefit of society," but Ball wanted to remind the Court that the measure might have been applied to the Amish in Green County for far less noble reasons.

After condemning the state's motive for enforcing the law, Ball proceeded to explain why the Amish had chosen to break it. Given an opening by an innocuous question posed by Justice Potter Stewart, Ball explained that the Amish traced their origins back to the Reformation, when their Anabaptist forebears broke with the Catholic Church in an attempt to "return to what they believe[d] to be the golden age of Christianity, in the early centuries of Christianity." He went on to discuss what he called "a basic doctrine of Amish religious teaching"— their commitment to keeping themselves apart from the corruption and sinfulness of the world at large. This desire for separation, Ball said, drove the Amish to form their own close-knit communities, and it also made them wary of extensive formal education. "The Amish," Ball told the Court, "do not want their children — and they do not want themselves — to be exposed to the spirit of luxury, of ostentation, of strife, consumerism, competition, speed, violence, and other such elements as are commonly found in American life." The Amish conceded that some basic education was desirable — they "believe[d] that a person should be able to read and write and communicate," Ball said — but they felt that an adolescent would be more harmed than helped by going to high school and being continuously exposed to the myriad vices of the world outside the Amish community.

As Calhoun had anticipated, Ball spent several minutes addressing the compelling state interest standard articulated in *Sherbert v. Verner* and its applicability to the prosecutions of Miller, Yoder, and Yutzy. He was nothing if not direct on this point, telling the Court that "there is no compelling state interest reflected in the state compulsory attendance laws, in having children attend school beyond the fourteenth birthday." In fact, when the Amish fathers had been tried in Green County, the state "never placed a single witness on the stand, produced any documentary evidence at all, one scrap of any study, which would give color to the charge that Amish non-attendance threatens some compelling state interest." In attempting to justify compelling Amish adolescents to attend high school, Calhoun had spoken "loosely about the disease of ignorance and opening the gateways of opportunity to these people," but he had offered little concrete evidence to support his position. Ball, in contrast, had produced several witnesses at the trial whose testimony indicated that there was nothing to be gained — and much to be lost — by forcing the Amish to comply with the state's compulsory school attendance law.

Ball did have to treat one matter gingerly, and that was his own involvement in the case. During oral arguments, the issue surfaced when Justice Blackmun questioned Ball about the willingness of the Amish to accept the help of professionals from outside their faith. Responding to a question from Blackmun about the Amish reliance "on medical knowledge [from] elsewhere," Ball stumbled through a brief explanation of how a case involving the Amish had wound up before the Supreme Court in the first place. "Right now," he said, "they are receiving legal help, though they did not seek it. It came to them through the National Committee for Amish Religious Freedom. But they do not—they would far rather suffer, personally, prosecution than make a test case—go to court and so on." Ball's comments might have raised red flags for those who suspected that outsiders had dragged the Amish into pursuing the case, but they apparently did not trouble the Court; Blackmun quickly moved on to another topic, and the issue did not come up again during oral arguments.

After outlining the case for the defendants, Ball closed his oral argument by reminding the Supreme Court of the stakes involved in *Wisconsin v. Yoder*. The survival of the Amish in New Glarus was hanging in the balance, he claimed, because their community surely would not endure if they were forced to comply with the state's compulsory school attendance law. Their wall of separation from the world having been demolished in Wisconsin, the Amish would have no real choice but to move elsewhere. "The question before this Court, then," Ball said, "is whether the State may destroy—because that's what it will come to if these children are forced into high school—a peaceable, self-sustaining community . . . on the grounds that the parents in that community cannot send their children, on account of the clear mandate of their religion, to one or two years of high school." Well aware that the Supreme Court's opinion was likely to have a far-reaching impact both practically and symbolically, Ball also touted the larger implications of the case. He told the Court that if the Amish fathers lost, "I fear that many people will feel that this Court has indicted our nation as too ossified, too brittle, too moribund to allow differences, innocent difference, to exist and to flourish in its midst."

Ball handled himself well. He even managed to endure the antics of Justice William Douglas, who was notoriously inattentive during oral arguments. Throughout Ball's presentation, Douglas "was just being extremely rude," recalled Joe Skelly, who had traveled from Pennsylvania to Washington to hear his law partner argue before the high court. "He was obviously working on another opinion. He was passing notes and having his law clerks come in and out." Ball noticed Douglas's mischief and made his displeasure known by briefly stopping his argument and glaring at the justice. Skelly, for one, was delighted that his law partner could register his disapproval of Douglas without losing his train of thought.

When he finished his oral argument, Ball was convinced that he had blundered terribly and would lose the case. As he collected his papers and prepared to leave the counsel table, Ball slipped Joe Skelly a brief, despairing note. It read: "We have lost." Skelly had practiced law with Ball for several years, and he had become accustomed to such responses from his colleague. "Any case he ever argued," Skelly later said, "he thought maybe he lost." Skelly thought the oral argument had gone well, and he did his best to reassure Ball that the Supreme Court might rule in their favor. Ball remained unconvinced. "He was really kind of down about it," according to Skelly.

Calhoun had saved time for rebuttal, and he now used it in a last-ditch effort to refute Ball's contentions. The state, he told the Court, had "absolutely no quarrel with the Amish way of life," which in fact seemed idyllic to many of those who were caught up in "the remorseless crunch of daily living." However, the state legislature had enacted compulsory education laws because its members firmly believed that "what is needed is more education to cope with the problems of society. More pride in intellect, not less pride." The Amish were defying the legislature's — and, by the extension, the people of Wisconsin's — commitment to that principle, but Calhoun saw a flaw in their claim for an exemption: their insistence that education beyond the eighth grade would violate the tenets of their faith. To Calhoun, it seemed to be an arbitrary demarcation, one that was not rooted in any particular passage of Scripture, and he pleaded with the Court not to give it sanction. "There can be no effort or no decision of this Court, it seems to me, that can say eighth grade is the cutoff point," he said. "There is nothing logical or constitutional about the cutoff."

After Calhoun finished his remarks, the waiting game began. It was now up to the nation's highest court to resolve *Yoder*, but no one involved in the case had any idea how the justices would rule, who would write their majority opinion, or when it would be handed down.

CHAPTER 9

The U.S. Supreme Court Rules in *Yoder*

On the day the U.S. Senate confirmed the nomination of William Rehnquist to the U.S. Supreme Court—December 10, 1971—his future colleagues met for their regular weekly conference. There they exchanged their views on *Wisconsin v. Yoder*, which had been argued before them two days earlier.

In keeping with tradition, Chief Justice Warren Burger spoke first when the seven justices began to share their preliminary views on the New Glarus school attendance case. Burger was unequivocal: he announced that he would affirm the lower court's ruling in this "very difficult case." The chief justice explained that despite the forceful arguments advanced by assistant attorney general John Calhoun during oral arguments, he had "difficulty in finding a compelling state interest" in mandating school attendance beyond the eighth grade. Education, to be sure, was part of the bedrock of modern society, but the state and its schools hardly possessed a monopoly on providing worthwhile instruction. With their emphasis on hands-on, practical teaching, the Amish did an exemplary job of educating their youngsters, and "the kind of discipline and training these [children] get from their fathers is as good as anything they'd get in Wisconsin schools." What's more, the Amish in New Glarus were part of an "ancient religion, not a new cult," Burger said. Given that their church was so well established, it was particularly important for the Court to protect their religious liberty from infringement by the state.

As the senior associate justice, William O. Douglas spoke after Burger. Then in his fourth decade of service on the Court, Douglas had long been one of the Court's leading advocates for safeguarding individual liberties from intrusion by the state. At the *Yoder* conference, Douglas indicated his willingness to shield the right of parents to direct the upbringing of their children. "I would affirm," he said. "*Pierce v. Society of Sisters* governs."

As the conversation about *Yoder* moved around the conference table, justices William Brennan and Potter Stewart spoke next. A stalwart of the Warren Court, Brennan had profoundly influenced First Amendment jurisprudence since joining the Court in 1956, authoring numerous opinions to expand the protection of individual liberties. (He had, for instance, written for the Court in *Sherbert v. Verner*, the landmark religious liberty case.) Stewart, a moderate, had been less influential, but throughout his career he provided a critical "swing" vote in many cases. Although their judicial philosophies differed, Brennan and Stewart agreed with Burger and Douglas that the Wisconsin Supreme Court's ruling in *Yoder* should be affirmed. Stewart added a caveat, telling the conference, "It would be difficult to sustain if the group merely did not want its children to be able to read."

Justice Byron White, appointed to the Court by President Kennedy in 1962, spoke fifth at the *Yoder* conference. White also indicated that the Court should rule in favor of the New Glarus Amish. He conceded, however, that one aspect of the case troubled him. White said that although many issues in *Yoder* had been exhaustively explored in briefs and during oral arguments, there had been "little talk of the interest of the children." Even though the "rights of children have independent standing," White pointed out, they had been largely overlooked throughout the case. The reservations expressed by White apparently did not provoke an extended debate among his colleagues, and the discussion moved on.

Justices Thurgood Marshall and Harry Blackmun followed White. A former solicitor general and the nation's first African American Supreme Court justice, Marshall had been a reliable advocate of minority and civil rights since joining the Court in 1967. Blackmun, in only his second term on the Court, had been expected to ally himself with Chief Justice Burger (so much so that they were dubbed "the Minnesota Twins" after the native state they shared), but over time, he cautiously developed a more liberal bent and often voted with Marshall and Brennan, particularly in civil liberties cases. Neither Blackmun nor Marshall spoke at length in the conference discussion of *Yoder*, but both indicated that they too would vote to affirm the Wisconsin ruling.

Blackmun did offer two brief comments on *Yoder*, and both were revealing. First, he acknowledged the power of the case put on at trial by attorney William Ball. "I would affirm," Blackmun said, "on this full and devastating trial record." But his admiration for Ball's work had its limits. Though he had been impressed by the expert testimony of witnesses John Hostetler and Donald Erickson, Blackmun apparently did not think that the Court should use *Yoder* as a vehicle for issuing a sweeping opinion on religious liberty or parental rights. The Court's most junior member said that if he were to write the opinion in *Yoder*, he "would not paint broadly for all cases." Given the uniqueness of the Amish claim, a narrow opinion was appropriate, Blackmun suggested.

The result of the conference discussion of *Yoder* seemed clear: all seven justices believed that the U.S. Supreme Court should affirm the ruling of the Wisconsin Supreme Court. Now, of course, the Court had to formulate an opinion to clarify the reasoning behind its decision. Chief Justice Burger had the prerogative to assign the writing of the *Yoder* opinion to any member of the Court's majority. In the end, he chose to give the job to himself.

Warren Burger's predecessor as chief justice had been the venerable Earl Warren. Even Warren's detractors — and they were legion — recognized that he had presided over one of the most important periods in the Supreme Court's history. Under his stewardship in the 1950s and 1960s, the Court had handed down a succession of landmark rulings to protect individual and minority rights, the most notable being *Brown v. Board of Education*. A towering figure, Warren was an almost impossible act to follow, and Burger suffered in comparison. Elevated to the Supreme Court in 1969 from the U.S. Court of Appeals for the District of Columbia, he was viewed by many as a "symbol of retrenchment," as one journalist later noted. Many observers of the Court assumed that he would do the bidding of Richard Nixon, the arch-conservative (and vehement Warren Court critic) who had nominated him.

But Burger's tenure as chief justice proved to be something of a surprise to those who had expected him to guide the Court in a conservative direction. "Contrary to the expectations of many, the advances of the Warren Court were not destroyed or even limited very much during [Burger's] years as Chief Justice," Justice Harry Blackmun observed. "Indeed, those precedents generally were accepted and were built upon and refined; perhaps it could even be said that such excesses as did exist were appropriately contained. Surely his seventeen years can be described, if not as a period of startling new developments in the law, at least as a period of settling and rethinking and stabilizing." With Burger's support, the Court established a constitutional right to abortion, approved court-ordered busing as a means of remedying racial segregation in schools, and rendered "the first decision in history ever to declare arbitrary discrimination against women unconstitutional," as Justice Ruth Bader Ginsburg put it. Burger was no Earl Warren, of course; during his tenure as chief justice, only William Rehnquist compiled a more conservative voting record. Liberal observers of the Court bemoaned Burger's conservatism, and they delighted in deriding him as an intellectual lightweight. But their worst fear — that he would undo the formidable accomplishments of his predecessor — never came to fruition.

Burger was not an especially prolific author of opinions. After tallying the majority, concurring, and dissenting opinions drafted by members of the Supreme Court during his tenure as chief justice, political scientist Charles Lamb came to the conclusion that Burger was the least productive writer among all the justices. According to Lamb's study, the opinions that Burger did produce were not often pathbreaking or profound. On the whole, they "tended to be short on constitutional theory and long on fine points required to dispose of cases. They were characteristically straightforward and matter-of-fact, workmanlike, reasonably well written but less than eloquent, and well grounded in precedent." Other commentators were somewhat less charitable in their assessment of the technical qualities of Burger's opinions. One wrote that "the quality of writing is uneven; the organization, sometimes incoherent; and the law, often vague."

Observers of the Court who tried to discern ideological trends in these opinions often expressed bewilderment at Burger's apparent lack of a broad and coherent constitutional philosophy. The chief justice obviously was no liberal: in criminal procedure cases, for instance, he gained a well-deserved reputation for being an unsparing law-and-order conservative by almost always voting to give wide latitude to police and prosecutors. Yet on civil rights, "Burger did not always assume the posture of an uncompromising conservative," Lamb wrote. To the surprise of many, he authored the Court's opinion in *Swann v. Board of Education* (1971), which upheld the constitutionality of school busing programs designed to promote desegregation.

James Volling, who served as a law clerk under Burger, suggested that when the chief justice wrote opinions in religion clause cases, he "sought reasoned balance and was a painstaking student of history." Burger's efforts in establishment clause cases — in which he appeared to be guided more by his famous pragmatism than by a consistent philosophy — constitute one of his most significant legacies as a jurist. But, as Volling pointed out, Burger also wrote several important free exercise clause opinions, and in them he showed himself to be "a staunch defender of religious liberty." In *McDaniel v. Paty* (1978), for instance, he wrote for the Court as it struck down a statute prohibiting clergy from serving as delegates to a state's constitutional convention. He also twice wrote opinions supporting claims by Jehovah's Witnesses that their religious liberty had been compromised.

Burger circulated the first draft of his opinion in *Yoder* — surely the most significant religious liberty opinion of his career — early in April 1972. (By that point, William Rehnquist and Lewis Powell had joined the Court, but they arrived too late to take part in deciding the case.) The chief justice began his draft by reviewing the facts of the case and briefly summarizing the arguments offered by both sides in the lower courts. Burger then launched into a lengthy and detailed examination of the history, beliefs, and practices of the Amish.

Nothing was more central to the Amish faith, according to the chief justice, than the concept of separation. Men like Jonas Yoder held a "fundamental belief," Burger wrote, "that salvation requires life in a church community separate and apart from the world and worldly influence." This article of their faith was the source of their objection to Wisconsin's compulsory school attendance law. "They object to the high school and higher education generally because the values it teaches are in marked variance with Amish values and the Amish way of life; they view secondary school education as an impermissible exposure of their children to a 'worldly' influence in conflict with their beliefs," the chief justice wrote.

The potential dangers posed to the Amish by these temporal influences were enormous, Burger claimed. Because it removed Amish youngsters "from their community, physically and emotionally, during the crucial and formative adolescent period of life," compulsory high school attendance had the potential to shatter Amish communities. In making this claim, Burger pointed to the trial testimony of John Hostetler, the leading scholarly expert on the Amish. According to the chief justice, Hostetler had testified that compulsory high school attendance "could not only result in great psychological harm to Amish children, because of the conflicts it would produce, but would . . . result in the destruction of the Old Order Amish community as it exists in the United States today." In short, the fate of the Amish faith was riding on the New Glarus case. If they were forced to comply with the compulsory school attendance law, Burger insisted, the communities of the Amish might very well disintegrate.

Burger then turned his attention away from the Amish and focused on the state's interest in enforcing the compulsory school attendance law. Burger did not deny that the state could, as he put it, "impose reasonable regulations for the control and duration of basic education," as the Court had acknowledged in such opinions as *Pierce v. Society of Sisters*. However, this power was not unlimited, particularly "when it collides with other fundamental rights, such as those specifically protected by the Free Exercise Clause of the First Amendment and the traditional rights of parents—antedating constitutions and even governments—with respect to the upbringing of their children." When an individual claimed that such a collision had taken place, Burger wrote, the state had a very clear burden. For the exercise of state power to be constitutionally valid in this context, the state was required to prove that it was not infringing on religious liberty or that "there is a state interest of sufficient magnitude to override the interest claiming protection under the Free Exercise Clause." As the chief justice framed it in his draft opinion, the New Glarus case in many ways hinged on the state's ability to show that it had satisfied these burdens.

To the chief justice, there was no question that the religious liberty of the Amish was being compromised by the application of the Wisconsin compulsory school attendance law. The Amish were still free to formally worship as they chose, but their "religious faith and their mode of life" were so "inseparable and interdependent" that the state's efforts to regulate their lifestyle inevitably circumscribed the exercise of their faith. Burger wrote:

> As the record strongly shows, the values and programs of the modern secondary school conflict with the fundamental mode of life mandated by the Amish religion, and modern laws requiring compulsory secondary education, have accordingly engendered great concern and conflict. The conclusion is inescapable that secondary schooling, by exposing Amish children to worldly influence in terms of attitudes, goals, and values in conflict with beliefs, and by substantially interfering with the integration of the Amish child into the way of life of the Amish faith community at the crucial adolescent state of development, contravenes the basic religious tenets and practice of the Amish faith, both as to the parent and the child.
>
> The record fully supports a conclusion that the impact of the compulsory attendance law on the practice of the Amish religion is not only severe, but inescapable, for the Wisconsin law affirmatively compels them, under threat of criminal sanction, to perform acts undeniably at odds with fundamental tenets of their religious beliefs.

The application of the compulsory attendance law, Burger concluded, "would gravely endanger if not destroy the free exercise of [the Amish] respondents' religious beliefs."

Given that substantial threat, the Court could not take at face value the state's rationale for applying the compulsory attendance law to the Amish. Instead, it had to "searchingly examine the interests which the State seeks to promote by its requirement for compulsory education to age 16." Throughout the New Glarus case, Wisconsin had attempted to justify enforcing the law against the Amish by arguing that "a brief additional period of formal education is imperative to enable the Amish to participate effectively and intelligently in our democratic process," Burger wrote. This additional training, it was suggested, would be particularly important for those youngsters who eventually left the faith and attempted to lead productive lives in "worldly" environments. Burger felt that this "highly speculative" line of reasoning was simply too flimsy. After all, nothing in the record of *Yoder* demonstrated that "persons possessing such valuable vocational skills and habits as Amish children are shown to possess are doomed to become burdens on society should they determine to leave the Amish faith." The hands-on training provided by the Amish to their children was different from what public high schools furnished, but this did not mean that it was so inferior as to permanently burden the youngsters who received it.

As he addressed the issue of the state's compelling interest, Burger acknowledged in the draft of his opinion that compulsory attendance laws had been established for noble purposes. "We should . . . note that compulsory education and child labor laws find their historical origin in common humanitarian instincts," he wrote, "and that the age limits of both laws have been coordinated to achieve their common objectives." These objectives included safeguarding the health of younger adolescents and keeping them from taking jobs "which might otherwise be held by adults," the chief justice observed. But in the case of the Amish, Burger asserted, these concerns were largely irrelevant. Employing Amish youngsters on farms as part of a vocational training program "presents none of the undesirable economic aspects" of taking jobs from worthy adults, and it in no way endangered their health.

The final major section of Burger's draft opinion in *Yoder* dealt with the rights of parents. "The history and culture of western civilization reflects a strong tradition of parental concern for the nurture and upbringing of their children," the chief justice wrote. "This primary role of the parent in the education and upbringing of his children is now established beyond debate as an enduring American tradition." The state of Wisconsin, however, was violating these rights in the name of ensuring that Amish youngsters received the purported benefits of an additional two years of high school. To halt this abrogation, Burger referred to one of William Ball's touchstones: the Supreme Court's opinion in *Pierce v. Society of Sisters.* That ruling, the chief justice wrote in his draft, stood "as a charter of the rights of parents to direct the religious upbringing and education of their children" free from interference by the state. "Until the child is capable of making his or her own decisions, the choices must be made by either the parents or the State, and we have come down firmly in favor of the parents."

Wrapping up his draft, Burger returned to a theme he had stressed in the Supreme Court's conference discussion of *Yoder:* the noble and "ancient" nature of the Amish faith. In his final paragraphs, the chief justice seemed to suggest that the religious liberty of the Amish was especially worthy of protection because their faith was so unique, all-encompassing, and stable:

> It cannot be over-emphasized that we are not dealing with a way of life and mode of education by a group claiming to have recently discovered some "progressive" or more enlightened process for rearing children for modern life. Aided by a history of three centuries as an identifiable religious sect and a long history as an exceptionally successful segment of American society, the Amish in this case have convincingly demonstrated the sincerity of their religious beliefs, the interrelationship of belief with their mode of life, the vital role which belief and daily conduct play in the continued survival of Old Order Amish communities and their religious organization, and the hazards presented by the State's enforcement of a statute generally valid as to others.

What's more, they had demonstrated "the adequacy of their alternative modes of continuing informal education in terms of precisely those overall interests that the state advances in support of its program of compulsory high school education." In other words, not only were the Amish practicing a well-established and admirable faith, but their effective vocational training of their children served the same interests promoted by the state. To the chief justice, these two factors made the claims of the Amish fathers all the more valid.

Justice Potter Stewart responded quickly after Burger circulated the draft of his opinion. In a memorandum dated April 10, 1972, Stewart praised the chief justice's "admirably thorough opinion" in *Yoder* but offered two suggestions to help clarify it. Stewart thought that the ruling should make clearer reference to the protections conferred by the Fourteenth Amendment in safeguarding religious liberty from infringement by the states. He also hoped that the chief justice would revise his discussion of parental rights. Stewart believed that Burger had overstated the protections afforded by the Constitution in that area. "I am enough of a disciple of Hugo Black to be unable to agree that 'parental direction' is a constitutional right," he wrote to Burger. "To be sure, our society has long been organized in terms of the monogamous family structure, and this Court's cases make clear that the interests arising from the structure enjoy procedural due process as well as equal protection immunity from governmental interference. But it is something else to say that those interests are substantive constitutional rights." Stewart hoped that Burger would change the sections of the *Yoder* opinion addressing the rights of parents "so as to make clear [that] the substantive reliance of the opinion is exclusively upon the right of free exercise of religion, conferred by the First and Fourteenth Amendments of the Constitution." Stewart's views were shared by Justice William Brennan, and he urged the chief justice to incorporate the revisions suggested by Stewart.

Burger seemed eager to accommodate his colleagues. "Your points give me no difficulty at all," he wrote to Stewart. The chief justice pledged to "make explicit what is now clearly implicit" with regard to the Fourteenth Amendment and to modify his comments on parental rights. His language on that point, he said, "can be converted into a looser observation as to the parental interest that, in this case, is linked with the Religion Clauses — also via the 14th."

For the final version of the Supreme Court's opinion in *Yoder*, Burger changed portions of the section addressing parental rights to reflect Stewart's concerns. At one point, the chief justice quoted perhaps the most famous passage from *Pierce:* "The child is not the mere creature of the State; those who nurture him and direct his destiny have the right, coupled with the high duty, to recognize and prepare him for additional obligations." Initially, Burger had written that "the *right* to prepare the child for 'additional obligations,' referred to by the Court, must be read to include inculcation of moral standards, religious beliefs and other elements of good citizenship." Sensitive to Stewart's worries about parental rights, he changed the beginning of that sentence to refer to "the *duty* to prepare the child for 'additional obligations'" (emphasis added).

Burger's final draft satisfied all his fellow justices except for William Douglas. Troubled by portions of the chief justice's opinion, the Court's senior member chose to craft a partial dissent. During the Court's conference discussion of the New Glarus case, Justice Byron White had grumbled that "the interests of the children" had been overlooked throughout the proceedings. It was the iconoclastic Douglas, however, who chose to pursue this point in a partial dissent.

Writing with his customary vigor, Douglas zeroed in on a point made by Nathan Heffernan, the only justice of the Wisconsin Supreme Court to dissent in *Yoder.* "The Court's analysis assumes that the only interests at stake in the case are those of the Amish parents on the one hand, and those of the State on the other," Douglas wrote. "The difficulty with this approach is that, despite the Court's claim, the parents are seeking to vindicate not only their own free exercise claims, but also those of their high-school-age children." By focusing so much of its attention on safeguarding the religious liberty of the parents, the Court was giving its imprimatur to the imposition of "the parents' notions of religious duty upon their children," something it had steadfastly refused to do in *Prince v. Massachusetts,* a Jehovah's Witness case from the mid-1940s. Douglas was willing to join the Court's ruling as it related to Jonas Yoder, because his daughter had testified about her religious beliefs during trial, but he balked at applying the ruling to Adin Yutzy and Wallace Miller, whose children hadn't testified about their religious faith. In their cases, "the question of their children's religious liberty" had been ignored, he maintained.

Whereas Burger's majority opinion focused on the rights of parents, Douglas's sharply worded partial dissent emphasized that "children themselves have constitutionally protectible interests." He pointed to several recent decisions in which the Supreme Court had acknowledged that children "are 'persons' within the meaning of the Bill of Rights." These precedents included opinions as old as *West Virginia Board of Education v. Barnette* (1943) and as recent as *In re Gault* (1967) and *Tinker v. Des Moines School District* (1969). Douglas condemned the majority opinion in *Yoder* because it seemed to completely ignore the Court's holdings in these earlier cases.

Douglas believed that the Court's opinion in *Yoder* might have dire consequences for Amish children who chose to leave the insular world of their religious faith. Deprived of schooling by their parents, they might not be sufficiently prepared to handle the myriad challenges of the modern world. "It is the future of the student . . . that is imperiled by today's decision," he wrote. "If a parent keeps his child out of school beyond the grade school, then the child will be forever barred from entry into the new and amazing world of diversity that we have today." In perhaps the most famous passage of his dissent, Douglas worried that an Amish boy's "entire life may be stunted and deformed" if he was deprived of an adequate education in the name of safeguarding his parents' religious liberty.

Douglas also quibbled with Burger over the chief justice's close inspection of Amish beliefs and practices. "I think the emphasis of the Court on the 'law and order' record of this Amish group of people is quite irrelevant," he wrote. "A religion is a religion irrespective of what the misdemeanor or felony records of its members might be." More troubling to Douglas were Burger's comments regarding which beliefs qualified as "religious" and thus merited protection under the First Amendment. In his majority opinion in *Yoder*, the chief justice commented that Henry David Thoreau's decision to isolate himself at Walden Pond was not analogous to the Amish decision to separate themselves from the modern world because Thoreau's "choice was philosophical and personal rather than religious, and such belief does not rise to the demands of the Religion Clauses." Douglas objected to this passage in particular — and to Burger's close scrutiny of Amish beliefs in general — because it seemed to put the justices in the position of judging the legitimacy of religious beliefs.

Burger revised the majority opinion in *Yoder* to refute some of the assertions made in Douglas's partial dissent. The chief justice downplayed Douglas's concerns about the rights of the Amish children. "The children are not parties to this litigation," Burger pointed out; only their parents had been charged under Wisconsin's compulsory school attendance law. "It is the parents who are subject to prosecution here for failing to cause their children to attend school," Burger wrote, "and it is their right of free exercise, not that of their children, that must determine Wisconsin's power to impose criminal penalties on the parent." The chief justice further deflected Douglas's assertions by suggesting that the state had no business mediating possible conflicts over religion that might arise between parents and children. Allowing the state to intrude "into family decisions in the area of religious training," he wrote, "would give rise to grave questions of religious freedom" and might very well "call into question traditional concepts of parental control over the religious up-bringing and education recognized in this Court's past decisions," including *Pierce*.

Justice Stewart buttressed the chief justice's refutation of Douglas with a brief concurring opinion. In addressing the matter of the rights of the Amish children, Douglas had explored an "interesting and important issue," Stewart wrote, but it simply had not been raised by the record in *Yoder.* Justice Brennan agreed with Stewart's argument on this point and joined the concurrence.

Both Stewart and Brennan also joined a concurrence written by Justice White. White apparently had overcome his earlier misgivings about the interests of the children being slighted; he did not review that issue at all in his concurrence. He did, however, discuss an aspect of the chief justice's majority opinion that would eventually draw fire from more than one critic. Acknowledging Burger's lengthy examination of the beliefs of the Amish and their way of life, White conceded that religious liberty cases like *Yoder* involved so many competing interests that they "will inevitably involve the kind of close and perhaps repeated scrutiny of religious practices . . . which the Court has heretofore been anxious to avoid." Perhaps anticipating that the Court would be accused of violating the First Amendment's establishment clause to resolve the free exercise claim, White argued that the Court's close scrutiny of the Amish faith "does not create a forbidden establishment of religion where it is essential to implement free exercise values threatened by an otherwise neutral program instituted to foster some permissible, nonreligious state objective." The Court was hardly taking a step toward establishing a religion, White suggested, if it merely stepped in to prevent a religious faith from being extirpated.

CHAPTER 10

Assessing the Supreme Court's Decision in *Wisconsin v. Yoder*

Americans of all faiths consider religious liberty to be one of the most important individual freedoms safeguarded by the Constitution. Chief Justice Burger's majority opinion in *Wisconsin v. Yoder* was a landmark because it protected that cherished right as it had never been protected before. As one scholarly commentator put it, Burger's majority opinion in the Amish school attendance case represented "the high water mark of religious liberty under the Free Exercise Clause of the First Amendment." The chief justice's analysis showed an unprecedented deference to the beliefs and practices of religious objectors, and his application of strict scrutiny placed a heavy burden on states to justify neutral laws that nonetheless infringed on those dissenters' right to the free exercise of religion.

The Supreme Court's religious liberty jurisprudence did not arrive at this peak overnight. A century earlier, in *Reynolds v. United States*, the Court essentially removed religious conduct from the purview of the First Amendment. In subsequent cases—including the Jehovah's Witnesses cases of the World War II era and *Sherbert v. Verner*—the justices gradually acknowledged that the Constitution protected many such actions from encroachment by the state. *Yoder* marked an important extension of this lengthy and slow-developing trend. Chief Justice Burger's analysis appeared to further circumscribe the power of states to regulate religious conduct.

Such a decision would have been unimaginable a century earlier. With matters relating to economic regulation dominating the justices' agenda well into the twentieth century, the Supreme Court had long overlooked minority rights and civil liberties. Thanks in part to the seeds planted in the 1930s and 1940s by litigants such as the Jehovah's Witnesses, a "rights revolution" bloomed under Earl Warren. During Warren's tenure as chief justice, the Supreme Court issued numerous opinions aimed at shielding individual rights and curbing the power of the state. Although Burger had resolved to quell this jurisprudential tumult, his majority opinion in *Yoder* seemed to put the Supreme Court back in the position of protecting individual freedoms from state intrusion.

The sterling character of the principals in *Yoder* made this task more palatable for the chief justice. The Amish humbly worked the land, devoted themselves to their religious faith, and asked for almost nothing from the state. (Indeed, they sought to dissociate themselves as much as humanly possible from all forms of government.) Although the piety of the Amish ostensibly had little bearing on the legal questions at the heart of *Yoder*, it clearly struck a chord with the straitlaced Burger. At one point in his opinion, the chief justice gushed that "the Amish communities singularly parallel and reflect many of the virtues of Jefferson's ideal of the 'sturdy yeoman' who would form the basis of what he considered as the ideal of a democratic society. Even their idiosyncratic separateness exemplifies the diversity we profess to admire and encourage." The fact that these superlative Americans seemed to embody many of the virtues exalted by social and political conservatives almost certainly made Burger more receptive to their legal claims.

That the Amish were exemplary Christians—and not, say, members of an obscure or disturbing religious cult—surely helped their cause as well. The Amish were by no means mainstream Protestants; their beliefs had not evolved considerably since the Reformation. Yet they still shared with members of most Christian denominations a set of core beliefs based on the teachings of Jesus Christ and the fundamental lessons of the Scriptures. The basic contours of their faith were thus easily discernible to Burger and his fellow justices. And the beliefs of the Amish seemed to be as laudable as they were familiar. With the world seemingly losing its moral bearings in the late 1960s and early 1970s, the durability and relative simplicity of their doctrines must have appeared quite admirable to Burger and his colleagues.

Moreover, adherence to these doctrines did not prompt the Amish to engage in outlandish behavior. In several notable cases, litigants appearing before the Supreme Court have asked the justices to protect uncommon religious conduct. Mormons (in *Reynolds*) argued that the First Amendment protected the practice of polygamy. Native Americans (in *Oregon v. Smith*) made a similar claim regarding the ceremonial use of peyote. The New Glarus Amish engaged in nothing so peculiar as ingesting hallucinogens or collecting multiple wives. They ran afoul of state authority simply by removing their children from school after the youngsters reached age fourteen. The relative inoffensiveness of this conduct probably made it easier for the Court to hold that the First Amendment shielded their actions.

While the Amish benefited from their image as virtuous but vulnerable Christians, the state of Wisconsin suffered greatly from perceptions regarding its motives and tactics in pursuing the school attendance case. The state was widely regarded as the villain in *Yoder* because it had prosecuted the New Glarus Amish only after they refused to help inflate the local public school census. (This point had been underscored early in John Calhoun's oral argument, when Justice Harry Blackmun asked him point-blank if the Amish had been the victims of retaliation.) The suspicion that the local school superintendent's main concern had been gaining a measure of retribution against the Amish — and not ensuring that their children received adequate schooling — seemed to cast a pall over the state's case. Throughout *Yoder*'s journey to the Supreme Court, the attorneys representing Wisconsin were burdened by credible accusations that the origins of the case were ignoble.

It is perhaps not surprising that a case involving tangled legal issues, an unusual group of litigants, and a dynamic attorney employed by an interest group yielded an imperfect result. One notable drawback of *Yoder* was its lack of scope. The protections it afforded to religious liberty were as narrow as they were strong. In his majority opinion, the chief justice focused almost exclusively on how the history, beliefs, and practices of the Amish made their religious liberty particularly vulnerable to encroachment by the state. Implicit in Burger's analysis of the threat posed to the Amish was the suggestion that these simple folk were uniquely qualified for special judicial protections.

The Supreme Court's narrow reasoning in *Yoder* left it open to charges that it had privileged members of a single religious faith and thereby violated the First Amendment's establishment clause. The conservative jurist and scholar Robert Bork maintained that the Supreme Court surely would have struck down, on establishment clause grounds, any law providing members of a particular religious group with an exemption from the compulsory school attendance law. Paradoxically, though, the Court provided just such a privilege to the Amish by judicial fiat. "Thus, in the name of the free exercise of religion," he wrote of *Yoder*, "the Supreme Court, according to its own criteria, itself established a religion."

Whatever the merit of Bork's criticisms, it seems clear that Chief Justice Burger struggled to fully harmonize the Supreme Court's often conflicting interpretations of the First Amendment's two religion provisions. Although he devoted a sizable portion of his majority opinion in *Yoder* to examining the litigants' faith and its many apparent virtues, Burger seemed less enthusiastic about explaining precisely how states could safeguard religion without appearing to establish it. At one point, he touted the benefits of "preserving doctrinal flexibility and recognizing the need for a sensible and realistic application of the religion clauses." Such vague language was not likely to provide a durable standard for future cases in which religious objectors claimed exemptions from generally applicable laws.

In a more general way, the *Yoder* opinion appeared to privilege religious beliefs over secular ones. Burger's majority opinion emphasized that the exemption being carved out for the Amish could not be claimed by members of groups who acted on the basis of sincere but nonreligious beliefs. Some critics find little fault with Burger for differentiating between religious and secular ideology, noting that religious beliefs are uniquely and prominently protected by the First Amendment. In drawing this distinction, however, Burger scrutinized nearly every aspect of the lives of the Amish, including their religious beliefs and the bearing of those doctrines on their conduct. As one scholarly critic noted, this comprehensive analysis came "perilously close to that examination of beliefs which, in itself, constitutes a violation of the right of free exercise." In fact, in *Braunfeld v. Brown*, the Supreme Court had highlighted the dangers of precisely such a searching inquiry.

Burger also might be faulted for failing to pay sufficient attention to the rights of Amish children. The chief justice maintained that the Court was not obliged to consider how the application of the school attendance law affected the welfare interests of Amish youngsters because they were not parties to the litigation. This rationale may have had some formal merit, but it obscured the fact that children plainly were the ultimate targets of Wisconsin's school laws. In the context of these statutes, the state concerned itself with parents only to the extent that they influenced — or dictated — the attendance patterns of their children. Given that fact, Burger's majority opinion in *Yoder* might have benefited from a more frank appraisal of how the interests of Amish youngsters would be affected by the disposition of the case.

And it appears that Burger might have erred in parroting William Ball's apocalyptic warning that application of the school attendance law would inevitably result in the destruction of the Amish community in New Glarus. Had Wisconsin's compulsory attendance statute required two additional years of education in a modern and "worldly" public high school, this assertion might have been credible; the Amish might have argued convincingly that their entire colony would be imperiled by the compelled exposure of their children to potentially corrupting influences outside their community. But the state school code clearly allowed the Amish to continue educating their children in their own parochial schools, sheltered from worldly influences. It was by no means certain that the New Glarus colony would have been ripped apart if the state had compelled Amish children to spend two additional years in such an isolated environment. "Surely there was no danger that the entire religious faith and practice of these convicted parents would be totally destroyed if their children attended two years of high school," one scholar wrote.

Burger's willingness to heed Ball's dire warnings is particularly intriguing in light of what ultimately transpired among the New Glarus Amish. Following Ball's lead, the chief justice reasoned that limiting the power of the state of Wisconsin to regulate the conduct of the Amish would help preserve their faith-based community. But what neither Ball nor Burger could predict was that the gravest threat to the Amish colony in New Glarus was not the heavy hand of the state but rather an ideological schism among the Amish themselves. The Supreme Court's landmark opinion hardly mattered when disagreements over church doctrine ripped the community apart in the mid-1970s.

Although the Supreme Court could not preserve the Amish community in New Glarus, it might have issued an opinion that provided a more careful assessment of the legal issues presented by *Yoder*. It is not difficult to imagine the Court handing down a decision that was devoted less to exalting the character of the Amish and more to considering how the rights of children reared in the faith might be affected by exempting their parents from the school attendance statute. The decision also might have provided a more thorough exploration of the state's interest in regulating education and a less hyperbolic analysis of the threat posed to the Amish by the state's efforts to mandate school attendance. After hearing *Yoder*, Wisconsin Supreme Court Justice Nathan Heffernan quickly wrote a dissenting opinion that forthrightly (if briefly) addressed such matters. His approach might have served as a useful blueprint when the highest court in the land heard the case.

The state of Wisconsin did a poor job of encouraging the Supreme Court to follow Heffernan's lead. It wasn't that the state's case in *Yoder* was inherently weak. In fact, its attorneys had several powerful lines of argument at their disposal. The courts had long deferred to states in matters relating to compulsory attendance, and the kind of exemption requested by the Amish appeared to be questionable under the First Amendment's establishment clause. What's more, had they simply added two more years to their own parochial schools, the New Glarus Amish might have been able to comply with the attendance statute without imperiling their faith-based community. But the attorneys who represented Wisconsin never fully developed such assertions. Throughout *Yoder*, they failed to match the continuity and coherence of William Ball's arguments on behalf of the New Glarus Amish. The NCARF lawyer laid the foundation for his constitutional claims at trial and then built on it, brick by brick, throughout the appeals process. The state put on a feeble case at trial and never fully recovered.

It's worth noting that the Supreme Court tackled the challenge of *Yoder* in peculiar circumstances. The Amish school attendance case arrived at the Court during a period of dramatic transition. Warren Burger was in only his second term as chief justice and had yet to emerge from the shadow of his formidable predecessor. More significantly, Justices Harlan and Black had recently been struck down by illness, and their departures temporarily left two seats vacant on the Court. (Some observers, pointing to the decline of aging Justice William O. Douglas, argued that a third seat was effectively empty.)

Had the full complement of nine justices heard the case, the Court might have adopted a different approach to *Yoder.*

The justices almost certainly would have benefited from the participation of Lewis Powell, Black's replacement. Prior to joining the Court in January 1972 (just a month after oral arguments in the Amish case), Powell sat on the Virginia State Board of Education and chaired the Richmond, Virginia, school board. Such experiences would have given Powell a uniquely informed perspective on such matters as the efficacy of school attendance laws, the state's interest in regulating education, and the right of children to obtain adequate schooling.

The Supreme Court handed down its opinion in *Wisconsin v. Yoder* on Monday, May 15, 1972. That afternoon, journalists flocked to New Glarus to gauge how the Amish were reacting to the news of their victory. Freelance reporter Ray Barth was the first journalist on the scene, and he helped break the news of the Supreme Court's decision to Jonas Yoder. After hearing that a ruling had been handed down in the Amish case, the freelancer sped to New Glarus and appeared at Yoder's front door with a transistor radio. Yoder invited the reporter inside, and along with several other Amish, they crowded around the dining room table and listened to a radio newscast describing the Court's decision. After he learned that his side had prevailed, Yoder told Barth that the case had been quite an ordeal for him and his codefendants. Given the choice, "he would not care to go through it again," the reporter wrote of the Amishman.

Later, some reporters approached Yoder as he unloaded grain in his barnyard. As news of the Supreme Court's decision sank in, he seemed to be more relieved than exultant. "I feel we had a miracle made for us, and I don't feel like making words," Yoder said. "I'm really glad to have it over with. It was a long struggle." As he tended to his farmwork, Yoder reflected briefly on the case and explained that he had never considered compromising his faith by giving in to the demands of local authorities. "There was no way I would have sent my children to the high school," he said.

The journalists who sought out Yoder in New Glarus apparently had expected him to rejoice over his triumph. Instead, they found him "reticent and uncomfortable in the limelight," as one of them later wrote. The Amishman obviously did not relish the attention generated by the case. A few months before the Supreme Court handed down its opinion, a reporter noted that Yoder "clearly has not liked the publicity that this case involves." Now, eager to get back to his chores and to the quiet life he had led before becoming embroiled in the court case, he quickly grew weary of addressing the members of the news media who had gathered at his farm. "I wish it had been anybody else," he said.

Throughout the compulsory education controversy in New Glarus, the Amish children at its center had remained largely silent. (This had been true even at the trial. Frieda Yoder, the only Amish youngster to testify, had done so in the most reserved manner imaginable, answering questions with a series of one-word replies.) After the Supreme Court issued its ruling, however, Frieda Yoder and Barbara Miller submitted to interviews with reporters. The two young women seemed eager to at last give their views on the case. "My father decided that it was best if I didn't go to high school," Miller said. "I trusted him and think it was the right decision." Jonas Yoder's daughter — who had become Frieda Hershberger after her marriage the previous fall — echoed Miller's comments and explained how she had been called upon to speak in court. "Barbara didn't want to testify, so I did. I was nervous at first but they only asked simple questions. They asked if I wanted to go to high school," she said.

Barbara's father was less talkative. Like Jonas Yoder, Wallace Miller seemed almost indifferent to the outcome of the case. Miller said that although he had known that the Supreme Court's ruling was imminent, he "didn't worry too much about it either way." He eventually conceded that he was "happy" and "glad" that the Court had ruled in favor of him and his coreligionists, but he was far from jubilant, at least in part because he too recoiled from the glare of the media's attention. At one point he told a persistent reporter that he simply didn't have anything to say about the decision.

The news that their coreligionists had prevailed pleased Amishman Melvin Kramer and his wife Katie. "Well, good for that," he said. "I figure that the Almighty will always see you through. You just have to be patient." Kramer reiterated that the Amish didn't have a blanket objection to sending their children to school. They simply believed that sending adolescents to high schools, especially worldly public high schools, would threaten the very foundations of their religious faith and community. "It isn't that we don't want them to have schooling. That isn't the point," he insisted. For her part, Katie Kramer did not feel compelled to reargue the Amish side of the *Yoder* case. "That's good news," she said of the Supreme Court's ruling. "I thought it was never going to come."

The neighbors of the Amish in New Glarus generally seemed satisfied with the Supreme Court's decision in *Yoder.* Although not everyone in the village fathomed the beliefs and practices of the Amish, most people recognized that they had broken the compulsory school attendance law because of their commitment to their religious faith. As one longtime resident put it, "Anyone who lived among the Amish knew that they were not breaking [the law] for grins and giggles to see if . . . they could bring down the New Glarus school district." Those who knew the Amish understood that "their breaking the state law was from the heart and not done in a malicious vein." Because they respected the motives of the Amish, "the local people for the most part agreed with the Supreme Court decision" in *Yoder.*

Attorney William Ball spent a torturous few months waiting for the Supreme Court to hand down its opinion. At one point early in 1972, he embarked on a long-overdue vacation cruise with his wife, Caroline. Before Ball departed, he gave a copy of his travel itinerary to his law partner Joe Skelly and instructed Skelly to contact him if the Supreme Court ruled in favor of the Amish. If he didn't hear from Skelly, Ball said, he would assume that he had lost the case. The cruise proved to be a glum one for Ball: Skelly never got in touch with him, and he came to believe the worst about the outcome of the case. (He was so convinced of this that he actually sent Skelly a postcard registering his disappointment at having lost.) It wasn't until he returned from vacation that Ball learned that the Court simply hadn't issued a decision yet.

When word of the Supreme Court's ruling in *Yoder* finally reached Ball, his reaction was relatively subdued. "Bill was not a guy to show a lot of emotion," Skelly later said. "Obviously, he was elated [about having won], but there wasn't a lot of slapping on the back or excessive jubilation." Asked by reporters to respond to the decision, Ball said that he was pleased by Chief Justice Burger's opinion because it assured that "our country will now protect these wonderful, good people we have in our midst." And not only the Amish would benefit from this "great victory for religious liberty," as Ball called it, for the *Yoder* ruling was sure to bolster the rights of millions of American parents.

A few years later, in a volume of essays devoted to compulsory education and the Amish, Ball elaborated on the significance of the Supreme Court's opinion in the New Glarus case. He wrote that in *Yoder* "a great crossing had been made in religious liberty in this country." In his mind, several aspects of the Supreme Court's opinion were particularly striking. First, the Court had refused to countenance the state of Wisconsin's shortsighted claim that "religion is worship — and that is all," but rather had acknowledged the all-encompassing nature of the Amish faith. Second, the Court had renounced the argument that "religious liberty consists simply of a freedom to believe." For Ball, this was a faulty and inherently dangerous premise, one that threatened to cloud the meaning of the free exercise clause, and the Court had been wise to reject it.

Ball's third point on *Yoder*'s significance related to what he termed "the role of religion in public education." To his profound dismay, there had developed "a strong prescription against any teaching of religion" in the public schools, thanks in no small part to the Supreme Court's controversial rulings in several cases relating to the establishment clause. In such an educational setting, Ball maintained, the religious liberty of children with deeply held religious beliefs — children like the Amish youngsters in New Glarus — was bound to be compromised. To illustrate this point, Ball offered a hypothetical example of a youngster raised in the Church of the Nazarene:

> He is taught to believe that the Bible is true, that the Bible is the Word of God. When that child today is placed in a public school environment in which the Bible is not referred to as the Word of God, there arises, I think, a serious problem of religious liberty because such a child is not readily able to maintain his religious faith in an environment in which the central belief of his religion is treated by his teachers as not necessarily true, or with indifferent "neutrality."

Yoder was limited to the Amish, of course, but its explicit safeguarding of religious liberty in the context of public education gave Ball hope. He believed that if the courts could be persuaded to read the decision more broadly, it would safeguard the religious liberty of other groups when their religious practices conflicted with laws governing public education.

Two of Ball's colleagues, Tom Eckerle and William Lindholm, also commented on the denouement of *Yoder*, and both seemed pleased. "Needless to say, we are tremendously happy on behalf of these people who have been persecuted for these last two decades," said Lindholm, the head of the National Committee for Amish Religious Freedom. Addressing the broader implications of the case, Lindholm claimed that Burger's opinion for the Court represented a resounding "victory for religious freedom." Eckerle offered a similar assessment. "It's just a matter of simple religious freedom," he said. "There are a lot of other overtones and ramifications to the case, but they all pale next to the religious freedom issue." With the dispute over the compulsory school attendance law at last resolved, Eckerle was hopeful that the Amish — "good, decent people who wanted to follow their conscience," he called them — would be able to live in peace.

John Hostetler, the Temple University professor whose extensive testimony had been a centerpiece of the Amish fathers' defense, echoed the comments offered by Ball, Lindholm, and Eckerle. In a lengthy statement, Hostetler applauded the Supreme Court's "landmark decision" in *Yoder*, claiming that it "finally puts an end to the years of harassment the Amish have suffered in one state or another." Thanks to Chief Justice Burger's opinion, "no longer must [the Amish] choose between criminal sanctions on the one hand and abandoning their religious practices and view of education which sustains their community on the other." Hostetler also remarked that the Amish were to be commended for standing up against infringement of their religious liberty and thereby helping to establish for members of other faiths "protection against the coercive powers of the state to obliterate cultural differences of no harm to anyone."

The losers in *Yoder* were not as voluble as the victors. Assistant attorney general John Calhoun barely concealed his disappointment over losing the biggest case of his career. "I don't see how the decision can avoid being important," he conceded. Calhoun told reporters that he would have to read and digest the ruling before he offered a more thorough public statement. (And this wasn't going to happen quickly, he explained, because the various opinions in the case totaled several dozen pages.) William Kahl, the state school superintendent, was no more eager than Calhoun to comment on the ruling. "We don't know what the wider implications of the decision are," he said. Kahl's strongest statement in defeat was a defense of his decision to support the prosecution of the Amish fathers under the compulsory attendance law.

Russell Monroe, who had replaced Kenneth Glewen as school superintendent in New Glarus, said that although the ruling "will have very little immediate impact on the school district," its "long-range effect on Wisconsin and the country may be great," presumably because it would weaken compulsory education laws across the United States. Monroe did his best to find a silver lining in the defeat. "At least our truancy officer will be able to quit making out reports on them," he said of the Amish.

Throughout 1972 and 1973, writers in a number of mainstream newspapers and periodicals commented on Yoder. These critical assessments were mixed. Several observers lauded the Supreme Court's decision both as a hard-won triumph for a people deserving protection and as a milestone for religious liberty in general. But other comments were far less favorable. Although no one seemed to have an unkind word to say about the Amish themselves, critics writing for popular audiences pointed out numerous apparent shortcomings in Chief Justice Burger's opinion for the Court in the New Glarus case.

The *Wisconsin State Journal* lauded the *Yoder* decision as "a victory for religious freedom and proof that the Bill of Rights is indeed a living, vital document." But the editors of Madison's other daily newspaper, the left-leaning *Capital Times*, offered a dramatically different view. In an editorial published a day after the *State Journal*'s, they decried the *Yoder* decision as "legal mischief." The newspaper acknowledged that its position might seem unduly harsh. "It is not easy to take sides against the god-fearing Amish," the editorial conceded. "We have seen their farms and their way of life and they are a compelling testament to the redeeming grace of honest toil." The *Capital Times* criticized the *Yoder* decision nonetheless, claiming that the Supreme Court had been "unduly swayed by the sentimental vision of some ennobling primitive, who having rejected the so-called benefits of modern civilization, has earned a right to legal privilege." The Court's respect for the commendable aspects of Amish culture apparently had blinded it to the profound — and potentially disastrous — consequences of allowing youngsters in the faith to reach adulthood without having received the kind of schooling they might need if they chose to live in more modern communities. As a result of this tendency to "oversentimentalize," the Court had made a grievous error and "consigned the Amish children to a life of ignorance — blissful as it may seem to the majority of the Wisconsin and U.S. supreme courts."

As had been the case when the state supreme court ruled in *Yoder*, newspapers throughout Wisconsin offered a wide range of opinions about the Supreme Court's decision in the New Glarus case. The *Sheboygan Press* maintained that "the Amish have won a victory in the courts that surely is approved by the majority of citizens." The same sentiment was voiced in nearby Milwaukee, where the *Sentinel* hailed the *Yoder* ruling as "a splendid victory for religious freedom in America." But the *Sentinel* also suggested that the Supreme Court had failed to put to rest all the "problems raised in connection with compulsory school attendance laws." The Amish had been exempted from such measures at least in part because of the age, stability, and size of their faith. Could members of newer, smaller sects expect similar protection? the *Sentinel* asked. The *Green Bay Press-Gazette* made much the same point in its editorial on *Yoder*. The reasoning of Burger's opinion for the majority in the New Glarus case seemed to suggest that "the age of a religious movement determines its validity and that there is order only in numbers," the newspaper argued. "This is dangerously close to a point of view in earlier times which the First Amendment was specifically written to safeguard against."

The decision drew comment from several publications outside Wisconsin as well. In an otherwise favorable editorial on *Yoder*, the *New York Times* reproved the Supreme Court for slighting the rights of Amish children. The newspaper expressed concern over the Court's failure to fully address the concerns raised in Justice William Douglas's partial dissent. "Stultifying tyranny can, of course, be exercised by parents as well as state authority," the *Times* observed. "The actual defection rate of a sizable minority of Amish youth from the 'simple life' suggests that this is not a purely hypothetical concern."

Several other major newspapers also commented on *Yoder*. The *Washington Post* registered its approval of modern society reaching a long-overdue "accommodation with the Amish." It termed Burger's majority opinion "a useful ruling both in underlining the country's commitment to the First Amendment and in reminding all of us that diversity is what [America] is all about." The *Chicago Tribune* also praised the Court's resolution of *Yoder*. As it applauded this "victory for the Amish," the *Tribune* claimed that "the United States is a bit more free for us all because the Amish won their case."

Hailing the justices' acknowledgment of "the right to be different," *Time* magazine extolled the Supreme Court for rendering a decision enabling "the religious freedom guarantee to override the state's right to set educational standards." In its account of *Yoder*, *Time* declared that the victorious Amish "can stand as heroes to laissez-faire conservatives" because of their dogged and ultimately successful opposition to the worldly entanglements of government regulation. This point was borne out just a few weeks after the Supreme Court handed down its opinion when a writer in the arch-conservative *National Review* offered a glowing evaluation of *Yoder*. "Praise be," Russell Kirk rejoiced, "the Old Order Amish won't have to migrate to Brazil." Kirk, a prominent conservative intellectual, noted that the efforts of William Ball, "a Pennsylvania lawyer (and a Catholic) who specializes in school cases," had been critical to the success of the Amish fathers; the arguments he had advanced on their behalf had been "utterly persuasive."

After commending Ball on a job well done, Kirk compared the New Glarus case with battles being waged by other deeply religious parents who objected to sending their children to public schools. The plight of these parents had become something of a cause célèbre among conservative critics of "big government," and Kirk seemed disappointed that the Court's opinion in *Yoder*, limited as it was to the Amish, might not be broad enough to offer them the help they so desperately needed. Although the emancipation of the Amish "from the tyranny of truant officers" clearly represented a ray of hope, Kirk was left to wonder, "Must everybody else submit to educational dragooning?"

The Catholic journal *America* also cheered *Yoder*, and it was more hopeful than Kirk that the ruling might have broad implications. Its editors argued that the decision should not "be viewed as mere judicial benevolence toward some quirky but harmless folk. For the case, the decision and the Amish themselves are all more significant than that." The New Glarus case mattered, they wrote, because it showed how forces within a democratic society could successfully combat the blundering oppression of "powerful, unimaginative bureaucracies." That this effort had been made on behalf of the Amish, who led such exemplary lives as Christians, made it all the more heartening. But perhaps the most promising aspect of *Yoder* was the Supreme Court's rationale for exempting the Amish from the compulsory school attendance law. *America* hinted that some of the principles undergirding the Court's ruling might bolster the efforts of those who were battling for public funding of private and parochial schools. According to the editorial, "The decision itself is significant because the Court has judged that when the principle of religious freedom conflicts with another principle such as the state's right to regulate education, religious freedom should, as the greater value, be given primacy. This is a point, incidentally, that defenders of governmental aid for church-related schools have urged within the context of a clash between religious freedom and the no-establishment clause." Although it neglected to mention that William Ball had long been a prominent champion of state funding for private and parochial schools, the *America* editorial called him a "distinguished Catholic lawyer" and cited his leading role in defending the Amish.

CHAPTER 11

The Aftermath and Legacy of *Yoder*

Roman Miller held a large auction before he moved away from New Glarus in the spring of 1974. Miller had operated both a sawmill and a dairy farm for several years, so he had plenty of livestock and equipment to sell before he left for his new home in Indiana. Among the items he put up for auction were fifty Hereford and Angus beef cows, a threshing machine, a power scythe, sixty Leghorn hens that were still "laying good," two washing machines, one hundred bushels of soybean for seed, "several good mares and geldings," twenty-five telephone poles, an eleven month-old Holstein bull, a sewing machine, and "one good buckboard." In addition to that array of animals and implements, Miller offered some real estate, including a home featuring "a modern kitchen with wood cabinets, dining room, living room, laundry and bath downstairs, five bedrooms plus bath upstairs and gas forced air heat." Miller might have had some sentimental attachment to the possessions he had accumulated in New Glarus, but he was determined to find buyers for most of his personal property before he moved. All of it was offered to the highest bidder on April 5, 1974, a Friday. An auctioneer named Ray Miskimon came up to Wisconsin from Winslow, Illinois, to conduct the sale.

Between 1973 and 1976, numerous Amish families such as the Millers packed up their belongings, auctioned off possessions they no longer needed or simply couldn't move, and headed for new homes. Some left New Glarus for other states — Missouri, Indiana, Ohio — while others chose destinations within Wisconsin. When Melvin Kramer moved early in 1975, a Madison newspaper commented that his exit was "the latest and not the last in a series of departures" that left the local Amish community on the verge of extinction. Drawn by cheap and available land, the Amish had begun arriving in the New Glarus area in 1964, and the community had expanded to include approximately thirty families by the early 1970s. But by the time Andrew Plank left in 1976, more than two-thirds of those families had moved away, and many of those remaining were thinking of following suit.

There were a number of theories about why the Amish abruptly left the New Glarus area in the mid-1970s. On the few occasions that they publicly explained their reasons for leaving, the Amish usually claimed that the land they had purchased was too hilly and thus unsuitable for their premodern farming methods. Jonas Hershberger, one of the Amish community's leaders, maintained that many families were leaving because they sought "better, flatter land. It is getting harder to work these hills with the horses, so some people are looking for flat land." (Horses were necessary, of course, because most Amish were generally unwilling to use tractors and other modern machinery on their farms.) Hershberger pointed out that a number of families had migrated to New Glarus from Iowa, where the land had been easier to work. "Some of the people who came here weren't ready for the land," he said. "They were spoiled by Iowa. You know, it's all flat land there."

There was also some speculation that the Amish moved because they had clashed once again with state authorities. The source of this rancor was the state's enforcement of barn sanitary regulations against Amish dairymen. After Roman Miller ignored warnings to clean up his barn and dairying equipment, a state dairy inspector filed charges against the Amishman in Green County Court for selling unsanitary milk to a local cheese factory. Miller pleaded no contest, and Judge Roger Elmer (who had presided over the *Yoder* trial) levied a twenty-five dollar fine. Shortly thereafter, Miller quit dairying and established a logging and pallet-making business. Some Amish dairymen reportedly believed that they might have to follow Miller's lead if the state continued to enforce sanitary regulations against them. To fully comply with the laws, they might be compelled to use electric equipment in their dairy barns, which most were reluctant to do.

Others maintained that internal dissension caused the Amish community in New Glarus to splinter. Over time, the colony centered in New Glarus had attracted both conservative and more progressive members of the faith. Though bound together by many core religious beliefs, conservatives and progressives sometimes failed to see eye to eye on such potentially divisive issues as the acceptability of modern technology. In general, the traditionalists — many of whom were among the colony's first settlers and lived north and west of New Glarus — abhorred the use of machinery powered by gasoline or electricity. Such equipment, they believed, was too worldly, and its use was a direct threat to their faith, which had always treasured simplicity. Progressive-minded Amish, however, were more open to technological innovation, and some of them used modern equipment on their farms. "The more progressive of the Amish could see that in order to survive, they would need the help of gas-powered horsepower," one longtime New Glarus resident later said. "Some eventually purchased small tractors and installed steel wheels. This, of course, was a great affront to the elders."

More than one observer claimed that the tensions between these two groups were brought to a head by the death of Amishman Dan Miller in the fall of 1973. The sixty-four-year-old Miller died after becoming entangled with a tractor-propelled forklift at Roman Miller's pallet-making operation. According to one account, some residents of New Glarus believed that Miller's demise "may have precipitated a split in the Amish community. According to this theory, some of the Amish believe that Miller should not have been working with machinery, and that he was punished by God for doing so." Addressing this hypothesis, a New Glarus resident speculated, "They were working with some modern machinery when the accident happened, and maybe they believed it was their punishment for using worldly things."

Jonas Hershberger vigorously denied that Dan Miller's death — or the frictions it might have catalyzed — helped bring about the breakup of the Amish community centered in New Glarus. Hershberger contended that the accident that claimed Miller's life was in no way connected to the exodus of the Amish that took place over the following three years. "Dan Miller's time was up, that's all," he said, dismissing the notion that the death had been interpreted as a sign of some kind. "He wasn't being punished for anything; it was just his time." When pressed to provide an explanation for the colony's disintegration, Hershberger claimed that the Amish were simply looking for better land.

But one surprisingly outspoken member of the Amish community contradicted Hershberger's assertions. The quality of land, Noah Kramer told a newspaper reporter, had nothing to do with the exodus of the Amish from New Glarus. "They'll tell you the land is too hard. But I don't believe it," he said. "Most of us hire out for plowing anyway. That's just an excuse." Kramer maintained that sharp disagreements among the Amish over doctrine caused members of his faith to leave New Glarus. "It's discord that's made them move," he said. "We've always gotten along in the past by compromise. But there's been no compromise here. When people couldn't agree, they left. . . . We had a split here — there were ones who wouldn't bend and others who wanted to bend a little."

Although few people could agree on why the Amish community in New Glarus broke apart in the mid-1970s, no one denied that the once-thriving settlement was in decline. According to federal census data, New Glarus lost nearly 20 percent of its residents between 1970 and 1980. A report on the drop in population explained that "almost all of it can be attributed to the decision of about 20 Amish families to find new homes." This was not news to anyone who read either of Madison's two daily newspapers in the mid-1970s. Throughout that period, the *Wisconsin State Journal* and the *Capital Times* routinely ran stories with headlines like "The Plain People Are Moving On" and "Auction Signals Continuing New Glarus Exodus." The departure of the Amish from New Glarus was so unexpected and dramatic that the *Chicago Tribune* dispatched a reporter to investigate. "There is an exodus from these hills," reporter Anne Keegan wrote. "A silent invisible trail of buggy wheels heading out. It is the Amish, bags packed and moving away — just as mysteriously as they moved in 13 years ago."

Jonas Yoder and his family were among the Amish to gather up their belongings and leave New Glarus. Participating in a landmark legal case had turned out to be something of a mixed blessing for the man who had lent it his name, and he seemed eager to put the whole experience behind him. Although *Wisconsin v. Yoder* helped shield Yoder's religious practices from interference by the state, it also made him a target for criticism from other Amish. What's more, the case brought him an extraordinary degree of notoriety — anathema for a member of a faith that valued humility. Reporters appeared at his farm and asked him to submit to interviews or, worse still, pose for photographs; tourists visiting New Glarus noted his presence when he came into the village to shop. The attention clearly distressed Yoder. "For me," he said at one point, "I wish it would be somebody else's name on this [case]."

Yoder's ambivalence about the school attendance case and its bearing on his decision to leave New Glarus were chronicled by Ray Barth, a talented freelance reporter who lived in nearby Monroe. In a series of articles published in the early and mid-1970s, Barth provided a remarkable account of how *Wisconsin v. Yoder*'s journey through the courts affected the people whose liberties were at stake in the case. After speaking with Jonas Yoder and several other New Glarus Amish, the reporter determined that the school attendance case had exacerbated tensions among them. "The truancy case which wound up in the United States Supreme Court," Barth wrote, "has had a disturbing effect upon the Amish settlement of New Glarus and on Amish everywhere."

Jonas Yoder found himself at the center of this controversy. The Amishman told Barth that many members of his faith supported his decision to litigate the case. "We hope you win," some Amish told him. But others were far less supportive. Yoder divulged that he faced sharp criticism for allowing the National Committee for Amish Religious Freedom to intervene and zealously represent the defendants in the courts. As Barth put it, some Amish expressed their belief that Yoder and his codefendants "should never have permitted a non-Amish legal committee to act as [their] legal counsel." These critics suggested that Miller, Yoder, and Yutzy should have followed the example of the Old Order Amish in Hazleton, Iowa, who had offered no defense to the charges leveled by local authorities during the schooling controversy there. This course of action, they suggested, would have been far more in keeping with the Amish tradition of nonresistance than allowing the NCARF and attorney William Ball to mount such a tenacious defense on their behalf. For some Amish, accepting this help was tantamount to "going to law."

There were consequences to these charges, Yoder told Barth. As a result of the defendants' controversial handling of the school attendance case, the entire New Glarus settlement was viewed differently by members of other Amish communities across the country. "We have become kind of a marked community among our people," Yoder said. "They are all watching us." Worse still, among the Amish in New Glarus, disagreement over the litigation pitted progressive members of the faith against their more conservative brethren. This friction prompted several prominent members of the community—including a bishop and a minister — to move elsewhere. To Barth's astonishment, it seemed that a case designed to preserve a community had actually helped tear it apart.

Some observers suspected that the publicity generated by the school attendance case, combined with the intramural squabbling to which it contributed, ultimately prompted Yoder to leave New Glarus. When he departed the settlement, a local newspaper went so far as to claim in a headline that "Unwanted Fame Forces Amish Leader to Move." A non-Amish neighbor doubted that assessment, later saying that Yoder's reasons for leaving were far more complex, but the fact remained that he was one of the first Amish to abandon the colony in New Glarus. He left late in 1973 for another Amish settlement in Missouri.

Wallace Miller was the last of the *Yoder* defendants to abandon New Glarus. He departed in the fall of 1977, when only a handful of Amish families remained. Miller held an auction and then moved his family to the burgeoning Amish colony in Evansville, Wisconsin, located just fifteen miles to the west. Barth visited Evansville around the time of Miller's move and found a thriving settlement. About a dozen families had preceded the Millers. Many of them had come from Indiana, Iowa, and Ohio, much like the settlers who had flocked to New Glarus a decade earlier. It was clear to Barth that the newcomers to Evansville had learned at least one valuable lesson from the declining New Glarus community: as soon as the settlement was on its feet, they formed a school board and erected a school.

As the success of the settlement in Evansville demonstrated, the Amish did not vanish from Wisconsin after their community in New Glarus fragmented in the mid-1970s. In fact, most of their communities thrived. By 1995, there were still more than two dozen Amish settlements in the state, and within them were more than fifty separate congregations (or church districts). The settlements were most heavily concentrated in Vernon County (which boasted more than a dozen congregations) and Clark County (with a half dozen). Researchers found it difficult to determine exactly how many people lived in these communities, but in 1990, the University of Wisconsin's Applied Population Laboratory estimated that the total exceeded six thousand women, men, and children.

In the 1980s and 1990s, the Amish living in these communities continued to seek judicial protections for their religious practices and beliefs. The *Yoder* precedent clearly benefited them when they opposed the application of a state law mandating the display of bright red and orange reflective triangles on slow-moving vehicles (SMVs). In 1996, the Wisconsin Supreme Court ruled that application of the SMV measure to the Amish — who had argued that placing the SMV emblem on their buggies was too "worldly" — violated their religious liberty. In determining that the state constitution's protections of conscience shielded the Amish, the court relied in part on the interpretive framework established by the U.S. Supreme Court in *Yoder* and its forebear, *Sherbert v. Verner*. *Yoder* had proved similarly important in earlier SMV emblem cases in Kentucky, Ohio, and Michigan.

Members of other faiths found that *Yoder*'s value as a judicial precedent was limited to a certain extent by the widely noted peculiarities of Warren Burger's opinion for the Court. The chief justice's analysis squared with the arguments made by attorney William Ball on behalf of Miller, Yoder, and Yutzy, but it was so narrowly tailored to the Amish that many courts later struggled to apply its holdings to members of different faiths.

In one instance, a group of fundamentalist Christian parents in Tennessee relied on *Yoder* when they asked to have their children excused from assignments involving a textbook they found objectionable on religious grounds. The Sixth Circuit Court of Appeals denied their claim. It asserted that the Supreme Court's opinion in the Amish case "rested on such a singular set of facts that we do not believe it can be held to announce a general rule" pertaining to the First Amendment protection of religious liberty. A New York case regarding home-schooling regulations yielded a similar result, with a federal district court judge maintaining that "the holding in *Yoder* must be limited to its unique facts and does not control the outcome" of the case at hand. Rulings such as these prompted one observer of *Yoder*'s legacy to assert that the opinion "has had a limited impact" in helping individuals who raised religious liberty claims. The opinion's promise, scholar Jay S. Bybee claimed, "has been long on rhetoric and short on substance."

In some contexts, however, *Yoder* proved to be an invaluable judicial precedent. The decision was particularly effective for attorney William Ball when he defended educators and parents affiliated with fundamentalist Christian schools. In the 1970s and early 1980s, according to one account, backers of these institutions "fought a holy war against state officials" who were attempting to enforce regulations pertaining to curricula and teacher certification. When they faced prosecution for failing to abide by these regulations, fundamentalist Christians in several states, including Ohio and Kentucky, called on Ball to defend them. In these clashes (which often involved, like *Yoder*, prosecutions under state compulsory school attendance laws), a main weapon in Ball's arsenal was the precedent he had helped establish in the New Glarus case. "In making their free exercise claim," commented an observer of Ball's efforts in Kentucky, "the fundamentalist schools rely heavily upon the landmark case of *Wisconsin v. Yoder*."

Ball's defense of pastor Levi W. Whisner typified his reliance on the *Yoder* precedent to free Christian schools from many of the constraints of state oversight. In the fall of 1970, Whisner opened a Christian school in Bradford, Ohio, that did not comply with the minimum state standards for elementary schools. Eventually, Whisner and more than a dozen other parents who had enrolled children at the school were indicted on charges similar to those leveled in the *Yoder* case. Ball defended them by essentially recycling the arguments and strategies he had used to defend the New Glarus Amish. (He even went so far as to reuse one of the expert witnesses from the *Yoder* trial, University of Chicago education professor Donald Erickson.)

At the fundamentalists' trial, Ball devoted part of his opening statement to stressing that the defendants, all of them deeply reverent Christians, were "committed by their consciences to enroll their children in a Christian Bible-oriented school." The First Amendment's protection of the free exercise of religion shielded their right to do so, Ball maintained, provided that the school of their choice operated in compliance with reasonable minimum education standards established by the state. In the case at hand, the state was encroaching on the parents' free exercise rights because it was attempting to enforce a dizzying array of unreasonable regulations on the Tabernacle Christian School. Here, Ball alleged, was another lamentable example of religious liberty being compromised by unwarranted state intrusion. Echoing his stance in *Yoder*, he reminded the court that Whisner and the other Tabernacle Christian School parents were not "attacking the compulsory attendance law on its face. Our complaint goes to the application of that statute. . . . A religious liberty claim has been raised."

The defendants were found guilty at trial. But the Ohio Supreme Court, in an opinion that relied in part on the standards articulated by the U.S. Supreme Court in *Yoder*, reversed the parents' convictions in July 1976. According to scholar James Carper, who has written the authoritative study of the case, backers of Christian schools came to view the *Whisner* ruling as "a keystone in their 'battle' to achieve freedom from state regulations and, indirectly, a measure of separation from the mainstream of society."

Advocates of home schooling have treasured the *Yoder* precedent as well. Launched in part by deeply religious parents who hoped to shield their children from the purported dangers of secularism in the public schools, the home-schooling movement took hold in the United States in the late 1960s and early 1970s. By some estimates, as many as one million children were being taught at home by the mid-1990s. The protections of religious liberty and parental rights afforded by *Yoder* helped spark that explosive growth. One scholarly commentator concluded that *Yoder* proved to be a "pivotal case" when home-schoolers were forced to defend their programs in court, allowing them to claim that the First Amendment protected their exercise of religion in their choice of schooling for their children.

Champions of parents' rights have also valued *Yoder*. Along with the Supreme Court's opinions in *Meyer v. Nebraska* and *Pierce v. Society of Sisters*, the *Yoder* ruling became a lodestar for those who believed that too many "innocent families have become the victims of overintrusive government action," as former Republican congressman Bob Dornan put it. Outraged by condom distribution and sex education in the public schools, Dornan helped spearhead the effort to enact federal parents' rights legislation by cosponsoring the Parental Rights and Responsibilities Act in the House of Representatives in 1995. According to Dornan, that measure (which ultimately failed to pass) was intended to establish "a legal standard to determine when the government may and may not interfere with the family. It would essentially prohibit any level of government from infringing on the right of parents to direct the upbringing of their children." As they urged passage of Dornan's bill and analogous measures, such as state parental rights amendments, a vocal coalition of conservative groups invoked

Yoder's protection of parents' rights to direct the upbringing and education of their children.

Although *Yoder* left an indelible mark on such areas as parents' rights, home schooling, and state regulation of religious schools, the core of its constitutional legacy did not prove to be especially durable. In a series of decisions in the final quarter of the twentieth century, the Supreme Court undercut the safeguards for religious liberty it had erected in *Sherbert v. Verner* and *Yoder.* In cases such as *United States v. Lee* (1982), *Goldman v. Weinberger* (1986), *Bowen v. Roy* (1986), and *Lyng v. Northwest Indian Cemetery Protective Association* (1988), the justices chipped away at the interpretive framework they had used to shield the religious liberty of the New Glarus Amish.

United States v. Lee demonstrated the limits of *Yoder's* usefulness as a shield for the Amish from the perils of modernity. Between 1970 and 1977, an Amishman named Edwin Lee farmed and worked as a carpenter in western Pennsylvania. Lee employed several of his coreligionists in his fields and in his carpentry shop, but he did not pay the Social Security taxes required of employers. Lee had religious grounds for refusing to participate in the Social Security System: the Amish faith stressed self-sufficiency, and its members had long spurned the largesse of the government's old-age pension program. In part because of their faith-based objections, self-employed Amish had been exempted by the federal government from paying Social Security taxes in the mid-1960s, but that privilege had not been extended to Amish who employed others, as Lee did. In 1978, the Internal Revenue Service informed Lee that he owed more than $27,000 in back taxes for the men who had been employed on his farm and in his workshop. The Amishman grudgingly paid a fraction of that total (the $91 he owed for the first quarter of 1973) and then filed a suit in federal court in which he maintained that the imposition of Social Security taxes violated his right to the free exercise of religion. His case found its way onto the U.S. Supreme Court's docket during its October 1981 term.

"To maintain an organized society of faiths requires that some religious practices yield to the common good," Chief Justice Warren Burger wrote for the Court's majority in *Lee.* "Religious beliefs can be accommodated . . . but there is a point at which accommodation would 'radically restrict the operating latitude of the legislature.'" According to the chief justice, whereas the circumstances of *Yoder* had lent themselves to permitting a narrow accommodation for members of one particular religious group, the complexities of the tax system involved in *Lee* made providing faith-based exemptions a hopelessly complicated endeavor. Burger noted that if Lee was exempted from contributing taxes to a government program simply because he had a religious objection to its operation, people who had faith-based reservations regarding war might demand an exemption from paying the portion of their taxes earmarked for defense programs. Opening the floodgates to such privileges might overwhelm the federal tax system, Burger warned. "The tax system could not function," he asserted, "if denominations were allowed to challenge the tax system because tax payments were spent in a manner that violates their religious belief."

In *Lee*, this fear of clogging the tax system with endless religious exemption claims tipped the balance in favor of the federal government. "Because the broad public interest in maintaining a sound tax system is of such high order," Burger wrote in reversing the lower court ruling, "religious belief in conflict with the payment of taxes affords no basis for resisting the tax." Adopting a scolding tone at the end of his opinion, the chief justice claimed that although legislators and judges had long recognized the paramount importance of protecting free exercise rights, "every person cannot be shielded from all the burdens incident to exercising every aspect of the right to practice of religious beliefs."

The trend that began in *Lee* reached its culmination in *Employment Division v. Smith* (1990), when the Supreme Court effectively sounded the death knell for *Yoder*. Prior to *Smith*, the justices had evaluated religious liberty claims by weighing the free exercise rights of individuals against the interests of the state. Within this framework, the application of a neutral law to a religious objector might be held unconstitutional if the state lacked a sufficiently compelling interest in enforcing the statute. (*Yoder* had turned on this very point: the state of Wisconsin had lost in part because it failed to demonstrate its interest in mandating an extra two years of schooling.) In *Smith*, the Court essentially scrapped the compelling state interest test. Indeed, in his opinion for the Court, Justice Antonin Scalia went so far as to claim that a society that abided by such a standard would be "courting anarchy." Although the Court did not explicitly overturn *Yoder* (it distinguished the Amish case by noting that it had involved both religious liberty and parental rights), its abandonment of the compelling state interest standard compromised one of the ruling's central constitutional legacies. Now, a statute's surface neutrality toward religion was enough to substantiate its constitutionality.

As *Smith* demonstrated, the overall direction of the Supreme Court's religious liberty jurisprudence changed dramatically in the two decades after *Yoder* was handed down. In the Amish school attendance case and its most significant forebear, *Sherbert v. Verner*, the Court forged stout constitutional protections for religious conduct. It did so by applying the highest level of judicial scrutiny to state actions that appeared to infringe on individuals' religious liberty. *Smith* marked the advent of a decidedly less rigorous level of review. Instead of undertaking a close inspection, the Court would now approach the claims of religious objectors by applying a rational basis or reasonableness test — the most permissive standard available — to the state actions at issue. With the justices looking less stringently at their actions, states would have wider latitude to regulate religious conduct.

Responding to claims that *Smith* gutted constitutional protections for religious liberty, Congress passed the Religious Freedom Restoration Act (RFRA) in 1993. There wasn't much doubt as to the measure's purpose: RFRA clearly was meant to circumvent *Smith* by making the compelling state interest test part of federal law. As one observer put it, "Congress believed that religious practice deserved more protection than *Smith*'s constitutional rule gave it," and it attempted to provide the necessary safeguards by essentially turning back the clock to *Yoder*.

A challenge to RFRA came quickly, in *City of Boerne v. Flores* (1997). Numerous individuals and groups, including the National Committee for Amish Religious Freedom, filed amicus curiae briefs when the case reached the U.S. Supreme Court. "The Religious Freedom Restoration Act states the principle of religious liberty set forth by the Court in *Wisconsin v. Yoder*," William Ball wrote for the NCARF. "The contrary principle stated in *Employment Division v. Smith* is unreasonable, unworkable and is threatening to religious freedom." Ball's arguments were not enough to save RFRA. The Supreme Court concluded in *Flo-*

res that the law was unconstitutional because it exceeded the powers granted to Congress by the Fourteenth Amendment. Congress did in fact possess broad powers under the enforcement clause of that measure, Justice Anthony Kennedy wrote for the Court's majority, but "RFRA contradicts vital principles necessary to maintain separation of powers and the federal balance." *Flores* inspired a spirited debate among several members of the Supreme Court regarding the soundness of its forebear, *Smith*, with Justice Sandra Day O'Connor stating flatly in dissent that the Court in that earlier case had "adopted an improper standard for deciding free exercise claims." Their sparring, however, could not resuscitate the compelling interest standard.

Undaunted by the failure of RFRA, some members of Congress continued to attempt to craft a federal law that would rejuvenate the heart of *Yoder*. While these efforts foundered in the late 1990s, many of the main characters in the *Yoder* drama were leaving the public stage. Robert Warren, for instance, died of cancer in August 1998. In 1974, Warren had left his position as Wisconsin's attorney general for a seat on the federal bench. (It was said that one of President Nixon's last official acts had been to sign the documents authorizing Warren's appointment.) His tenure as a federal district court judge did nothing to diminish Warren's reputation as a defender of law and order. He was perhaps best known for issuing an order restraining *The Progressive* magazine from publishing articles explaining how to assemble a hydrogen bomb.

Attorney William Ball died five months after Warren. Like his adversary in *Yoder*, Ball had continued to flourish after his involvement in the New Glarus case. He argued seven more cases — all of them dealing with free exercise or establishment clause issues — before the U.S. Supreme Court. Recognizing Ball's tireless efforts in this realm, an admirer mourned that "his passing on certainly takes away a major spokesman and leading promoter of accommodation between church and state."

Most of the jurists who wrote opinions in *Yoder* preceded Warren and Ball to the grave. William O. Douglas died in 1976. Warren Burger remained on the Supreme Court until 1986, when he left to head the Commission on the Bicentennial of the United States Constitution. He passed away in 1995. Green County Court judge Roger

Elmer and Harold Hallows, chief justice of the Wisconsin Supreme Court, both died in 1974. Following a long illness, Elmer used a shotgun to take his own life; Hallows succumbed to leukemia. At the latter's memorial service, a longtime friend observed that Hallows could now look forward to sparring with the other great jurists — men like John Marshall and Louis Brandeis — who had already made the journey to heaven. "They will welcome him," the friend said of Hallows, "because he matched them in merit and in nobility of purpose."

Among those who mourned Hallows's passing was Nathan Heffernan, his colleague on the Wisconsin Supreme Court. Not long before he stepped down from the bench, Heffernan expressed his lingering dismay over the outcome of *Yoder.* "I still think the U.S. Supreme Court was all wet on that one," he said. The turn of the century found Heffernan leading an active retirement in Madison. He lived not far from Tom Eckerle, the attorney who had helped William Ball in the early stages of the *Yoder* case.

Under the stewardship of Lutheran minister William Lindholm, the National Committee for Amish Religious Freedom continued to operate in the decades after it shepherded *Yoder* to the U.S. Supreme Court. Despite its much-heralded success in the New Glarus case, the NCARF never reprised its role as an important mediator between the Amish and the state. The organization struggled to forge and maintain strong connections with the very people to whom it was providing assistance. One scholarly expert concluded that "the Amish have been perplexed by and indifferent toward the NCARF. They don't view it as their organization, don't know much of anything about it, and aren't sure what its purpose or motives might be when the group is explained to them." Today, the Amish rely on the Amish Steering Committee, a group controlled by members of their own faith, to negotiate on their behalf with state authorities.

By the late 1990s, the Amish principals in *Yoder* had returned to the quiet lives they had led before the landmark case thrust them into the national spotlight. Jonas Yoder settled on a farm in Missouri, and Wallace Miller lived with his family outside the town of Evansville, Wisconsin. The Millers' farm, nestled in sloping terrain, can be reached only by a narrow, winding country highway that is scarcely wide enough to accommodate the sports utility vehicles and pickup trucks that constitute the bulk of local traffic. Racing between destinations, these vehicles occasionally decelerate and share the road with less modern means of conveyance — horse-drawn carriages. As the modern world zooms past, Amish drivers guide the buggies slowly but steadily through the countryside. They remain unhurried.

CHRONOLOGY

1693–1697	Amish break from Swiss Brethren
1720s	Amish settlers begin arriving in Pennsylvania from Switzerland
1852	Massachusetts enacts first compulsory school attendance statute
1865	Schism between conservative and progressive Amish factions leads to emergence of Old Order Amish
May 5, 1879	U.S. Supreme Court articulates belief-conduct distinction in religious liberty claims in *Reynolds v. United States*
1889	"Bennett Law" enacted in Wisconsin
June 4, 1923	U.S. Supreme Court rules in *Meyer v. Nebraska*
June 1, 1925	U.S. Supreme Court rules in *Pierce v. Society of Sisters*
May 20, 1940	U.S. Supreme Court incorporates protections of religious liberty into Fourteenth Amendment in *Cantwell v. United States*
June 17, 1963	U.S. Supreme Court articulates three-tiered standard for religious liberty claims in *Sherbert v. Verner*
January 1964	Old Order Amish families begin settling in New Glarus, Wisconsin
January 1966	Adin Yutzy moves from Hazleton, Iowa, to New Glarus
Winter 1966	Jonas Yoder and Wallace Miller move from Plain City, Ohio, to New Glarus
1966	New Glarus Amish clash with local school authorities over gym uniforms; school board agrees to permit Amish to wear modified uniforms
Autumn 1966	Amish school's controversy in Hazleton reaches its height
November 5, 1966	Kansas Supreme Court rules against Amish in *Garber* school attendance case
January 19, 1967	Assembly Bill 59, designed to exempt Amish youngsters from physical education courses, introduced in Wisconsin legislature

March 1967	National Committee for Amish Religious Freedom formed
March 8, 1967	Assembly Bill 358, under which Amish children would be permitted to fulfill the state compulsory school attendance law by attending school up to eighth grade, introduced in Wisconsin legislature
April 20, 1967	Assembly Bill 358 tabled
October 1967	U.S. Supreme Court denies certiorari in *Garber*
December 7, 1967	Assembly Bill 59 tabled
August 1968	New Glarus Amish open their own schools
August 30, 1968	School superintendent Kenneth Glewen dispatches letters warning Amish parents that they might be violating the state's compulsory school attendance law
September 18, 1968	Glewen dispatches second round of warning letters to Amish parents
October 23, 1968	Criminal complaints filed against Wallace Miller, Jonas Yoder, and Adin Yutzy
December 1968	*Yoder* defendants make their first court appearance
January 1969	Miller, Yoder, and Yutzy formally agree to permit representation by National Committee for Amish Religious Freedom
January 20, 1969	Attorney William Ball writes to state school superintendent William Kahl and asks for exemption to state school code for Amish
February 11, 1969	*Yoder* defendants enter formal not-guilty plea
April 2, 1969	Green County Court trial in *Wisconsin v. Yoder*
June 23, 1969	Earl Warren resigns as chief justice of the United States; Warren Burger takes oath of office to replace him
August 15, 1969	Green County Court judge Roger Elmer rules for state in *Yoder*
November 13, 1969	Green County Circuit Court judge Arthur Luebke rules for state in *Yoder*
December 1, 1970	Wisconsin Supreme Court hears oral arguments in *Yoder*
January 8, 1971	Wisconsin Supreme Court rules for Amish defendants in *Yoder*

March 30, 1971	State of Wisconsin applies to U.S. Supreme Court for certiorari in *Yoder*
May 24, 1971	U.S. Supreme Court grants certiorari in *Yoder*
June 18, 1971	Wisconsin Assembly passes nonbinding resolution asking attorney general Warren to drop *Yoder* appeal
June 28, 1971	U.S. Supreme Court articulates three-tiered standard for evaluating establishment clause claims (known as "the *Lemon* test") in *Lemon v. Kurtzman*
September 17, 1971	U.S. Supreme Court justice Hugo Black retires
September 23, 1971	U.S. Supreme Court justice John Marshall Harlan retires
December 8, 1971	U.S. Supreme Court hears oral arguments in *Yoder*
December 10, 1971	Members of U.S. Supreme Court discuss *Yoder* in conference
January 7, 1972	Lewis Powell and William Rehnquist sworn in as U.S. Supreme Court justices
May 15, 1972	U.S. Supreme Court rules for Amish in *Yoder*
1973	Jonas Yoder and family leave New Glarus for Missouri
September 12, 1974	E. Harold Hallows, former chief justice of the Wisconsin Supreme Court, dies at age seventy
July 28, 1976	Ohio Supreme Court rules in favor of William Ball's clients in *State v. Whisner*
1977	Wallace Miller and family leave New Glarus for Evansville, Wisconsin
February 23, 1982	U.S. Supreme Court rules against Amish in *United States v. Lee*
April 17, 1990	U.S. Supreme Court undercuts the heart of its *Yoder* precedent in *Employment Division v. Smith*
November 16, 1993	President Clinton signs Religious Freedom Restoration Act (RFRA) into law
June 19, 1996	Wisconsin Supreme Court rules in favor of Amish in *State v. Miller*
June 25, 1997	U.S. Supreme Court rules RFRA unconstitutional in *City of Boerne v. Flores*
August 20, 1998	Former Wisconsin attorney general Robert Warren dies at age seventy-two
January 10, 1999	Attorney William Ball dies at age eighty-three

BIBLIOGRAPHICAL ESSAY

What follows is a survey of the primary and secondary source materials I relied on as I researched the *Yoder* case. Readers interested in more comprehensive treatments of individual subjects, people, or events mentioned in this book are encouraged to refer to these accounts.

A number of perceptive studies have examined the history, doctrines, and practices of the Amish. Among the best of these general works is John Hostetler's *Amish Society*, 4th ed. (Baltimore: Johns Hopkins University Press, 1993), which provides a solid overview of the faith. Also worth noting are Steven Nolt's excellent *A History of the Amish* (Intercourse, Pa.: Good Books, 1992) and two outstanding works by Donald Kraybill: *The Riddle of Amish Culture*, rev. ed. (Baltimore: Johns Hopkins University Press, 2001), and *On the Backroad to Heaven: Old Order Hutterites, Mennonites, Amish, and Brethren* (Baltimore: Johns Hopkins University Press, 2001).

Several collections of essays have focused on particular aspects of Amish culture. Two works that might be of particular interest to anyone interested in the *Yoder* case are Albert Keim, ed., *Compulsory Education and the Amish: The Right Not to Be Modern* (Boston: Beacon Press, 1975), and Donald Kraybill, ed., *The Amish and the State*, 2d ed. (Baltimore: Johns Hopkins University Press, 2003). The latter volume includes compelling essays on *Yoder* by attorney William Ball and William Lindholm of the National Committee for Amish Religious Freedom. Other informative essay collections include Donald Kraybill and Steven Nolt, eds., *Amish Enterprise: From Plow to Profits* (Baltimore: Johns Hopkins University Press, 1995), and Donald Kraybill and Marc Olshan, eds., *The Amish Struggle with Modernity* (Hanover, N.H.: University Press of New England, 1994). For an excellent collection containing essays written by the Amish themselves, see Brad Igou, ed., *The Amish in Their Own Words: Amish Writing from 25 Years of* Family Life *Magazine* (Scottdale, Pa.: Herald Press, 1999). Another informative collection is John Hostetler, ed., *Amish Roots: A Treasury of History, Wisdom, and Lore* (Baltimore: Johns Hopkins University Press, 1989).

My research on the issue of the Amish reluctance to "go to law" was informed by John Hostetler's "The Amish and the Law: A Religious Minority and Its Legal Encounters," *Washington and Lee Law Review* 41 (1984): 33–47. I also benefited from a review of John Oyer's *Anabaptists, the Law, and the State: Some Reflections Apropos North American Mennonites* (Washington, D.C.: Marpeck Academy, 1985). Despite the Amish aversion to "going to law," they have been involved in several notable legal cases besides *Yoder*. These include *Kansas v. Garber* (419 P. 2d 896 [Kan. 1966]), *United States v. Lee* (455 U.S. 252 [1982]), and *Wisconsin v. Miller* (538 N.W. 2d 573 [Wisc. 1995]). For an analysis of *Garber*, see Robert Casad's "Compulsory High School Attendance and the Old Order Amish: A Commentary on *State v. Garber*," *Kansas Law Review* 16 (1968): 423.

The schooling controversy involving the Old Order Amish in Hazleton, Iowa, occasioned numerous magazine and newspaper articles. The *Des Moines Register* provided thorough daily coverage of the dispute. A more scholarly treatment can be found in Harrell Rodgers's *Community, Conflict, Public Opinion and the Law: The Amish Dispute in Iowa* (Columbus, Ohio: Charles E. Merrill, 1968). Other accounts include Franklin Littell's "The State of Iowa vs. the Amish," *Christian Century*, February 23, 1966, 234–35.

Surprisingly little has been written about the Amish in Wisconsin. Perhaps the most reliable source of information in this area is Harvey M. Jacobs and Ellen M. Bassett's excellent overview *The Amish: A Literature Review* (Madison: University of Wisconsin–Extension and University of Wisconsin–Madison School of Natural Resources, 1995). Also helpful is the Wisconsin Legislative Council's "Staff Report to the Education Committee on the Amish Community in Wisconsin and Selected Other States," submitted in February 1968.

Of the major figures involved in the *Yoder* case, attorney William Ball was by far the most prolific writer. His book *Mere Creatures of the State? Education, Religion and the Courts: A View from the Courtroom* (Notre Dame, Ind.: Crisis Books, 1994) includes several lengthy passages describing his involvement in *Yoder*. Other works by Ball that shed light on his role in the case include "Accountability: A View from the Trial Courtroom," *George Washington Law Review* 60 (1992): 809; "Keynote Address: 1981 Seminar on Church, Family, State, and Education," *Journal of Christian Jurisprudence* (1982): 17–18; "Law and Religion in America: The New Picture," *Catholic Lawyer* 16 (winter 1970): 3–14; "Legal Religion in the Schools," *Catholic World*, September 1963, 366–71; and "On Hoping to Be, Being, and Having Been," *Texas Tech Law Review* 27 (1996): 1005–9.

I learned a great deal about Ball and his career by reading the many tributes published after his death in 1999. These include "Editor's Note," *Crisis*, March 1999, 53, and Edward McGlynn Gaffney's "William Bentley Ball (1916–1999)," *First Things*, April 1999, 71–88. For a reliable account of Ball's post-*Yoder* activities on behalf of fundamentalist Christian schools, see Michael D. Baker's "Regulation of Fundamentalist Christian Schools: Free Exercise of Religion v. the State's Interest in Quality Education," *Kentucky Law Journal* 67 (1978–1979): 415. These matters are also discussed in James Carper and Thomas Hunt, eds., *Religious Schooling in America* (Birmingham, Ala.: Religious Education Press, 1984). For an excellent account of the *Whisner* case, see James Carper's "The *Whisner* Decision: A Case Study in State Regulation of Christian Day Schools," *Journal of Church and State* 26 (1984): 281–302.

One of Ball's allies in *Yoder*, Donald Erickson, wrote dozens of articles examining such issues as Amish educational practices and public funding for nonpublic schools. Among them are "Public Funds for Private Schools," *Education Digest*, December 1968, 9–12, and "The Supreme Court on Aid to Private Schools," *Theory into Practice* 17 (1968): 291–302. Erickson also contributed to and edited the collection of essays inspired by the nonpublic schools conference at which the National Committee for Amish Religious Freedom was formed: *Public Controls for Nonpublic Schools* (Chicago: University of Chicago Press, 1969).

The U.S. Supreme Court during Warren Burger's tenure as chief justice has been most famously examined in Bob Woodward and Scott Armstrong's controversial *The Brethren: Inside the Supreme Court* (New York: Simon and Schuster, 1979). A more scholarly (and perhaps more substantive) study is Bernard Schwartz's *The Ascent of Pragmatism: The Burger Court in Action* (Reading, Mass.: Addison-Wesley, 1990). Similarly perceptive is Charles Lamb and Stephen Halpern, eds., *The Burger Court: Political and Judicial Profiles* (Urbana and Chicago: University of Illinois Press, 1991). A number of law review articles have examined Burger's career on the bench. Among the more useful of these studies are Philip Craig Zane, "An Interpretation of the Jurisprudence of Chief Justice Warren Burger," *Utah Law Review* 1995 (1995): 975–1005; Henry J. Reske, "The Diverse Legacy of Warren Burger," *American Bar Association Journal* 81 (August 1995): 36; and A. E. Dick Howard, "Chief Enigma," *American Bar Association Journal* 81 (October 1995): 66. Anyone curious about Burger's standing with his colleagues on the bench might consult the numerous tributes occasioned by his death. These include Harry A. Blackmun's "A Tribute to Warren E. Burger," *William Mitchell Law Review* 22 (1996): 15–17, and William Rehnquist's "A Tribute to Chief Justice Warren E. Burger," *Harvard Law Review* 100 (1987): 969–71.

The published opinions in *Yoder* are available in most law libraries. The Wisconsin Supreme Court's decision can be found at 182 N.W. 2d 539 (1971). The U.S. Supreme Court's decision is located at 406 U.S. 205 (1972). A transcript of oral arguments before the U.S. Supreme Court is furnished in Philip B. Kurland and Gerhard Casper, eds., *Landmark Briefs and Arguments of the Supreme Court of the United States: Constitutional Law*, vol. 71 (Arlington, Va.: University Publications of America, 1975). That same volume also reproduces all the briefs in the case. For a transcript of the Supreme Court's conference discussion of *Yoder*, see Del Dickson, ed., *The Supreme Court in Conference (1940–1985): The Private Discussions behind Nearly 300 Supreme Court Decisions* (New York: Oxford University Press, 2001).

Several Wisconsin newspapers provided thorough coverage of the *Yoder* case. Madison's two daily newspapers, the *Wisconsin State Journal* and the *Capital Times*, published dozens of articles chronicling the case's progress through the courts and the subsequent breakup of the Amish community in New Glarus. (Many of these articles were written by Ray Barth, the freelance journalist who closely followed the case and its impact.) The *New Glarus Post*, a small weekly, also covered the case, as did *The Budget*, a newspaper published in Sugar Creek, Ohio.

Yoder drew the attention of the national media in the early 1970s, and it was analyzed in several informative magazine articles. Perhaps the most controversial of these were studies examining the motives of attorney William Ball and his colleagues in the NCARF: "Using the Amish?" *Christianity Today*, January 7, 1972, 26–27, and writer James Castelli's follow-up, "Catholics and the Amish," *Commonweal*, June 16, 1972, 331–32. The potential links between the New Glarus case and public funding for nonpublic schools were explored in Russell Kirk's "The Amish Case," *National Review*, July 7, 1972, 747, and "The Court Finds for the Amish," *America*, May 27, 1972, 554. Walter Burns's "Ratiocinations: The Importance of Being Amish," *Harper's*, March 1973, 36–42, provided an early critique of the U.S. Supreme Court's opinion in *Yoder*. For a more general account of the facts of the case and its impact, see "The Right to Be Different," *Time*, May 29, 1972, 67.

Dozens of scholarly studies have assessed the constitutional issues at play in *Yoder* and Chief Justice Burger's treatment of them in his majority opinion. Among the most helpful of these works are Anthony J. Basinski, "The Amish Exemption," *University of Pittsburgh Law Review* 34 (1972): 274–89; Jay S. Bybee, "Substantive Due Process and Free Exercise of Religion: *Meyer*, *Pierce* and the Origins of *Wisconsin v. Yoder*," *Capital University Law Review* 25 (1996): 887–932; James D. Gordon III, "*Wisconsin v. Yoder* and Religious Liberty," *Texas Law Review* 74 (1996): 1237–40; Robert J. Seminara, "Case Comments," *Notre Dame Lawyer* 48 (1973): 741–50; Steven D. Smith, "*Wisconsin v. Yoder* and the Unprincipled Approach to Religious Freedom," *Capital University Law Review* 25 (1996): 805–18; and Laura S. Underkuffler-Freund, "*Yoder* and the Question of Equality," *Capital University Law Review* 25 (1996): 789–803. Robert Bork expressed his sentiments on the case in his book *The Tempting of America: The Political Seduction of the Law* (New York: Free Press, 1990).

Many primary documents relating to *Yoder* can be found in either the Wisconsin State Law Library or the State Historical Society of Wisconsin (both of which are located in Madison). The historical society's collections, for instance, contain materials on the case accumulated by the state Department of Public Instruction. These documents include the trial transcript, the decisions written by trial court judge Roger Elmer and Judge Arthur Luebke of the Green County Circuit Court, memoranda prepared by the state Department of Justice, and correspondence between the state's attorneys and those representing the Amish. Also available are the papers of several members of the Wisconsin Supreme Court, including Justice Nathan Heffernan. The state law library's holdings including all the briefs filed when *Yoder* reached the state supreme court.

Many of the surviving principals in *Yoder* submitted to lengthy interviews for this book. I benefited greatly from my contacts with William Lindholm, Nathan Heffernan, Tom Eckerle, Don Showalter, and Wallace Miller. Other people who had less direct involvement in *Yoder* also provided valuable insights during interviews and through correspondence. Longtime New Glarus residents Kim Tschudy and Kay Roth shared their memories of the Amish. Joe Skelly recalled his experiences with William Ball, his friend and law partner. Betty Brown and LeRoy Dalton discussed the operation of the Wisconsin Department of Justice.

The history of compulsory school attendance laws is covered capably in David B. Tyack's "Ways of Seeing: An Essay on the History of Compulsory Schooling," *Harvard Educational Review* 46 (1976): 355–89. For another scholarly study of the topic, see David Edward Ramsey's "A Historical Review of the Origins, Developments, and Trends in Compulsory Education in the United States, 1642–1984" (Ph.D. diss., East Tennessee State University, 1985). My understanding of the controversy in Wisconsin over the Bennett Law was shaped by Thomas C. Hunt's "The Bennett Law of 1890: Focus of Conflict between Church and State in Education," *Journal of Church and State* 23 (1981): 69–93. The definitive account of the school law controversies in Nebraska and Oregon that gave rise to the *Pierce* and *Meyer* cases is William G. Ross's excellent *Forging New Freedoms: Nativism, Education, and the Constitution, 1917–1927* (Lincoln: University of Nebraska Press, 1994). Another helpful study of *Pierce* is David B. Tyack's "The Perils of Pluralism: The Background of the *Pierce* Case," *American Historical Review* 74 (1978): 74–98.

This book touches only briefly on the topic of interest-group litigation. Readers interested in a more thorough treatment of that subject might consult Lee Epstein and C. K. Rowland's "Interest Groups in the Courts: Do Groups Fare Better?" in Allan J. Cigler and Burdett A. Loomis, eds., *Interest Group Politics*, 2d ed. (Washington, D.C.: Congressional Quarterly Press, 1986), 275–88. An excellent study that also discusses this issue is Charles Epp's *The Rights Revolution: Lawyers, Activists, and Supreme Courts in Comparative Perspective* (Chicago: University of Chicago Press, 1998).

The U.S. Supreme Court's significant religion clause decisions are reviewed in most constitutional law casebooks. Among the most comprehensive and perceptive of these is Lawrence Tribe's *American Constitutional Law*, vol. 2, 3d ed. (New York: Foundation Press, 2000). One volume that focuses more specifically on the free exercise and establishment clauses is Francis Graham Lee, ed., *All Imaginable Liberty: The Religious Clauses of the First Amendment* (Lanham, Md.: University Press of America, 1995). Useful articles in law journals include William Buss, "Federalism, Separation of Powers, and the Demise of the Religious Freedom Restoration Act," *Iowa Law Review* 83 (1998): 391; Jesse H. Choper, "A Century of Religious Liberty," *California Law Review* 88 (2000): 1709–41; Philip Kurland, "The Irrelevance of the Constitution: The Religion Clauses of the First Amendment and the Supreme Court," *Villanova Law Review* 24 (1978): 3–27; Michael McConnell, "The Origins and Historical Understanding of Free Exercise of Religion," *Harvard Law Review* 103 (1990): 1409–76; and Herbert W. Titus, "The Free Exercise Clause: Past, Present and Future," *Regent University Law Review* 6 (fall 1995): 7–63.

Several books have illuminated the meaning of the religion clauses by examining individual cases or sets of cases in some detail. Carolyn Long's *Religious Freedom and Indian Rights: The Case of* Oregon v. Smith (Lawrence: University Press of Kansas, 2000) provides the most original and insightful account of the landmark *Smith* case and the subsequent battle over the Religious Freedom Restoration Action. The legal campaign of the Jehovah's Witnesses during the World War II era is explored in my book *Judging Jehovah's Witnesses: Religious Persecution and the Dawn of the Rights Revolution* (Lawrence: University Press of Kansas, 2000). Although the constitutional issues in the case are not its primary focus, the facts of the *Reynolds* case are capably described in Bruce Van Orden's *Prisoner for Conscience' Sake: The Life of George Reynolds* (Salt Lake City: Deseret Book Company, 1992).

The following U.S. Supreme Court opinions are among its most important relating to religious liberty: *Reynolds v. United States* (98 U.S. 145 [1878]), *Cantwell v. Connecticut* (310 U.S. 296 [1940]), *Sherbert v. Verner* (374 U.S. 398 [1963]), *Oregon v. Smith* (494 U.S. 872 [1990]), and *City of Boerne v. Flores* (521 U.S. 507 [1997]). Other important decisions include *Goldman v. Weinberger* (475 U.S. 503 [1986]), *Bowen v. Roy* (476 U.S. 693 [1986]), and *Lyng v. Northwest Indian Cemetery Protective Association* (485 U.S. 439 [1988]).

A number of fine scholarly studies have examined the complex field of parents' rights and children's welfare. An excellent work in this area is James G. Dwyer's "Parents' Religion and Children's Welfare: Debunking the Doctrine of Children's Rights," *California Law Review* 82 (1994): 1371–447. Other analyses include Katheryn D. Katz, "Majoritarian Morality and Parental Rights," *Albany Law Review* 52 (1988): 405, and Francis B. McCarthy, "The Confused Constitutional Status and Meaning of Parental Rights," *Georgia Law Review* 22 (1988): 975. Among the U.S. Supreme Court's most significant rulings in this area are *Meyer v. Nebraska* (262 U.S. 390 [1923]) and *Pierce v. Society of Sisters* (268 U.S. 510 [1925]).

This book touches only briefly on the far right movement and its attitudes toward the public schools. A more thorough account of these matters is furnished in Chip Berlet and Matthew N. Lyons's *Right-Wing Populism in America: Too Close for Comfort* (New York: Guilford Press, 2000). For an example of ultraconservative opinion regarding the purported dangers of compulsory school attendance laws, see Medford Evans's "Our Schools: Education as Witchdoctor," *Public Opinion*, June 1967, 29–39, and Blair Adams and Joel Stein's *Who Owns the Children? Compulsory Education and the Dilemma of Ultimate Authority* (Grand Junction, Colo.: Truth Forum, 1984).

INDEX